"Osheta Moore has given us all the gift *Dear White Peacemakers*. Her perspective and hope into discussions on racism. H. provide real-life restoration. May the scales fall from our eyes. May restoration and healing come. A must-read for my brothers and sisters in Christ."

—**LECRAE**, Grammy award–winning artist and *New York Times* bestselling author of *I Am Restored*

"Every white person should read *Dear White Peacemakers*. Osheta Moore serves as the best of guides for how white people, growing in their racial awareness, can both engage the issue of racism and embody a peacemaking ethic moving forward. She will challenge you, shock you, inspire you. After reading this book, you'll feel all the more equipped to seek shalom and healing instead of hate and retribution in our racially torn world."

—**MICHELLE AMI REYES**, vice president of the Asian American Christian Collaborative, co-executive director of Pax, and author of *Becoming All Things: How Small Changes Lead to Lasting Connections across Cultures*

"In the wonderful *Dear White Peacemakers*, Osheta Moore gives us the gift of insight, offered from a loving sister wanting all the best for her spiritual family. With Jesus at the center, we can move forward with hope in him as our healer of broken relationships and inadequate identities as mere victims and victimizers. Thank you, my sister, for this compelling labor of love. As you say, 'Let us come together and be free.' Amen!"

—**BRUXY CAVEY**, teaching pastor at The Meeting House and author of *The End of Religion*

"This book is our North Star, bright enough to illuminate the anti-racism path and bold enough to offer love for our souls along the way. This book transformed my weariness into a howl of hope in my chest. Osheta Moore challenges us to build peacemaking into our anti-racism work because there is no peace and no justice without the constellation of love."

—**DIANA K. OESTREICH**, soldier turned peacemaker and author of *Waging Peace: One Soldier's Story of Putting Love First*

"Osheta Moore's letter to her white siblings is a gift that we don't deserve. It's a labor of love straight from the soul of a Black woman who dares to believe that white folks can become peacemakers. This book is a one-of-a-kind pastoral invitation for you and me to come to the table as participants in the restorative revolution. I needed this, and I commend it with hope!"

—**JER SWIGART**, cofounder of the Global Immersion Project, coauthor of *Mending the Divides*, and cohost of the *Everyday Peacemaking* podcast

"*Dear White Peacemakers* is a textbook of tender tenacity: never shaming, always truthful. Not content to be convicting without a way forward, Osheta is committed to seeing everyone around her as God's Beloved (even those who remain committed to a life of violence and prejudice against her), and this perspective will change your own lens for viewing the world. *Dear White Peacemakers* is not just a book, it's a calling and an invitation to drink from the bottomless well of God's shalom. I cannot imagine a more gracious invitation, nor a more compassionate host."

—**ERIN HICKS MOON**, senior creative for The Popcast Media Group and resident Bible scholar on *The Bible Binge* podcast

"Osheta Moore has written not only an important book, but what some may consider an impossible book. In *Dear White Peacemakers*, Osheta calls us to fight racism while remaining true to the peacemaking ethic set forth by Jesus in the Sermon on the Mount. This is a smart and compelling work, and Osheta's voice is both honest and hopeful. I benefited greatly from *Dear White Peacemakers*."

—**BRIAN ZAHND**, lead pastor of Word of Life Church in Saint Joseph, Missouri, and author of *Sinners in the Hands of a Loving God*

"As a white woman, I believe every white Christian needs to read *Dear White Peacemakers*. Osheta Moore's vulnerability, authenticity, and call to action is a rare gift, and we are lucky to have her leadership in this space. I felt uncomfortable, challenged, and empowered to take steps in my own work around anti-racism."

—**JESSICA TURNER**, *Wall Street Journal* bestselling author of *The Fringe Hours*

"This is a love letter void of shallow sentiments, and is one steeped in honesty, authenticity, storytelling, challenge, and faith-filled conviction. Readers will find Osheta Moore is a theologian, pastor, practitioner, and companion on the journey. *Dear White Peacemakers* is both invitational and incarnational in every story—evoking the true substance of anti-racism in the way of Jesus. I've no doubt this book will become a pillar in anti-racism work for subversive, holistic kingdom advancement."

— **ROSE LEE-NORMAN**, formation pastor at Sanctuary Covenant Church in Minneapolis, Minnesota

"I know of no other book on racial reconciliation that embodies the humble cruciform beauty of Jesus' 'third way' kingdom as beautifully and as powerfully as *Dear White Peacemakers*. My fellow White American Christians, wherever you may be at in your awareness of White superiority and of systemic racism in our country, and even if you currently aren't convinced these things are present realities in this country, I implore you to read this informative, insightful, moving, down-to-earth, often funny, remarkably vulnerable, and certainly impactful book!"

— **GREGORY A. BOYD**, theologian, author, and senior pastor of Woodland Hills Church

"In *Dear White Peacemakers*, Osheta Moore brilliantly brings our lives with God into direct contact with anti-racism. This book is grace-oriented, Jesus-centered, truth-driven, shame-defying, and shalom-seeking. Osheta Moore refuses to dehumanize White readers, and with the same stroke of the pen calls White peacemakers to put to practice 'the things that make for peace' (Luke 19:42). Osheta is the vulnerable, wise, pastoral voice the church needs as we discern a better path forward for resisting racial injustice. I hope church leaders and attenders in the United States and beyond will ponder her words and put them into practice. I can't recommend this book enough!"

— **KURT WILLEMS**, pastor and author of *Echoing Hope: How the Humanity of Jesus Redeems Our Pain*

"In her extraordinary book, Osheta Moore invites white peacemakers to embody the fierce and tender way of anti-racist peacemaking. We do this, Osheta reminds us, by first owning our Belovedness so that we can access the call to courage that true shalom requires. *Dear White Peacemakers* is both a love letter and a sacred call to action as we navigate this important time in the world."

—**AUNDI KOLBER**, MA, LPC, therapist and author of *Try Softer*

"Painfully vulnerable, Osheta Moore's *Dear White Peacemakers* reads as both her personal testimony and a confession of her deepest convictions. Moore beautifully uses African American spirituals as a healing balm in the tenuous topic of race in American Christianity. Whether she is addressing Black hairstyles in the movie *Black Panther* or racial slurs at her son's school, Moore is a brilliant guide and teacher. She's a generous host inviting us into her inner sanctuary, making readers feel well cared for—the true gift of a dedicated peacemaker."

—**MARCIE ALVIS-WALKER**, creator of *Black Coffee with White Friends*

"*Dear White Peacemakers* strikes a delicate, beautiful balance between enduring compassion and the relentless pursuit of justice. With wisdom and grace, Osheta Moore guides readers through the arduous journey of being actively anti-racist, and her approach overflows with a love that cultivates empathy without sacrificing truth. Her words have both refreshed my soul and challenged my posture in this work, and I'm certain that they will do the same for readers everywhere!"

—**DANIELLE COKE**, illustrator and activist

"While many books on race have filled me with knowledge about the depth, complexity, and wickedness of racism, and of white supremacy, *Dear White Peacemakers* is the first book that has filled me with hope. If you hope for racial reconciliation and holistic restoration, get Osheta's book. If you hunger for a path toward meaningful racial peace and kingdom shalom, buy Osheta's book."

—**DAN KENT**, community engagement pastor at Woodland Hills Church and author of *Confident Humility*

# dear
# white
# peacemakers

# dear
# white
# peacemakers

## DISMANTLING RACISM WITH GRIT AND GRACE

# Osheta Moore

FOREWORD BY JEN HATMAKER

## HERALD
### P R E S S

Harrisonburg, Virginia

Herald Press
PO Box 866, Harrisonburg, Virginia 22803
www.HeraldPress.com

Study guides are available for many Herald Press titles at www.HeraldPress.com.

DEAR WHITE PEACEMAKERS
© 2021 by Herald Press, Harrisonburg, Virginia 22803. 800-245-7894.
  All rights reserved.
Library of Congress Control Number: 2021933133
International Standard Book Number: 978-1-5138-0766-9 (paperback);
  978-1-5138-0767-6 (hardcover); 978-1-5138-0768-3 (ebook)
Printed in United States of America
Cover art by Marian Bailey

All Scripture quotations, unless otherwise indicated, are taken from the *Holy Bible, New International Version*®, NIV®. Copyright ©1973, 1978, 1984, 2011 by Biblica, Inc.™ Used by permission of Zondervan. All rights reserved worldwide. www.zondervan.com The "NIV" and "New International Version" are trademarks registered in the United States Patent and Trademark Office by Biblica, Inc.™

Scripture quotations marked (ESV) are from the ESV® Bible (*The Holy Bible, English Standard Version*®), copyright © 2001 by Crossway, a publishing ministry of Good News Publishers. Used by permission. All rights reserved.

Scripture quotations marked (KJV) are taken from the *King James Version*.

Additional Scripture taken from *The Message*. Copyright © 1993, 2002, 2018 by Eugene H. Peterson. Used by permission of NavPress, represented by Tyndale House Publishers. All rights reserved.

Scripture quotations marked (NLT) are taken from the *Holy Bible, New Living Translation*, copyright © 1996, 2004, 2015 by Tyndale House Foundation. Used by permission of Tyndale House Publishers, Inc., Carol Stream, Illinois 60188. All rights reserved.

Scripture quotations marked (NRSV) are taken from the *New Revised Standard Version Bible*, copyright © 1989, Division of Christian Education of the National Council of the Churches of Christ in the United States of America. Used by permission. All rights reserved.

Scripture quotations marked (RSV) are taken from the *Revised Standard Version of the Bible*, copyright © 1946, 1952, and 1971 the Division of Christian Education of the National Council of the Churches of Christ in the United States of America. Used by permission. All rights reserved.

25 24 23 22 21          10 9 8 7 6 5 4 3 2 1

## DAKOTA LAND ACKNOWLEDGMENT

This book is written to you, a White Peacemaker, from me, a Black Peacemaker, living in Minnesota (Mni Sota Makoce), the homeland of the Dakota people. I would like to acknowledge their faithful stewardship throughout many generations. The Dakota are still here! Every day, they are teaching their language and way of life to the next generation—a thing that was once illegal. I hold space to lament the trauma they've experienced when they were forcibly and violently removed from their ancestral land.

Here's another old saying that deserves a second look: "Eye for eye, tooth for tooth." Is that going to get us anywhere? Here's what I propose: "Don't hit back at all." If someone strikes you, stand there and take it. If someone drags you into court and sues for the shirt off your back, giftwrap your best coat and make a present of it. And if someone takes unfair advantage of you, use the occasion to practice the servant life. No more tit-for-tat stuff. Live generously.

 —**JESUS**, PRINCE OF PEACE (MATTHEW 5:38-42 *THE MESSAGE*)

    ❀  ❀  ❀

If we merge mercy with might, and might with right, then love becomes our legacy and change our children's birthright.

 —**AMANDA GORMAN**, NATIONAL YOUTH POET LAUREATE, "THE HILL WE CLIMB"

# Contents

# Foreword

Fourteen years ago, I was teaching at a weekend event for young adult women in Virginia. That Saturday morning, I headed into the hotel restaurant for breakfast by myself. A vibrant, attractive Black woman, an attendee, introduced herself to me, and however it went down, we ended up eating breakfast together. I remember listening to her story with clear eyes—White husband, ministry in Boston, brand-new baby, one of very few Black women at a conservative conference—and knowing instantly: "This is a special leader with an important space in this world." I remembered her name, because I knew.

Osheta.

This book is going to drive you crazy one way or another, White folks. Let's just lay those tracks right out of the gate. Women committed to the ways of peacemaking in a violent world always confound. For some of you, her posture will be too gracious, too generous, too resistant to anger and revenge.

For others, Osheta will challenge tenets that have held your whole white life together, and you might rail and reel and rage. The way of shalom is wildly misunderstood. Peacemaking is typically seen as noble only in hindsight; its real-time response is far too "third way" to be endorsed by the sides. You'll feel the push and pull, reader, and that is how you know it is working.

Here is what you should know as you open these pages: First, Osheta is a trustworthy guide led by faithfulness, practice, and deep wisdom. This matters. Whom we listen to matters. Whose knowledge and experience we learn from matters. Our teachers lead us toward their own North Stars, and hers is the Beloved Community. What do our leaders care about? That is where they will take us. With certainty, I can tell you that Osheta cares about justice and goodness, community and healing, even inside the constructs of white supremacy and all its evils. She doesn't leave her readers in the grip of its control but leads us out with faithful authority. Check her receipts. This is her work, and she has earned these pages.

Second, you can handle this discomfort, White Peacemakers. Indeed, we must. This is a chosen labor, this setting of a table by a Black Peacemaker for the sake of all her siblings. I honor it. Pull up a chair, because by some miracle of giftedness, Osheta has created a safe space for the work here. Don't get it wrong: "safe" does not mean the protection of our white feelings at the expense of anti-racism. But it does mean the Beloved Community includes every human person, and that belovedness is never in question. You'll see. As Osheta writes: "Love is the reason we offer each other grace and dream of reconciliation, but love is also the reason we relentlessly pursue justice and equity. Both . . . with grit and grace."

The work of anti-racism sets us all free, as Osheta saliently explains. This is the pathway to shalom for the whole earth. In the work of anti-racism, we are all liberated from the deception of white supremacy and the ten million ways it holds our communities in bondage. The predictable result of anti-racism peacemaking is *flourishing*—all-encompassing, boundless, rooted. It is activated not by shame but by truth, which has always set us free. This is good and holy work with great consequence. Its ripple effects will span generations.

Finally, to my friend Osheta, breakfast companion that long-ago day, it is with a deep bow that I honor your work here. I see what it cost you, I recognize the labor, and I am a grateful recipient. Your faithfulness is evident and your leadership invaluable. I bless you, my friend and sister. May the fruit of your work create shalom in hearts and lives. It is with true integrity you have brought it forth.

—Jen Hatmaker

# Markers on My Hand, a Call to Empathy

The night I decided to confront the middle school coach who called my son the N-word, my hands were stained with permanent marker from making signs for the Special Olympics. While my son, the very one called a n***** by a White forty-something grown man, slept in the next bedroom, I obsessed over two things: the exact dressing-down I'd give the coach and the fact that I would go into this meeting with dirty hands—which would be an enormous problem because I talk with my hands. How will I adequately communicate to this man how completely he messed up if I can't gesticulate wildly? It felt as if I'd been robbed of one of my essential weapons for battle. So I got up and washed my hands for oh maybe the third time and went back to bed to toss and turn and wait for morning.

We had decided to go to the Special Olympics because of something my friend Margot told me—that we belong to each other. Every single person whom God has made is immediately a member of this large, messy family. We're siblings, and siblings show up for one another. That weekend my disabled siblings were running and playing their hearts out, so I decided to gather the kids, make some signs, and spend a Saturday cheering them on. Having three children who are grossly labeled as "typical," I was challenged by Margot's encouragement to show up because I rarely if at all make space to consider how people with disabilities move through their lives. Because I don't have to, it's easy to not grieve their losses, celebrate their joys, or learn how they perceive this big, vast, challenging world. For over thirty years of my life, I've lived with them, but never for them, and most definitely not among them. And so I decided to pay attention, first to their joys at the Special Olympics and then to their perspective by learning from Margot, whose intentional community gathers people of all abilities to truly become that large, messy family.

I finally fell asleep with thoughts of family and empathy, anger and revenge, inadequacy and fear swirling in my mind.

The day of the Great Dressing-Down of the Racist Coach, I wore white. It made me feel confident and righteous. My husband, a White pastor, and I showed up early and were ushered into an office, where we sat across from the coach, the principal, who was a Latina woman, and my son's homeroom teacher, a White woman.

I listened to them deflect and demur.

"It's unclear that Coach Nelson said this, but *it is* clear that Tyson is upset."

Read: We don't really believe this happened, but we're afraid of your Black son's anger, so we're addressing the so-called event.

"From our investigation it seems there was a misunderstanding."

Read: We have a way of dealing with these types of kids. Your request for a meeting to get to the bottom of the issue is solidly getting in the way of our status quo.

"A misunderstanding we hope will clear up so that Tyson can go on to thrive here at Racist Coach–Hiring Junior High."

Read: This is all you'll get, Black mother, and you should be grateful. Get your child in order, or next time we won't be as nice.

The White homeroom teacher pulled out a few documents to show us that the students were learning about "diversity and the civil rights movement." She stumbled and paused every now and again, trying to avoid the land mines of a racially charged conversation. Then I noticed a small pen mark on the side of her hand as she turned the pages. I saw numbers and notes in black ink in her right palm, and when she placed those hands atop those papers on her lap, all I could think was, "Me too . . . I've got ink on my hands and too many thoughts in my mind and I'm showing up for this important meeting feeling completely overwhelmed. Maybe, just maybe, you're trying your best too."

I looked over at the coach, who honestly didn't emote at all, not a single wrinkle or frown. Hidden under his hat and fortified with his whistle and emboldened by his Whiteness, he just shrugged and said, "I'm sorry if Tyson thinks I don't like him; that's just not the case."

Read: This conversation makes me so uncomfortable. Make it stop. In fact, let me end it now with empirical truth and final statements.

As my White husband went toe-to-toe with the White coach about the history of that word and setting an example for the White students in that school, I zoned out and began thinking about something Margot has said about her diverse and deeply compassionate community. They decided early on to be intentionally diverse not for diversity's sake but because living with each other in their distinct differences teaches them how to be human. Fully. One hundred percent human. That's why we were in that room—the coach said a racist word to my son that dehumanized him and we were there to figure out how to restore some shred of my son's humanity so that he could continue attending that school in peace. Even still, the coach was human and I, clothed in my white sundress and mama fury, was not remembering that. I was curious—what would happen if I was fully human in this meeting? What would happen if I treated the coach as a potential friend and not a current enemy?

"Coach Nelson," I started, "I want you to know that it's been a hard year for Tyson. We've moved here from Boston and he's trying so hard to find his way. We're adjusting and he's looking to his teachers to know whether he's safe. I can't imagine when you became a teacher you ever intended to call a child a racial slur, but your comment made him feel unsafe. I'm just wondering, what would cause you to say something like that to a thirteen-year-old boy?"

Coach Nelson looked down and shrugged. "I honestly don't remember making that comment, but according to Tyson and other students, they heard me say it, so I'll accept responsibility. Listen: I'm a dad too. I never want any kid to feel unsafe at school. Will you tell Tyson I'm sorry for his pain?"

Read: I don't think I can give you what you want. Clearly something terrible is going on here, but I don't feel adequate to fix it, so here's a small offering.

I nodded in acceptance and we said our farewells while shaking hands and stapling documents.

On the drive home, we had to make a detour and we ended up passing the field where the Special Olympics had been held that past weekend. I remembered one kid's reaction to our standing on the sidelines cheering him on. We didn't know him and he didn't know us, but still his gratitude and acceptance were evident. He ran up to us for high fives and side hugs. This sweaty, beautiful teen was just so happy to see us, and we really didn't deserve it. We were not allies to the disabled community, we were not activists, or academics—we simply brought what little we had and he responded with open arms. The coach's apology was like our signs for the Special Olympics. It was all he had to offer, and I wondered—could I, an angry Black mama, invite him, an oblivious White man, in with open hands and acceptance? Could I be a peacemaker, seeking to believe the best and give the benefit of the doubt to this White man who had hurt me and my son?

❀　❀　❀

Lindsey paced on my porch with her hands thrown in the air. I'd frustrated her.

"Are you freaking kidding me, Osheta?"

"No, I've decided."

Lindsey was one of the only other Black parents at our middle school, and when I texted her that I wasn't going to pursue termination for Coach Nelson, she rushed right over because her pleas over text were left without a response from me. She could see I'd read them, but I didn't know how to tell her any more clearly— I was going to try to love the coach who called my son a horrific word. I was convinced that in this instance, grace was required of me. When I told her this to her face at my door, she stared at me with disbelief in her wide brown eyes. With her natural hair often pulled back in a colorful African print wrap, Lindsey always made me feel a little more proud of my Blackness and a little bit inadequate in my expression of it. Today, though, I was unmoved. Even by her righteous anger at the racism hurled at my biracial son.

"Osheta, how can you be so freaking irresponsible?! If you don't go to the school board, I will. Our kids cannot be subjected to this man."

"Lindsey, listen. Listen. I believe him that he wants to take responsibility. I believe them that they're going to try to do better. I want to give them a chance to make it right. Can you at least respect me enough to let me make the call about Coach Nelson? I'm trying to do what I believe is best here."

Lindsey shook her head and pulled out her phone. "I can find at least five other Black families who disagree with your 'wait and see' approach, and we'll be at the school door within an hour to demand Coach Nelson's job. We'd make the news! We'd make an example of him! Why don't you care enough about our people to rise up against this White nonsense?"

Lindsey scoffed and threw her phone back into her leather tote. "Osheta! People have died for our kids to go to public school and be safe and educated. You're wasting this moment. You're wasting an opportunity for change. What's the point of meeting with them if you weren't going to nail him to the freaking wall!"

I wish I could say that I gave some impassioned speech to Lindsey on my porch. One that spoke to my love for my Black community and my commitment to Jesus' nonviolent, enemy-love ethic. And how those values are not antithetical. I wish I told her about the pen on the teacher's hand and the shame in the coach's eyes and how the only thing I could offer with integrity was a peaceable, empathic response to those White authority figures who made terrible choices, but I didn't.

Maybe more accurately, I couldn't. This new peacemaking ethic toward White people was just blossoming within me. It wasn't even through its first trial run.

I was so disappointed by her anger directed toward me, another Black mother, that I shrugged and said something about needing to get a few essays edited or dinner in the oven, or my dog being needy. . . something, anything, to get me back into the safety of my apartment and my own thoughts. Curling up on my couch, I wondered:

*Am I being naive and stupid to give the administration the benefit of the doubt?*

*Should I go to the school with the other Black families and protest?*

*Was the coach sincere? Sincere enough?*

*What would Martin Luther King Jr. do?*

*Or maybe more importantly but equally cheesy, what would Jesus do?*

My dog joined me on the couch because I was the actual needy one. Fenway, with his impossibly short coat and adorable little face, wishes he were a bigger, fluffier dog. He nuzzled under my cheek as if to say, "It's okay, Doggy Mommy, cry right into the thinning, patchy terrier coat." I patted him with my markered hand and wondered, not for the first time, if

God's grace comes to us through creation more often than we give it credit for.

The tears fell because I honestly didn't know what to do: engaging with racism while trying to maintain my value of peacemaking is the hardest thing I've ever done. But I would not budge. I loved Lindsey and understood her very valid anger. I'd felt that anger just hours before in the principal's office, but one thing differs between me and Lindsey. I had spent the last ten years studying and committing myself to the peacemaking way of Jesus. I try my hardest to seek shalom and healing when I face conflict. Hate or retributive anger toward White people has no room in my heart.

Only love.

# Come to the Table

Dear White Peacemakers,

I have begun this introduction letter three times and deleted it three times. I keep seeing your faces. Mostly I keep seeing your eyes and the emotions you bring to this conversation on race at this moment of racial uprising. I see the fear. I see the confusion. I see the shame. I see the defensiveness. I see the fog of disinterest and the storm of discomfort. I see you. I also worry about you.

You watched George Floyd murdered before your eyes by a White police officer, you watched a viral video of Ahmaud Arbery hunted down and shot by a White father and his son, you held your phones in your hands doom-scrolling Twitter on January 6, 2021, as White supremacists stormed the U.S. Capitol holding Confederate flags and erecting a noose. And these are just the racialized events I can think of within the past six months.

With over four hundred years of the violence of white supremacy interwoven into American DNA, I'm sure your eyes may also have been filled with terror in response to learning about hundreds of instances of racism—the lynchings, the rapes, the expulsion of Black residents to create all-White communities, the silence of the White evangelical church, and so many more acts of harm toward Black, Indigenous, and people of color (BIPOC). America is sick with the sin of white supremacy, and when I sit across from you, White Peacemaker, and look into your eyes, I clearly see how overwhelmed you are. What you do in the dawn of racial awareness, when the scales fall from your eyes and you are beginning to see clearly, matters. I'm here to be your honest Black friend, your cheerleader, your companion, your sounding board. As I process how I've come to terms with my calling to practice peace as a Black woman, I hope the Holy Spirit meets you and inspires you, as a White person, to be a peacemaker for anti-racism. I hope you know that here you are loved and wanted.

I have spent my life in this unique ministry as a pastor, and as a teacher to White people at various places in their anti-racism journey, and have fielded questions of "Why?" "How?" "Is it really that bad?" "What can I do next?" This book is a collection of my answers, shared to encourage you along the way.

My friend Marcie is an anti-racism educator I look up to, and one thing I learned from her is that anytime she does the hard work of racial justice cross-culturally, she not only invites, but requires, her White friends to spend time in her home as they unpack concepts like white supremacy, white fragility, white saviorism, and white guilt. When I asked her why, she said, "Learning to sit in a space specifically curated by a Black woman with Black art and Black food and a

Black teacher is part of their dismantling of white supremacy. Not often are they expected to adjust to our ways of living, but you and I, as Black teachers to White people, are always adjusting to them. As an act of radical hospitality, we can offer them the comfort of our homes as they begin this uncomfortable work."

Consider this book an invitation to join me in my home for a few hours. If you were here in my home, we'd curl up on my couch with the fireplace going, and my two pets, Fenway, the most spoiled dog in the world, and Broadway, the most entitled cat in the world, would sit with us. I'd hand you books from my shelves from my favorite Black peacemaking thinkers: Toni Morrison, James Baldwin, Audre Lorde, Howard Thurman, and of course, Dr. Martin Luther King. Then we'd go to the table, where I'll serve you, not because I have to, but because I want to. At this table I'll serve you White Ally gumbo and rice. We'll take communion with honey cornbread and sweet tea. We'll celebrate the small wins with ice cream and apple cobbler. This is a space where you'll need to be fortified with good recipes and good humor because we're also going to be honest, breathtakingly honest, about the ways the knee of white supremacy has been on both our necks for centuries. At this table, you are seen as Beloved and your curiosity is honored. At this table, I'll be patient and I won't patronize you.

We'll talk about our collective calling to dismantle racism as we become Dr. King's vision for a community fully invested in each other because of a commitment to agape love: the Beloved Community. We'll spend more time on this later in the book, but making the Beloved Community my North Star in my anti-racism work has changed everything. It's the single most impactful and Christ-centering adjustment I've made in all my years of practicing shalom.

I've spent the last decade calling in the peacemakers to view their peacemaking in light of the Hebraic concept of shalom. I define it as God's dream for the world as it should be, nothing missing, nothing broken, everything made whole. Because shalom is God's dream and God is love, our shalom practices must be rooted in love. Therefore, I've invited peacemakers to resist peacekeeping that is rooted in anxiety and to choose peacemaking out of a posture of love. When love enters the equation, everything changes. We begin to ask ourselves what we're *for* instead of what we're *against*. We stop seeing other people as enemies. We let empathy tenderize our hearts. Our skin gets clearer, our hair gets shinier, and the Nobel Peace Prize committee comes knocking at our door. Okay, well maybe not those last three—I'm still waiting on all that. But from my experience, if I do not have love, if it's not the foundation on which I build my peacemaking practice, then I'm in grave danger.

This book you're holding in your hands is incredibly personal; I wrote it from my core conviction that peacemaking is partnering with God to create shalom and that the greatest calling for peacemakers in this moment is to practice anti-racism.

I am anti-racist because I want to actively dismantle ideas, thoughts, beliefs, and actions that say White people are superior to people of color and our ideas, thoughts, beliefs, and actions. This belief is called white supremacy, and it's dangerous not just to me, but to you as well, White Peacemaker.

I am a peacemaker because I want to embody these three paradigm-shifting teachings from Jesus:

1. "Love the Lord your God with all your heart and with all your soul and with all your mind" (Matthew 22:37). Peacemaking requires me to be my full, whole self. Shalom is

God's dream for me to be transformed by his love so that all aspects of myself, even myself in this Brown body, can flourish. My thoughts, my heart, my experiences, my perspective as a Black woman can be used to proclaim the love of God, but first peace and the making of it begins within. It begins with me dismantling any internalized racism—the sense that I am not good enough because I am not White. It begins with me looking at myself in the mirror as a Black woman and saying, "God did not make a mistake when he made you Black. Your Blackness is a gift from a God who loves you and desires to reveal more of himself to the world through you."

2. "Love your neighbor as yourself" (v. 39). My core dignity as a human is restored first by fully loving myself because God loved us first, and then from that overflow being able to truly, wholeheartedly love you, my White neighbor. This is why I've decided to treat you, White Peacemaker, just as Beloved as I treat myself. I want to create an environment where we can make peace together. This common bond of unity based on our love makes our peacemaking spectacular because we are becoming the Beloved Community in this world so influenced by white supremacy that our cross-cultural relationships are often expected to be dotted with vitriol and mistrust.

3. "Love your enemies, do good to those who hate you, bless those who curse you, pray for those who mistreat you" (Luke 6:27-28). This third way of approaching an enemy, someone who is just beyond my empathy, is a way that rejects passivity and violence. It requires courage to maintain my dignity and call it out in someone whom I want to humiliate. When White people do something that enacts harm on me and reveals how influenced by white supremacy they are, I will choose to love them. Love will look like addressing their actions, holding them accountable, and expecting change. Love may also look

like praying for them, encouraging them to do better, and setting healthy boundaries while they are still in-process around race and justice. Peace and the making of it transform the way I think of enemies, from monsters to fellow wounded humans trying to make their way in a dangerous world.

An anti-racism peacemaker, then, is a person who actively works toward a holistic restoration of the interpersonal and systemic effects of white supremacy through nonviolence and empathy. It's a way of doing this work that holds in tension systemic change and relational unity—grit and grace. When I think of grit, I lean into Angela Duckworth's work that describes grit as "passion and perseverance for very long-term goals."[1] Grace is both a posture and a promise to seek to understand and choose to love—even if it is costly. We'll talk more about how this third-way approach is necessary and how the current anti-racism frameworks don't always make room for this tension.

This book is an invitation to approach your anti-racism work in a way that follows Jesus, Prince of Peace, man acquainted with sorrows, flipper of tables, and King of kings, who overcame sin and death on the cross not by power-over dominion but by power-under love. As a person devoted to understanding why Jesus was so obsessed with the kingdom of God, it only makes sense that I would want to find some way to map kingdom ethics onto our current call to become anti-racists.

Jesus lived, taught, and modeled the way of his kingdom. He began his ministry proclaiming, "The kingdom of God has come near. Repent and believe the good news!" (Mark 1:15). This was good news indeed—the peacemaking kingdom had come and Jesus was prepared to teach us how to live its countercultural ways.

White supremacy is a cultural influence that has invaded every aspect of Western life—healthcare, education, housing, and policing are just a few areas where we've seen it flare up in the past few years. We've seen how it not only affects Black and Brown people in our lived experiences, but also blinds and buffers White people from reality. It keeps you blissfully ignorant of the suffering of non-White peoples and brashly arrogant when we deign to ask to be treated as fellow Beloveds.

It's pernicious and insidious, and in this book I hope I give you the nudge you need to say, "No more will I be duped."

In the summer of 2020, an Atlanta pastor revealed how white supremacy can influence even a good, godly, well-meaning man. "We understand the curse that was slavery," he said in a panel called "The Beloved Community." "White people do, and we say that was bad. But we miss the blessing of slavery, that it actually built up the framework for the world that White people live in."

And the Internet went wild. The backlash was swift. Many thoughtful pastors pushed back on him to help him consider the harmful impact of his statement. As I watched the whole thing unfold, I had a deep desire to come alongside this White Peacemaker, a man who truly loves Jesus, is committed to justice, and cares about the kingdom of God.

The problem I saw in the ways he spoke about racism in our country was that he talked about it within a curse/blessing framework, or a reframing of words and concepts that make us uncomfortable in order to make this hard work palatable—when that's not what we're dealing with at all. We are partnering with Jesus to do the work of the cross—bringing an end to enmity and restoring relationships. This is gonna be hard, it's gonna be scary, and we have to call it what it is. In all my years of study and conversations about racism,

I've learned that unless we address the issue as it truly is, we cannot dismantle it.

We are dealing with a culture formed for, reinforced by, and built to protect the lie of white supremacy.

Mark Charles and Soong-Chan Rah, in *Unsettling Truths: The Ongoing, Dehumanizing Legacy of the Doctrine of Discovery*, say,

> Many authors, professors, pastors, and social justice leaders and organizations (both Christian and secular) who are considered to be on the forefront on the racial dialogue frequently use the term "white privilege." However, the word *privilege* suggests that the inequality that favors white people is actually a blessing which they must learn to share. The term white privilege perpetuates an implicit bias. Whiteness is neither a privilege nor a blessing to be shared, it is a diseased social construct that needs to be confronted.[2]

White supremacy has informed our culture to ensure that everything White is right. White forms of communication are validated as intelligent and clever, White bodies are worth celebrating and protecting, White legacies must be passed on, White wealth must be generated and shrewdly managed. Because European settlers built this country, white supremacy culture is the American culture. Nestled in every aspect of American culture is the preservation of the social construct of Whiteness.

We cannot adequately address any of the systematic problems we see: the police brutality, the wealth gap, the lack of trust between communities of color and White authority figures, the intended segregation of the Sunday hour or even worse, the lack of cultural diversity in our "multiethnic" churches, unless we call out white supremacy as the primary influencer of this culture. And if we want to dismantle it, then we need a countercultural strategy to do so. A strategy that celebrates all people, a strategy that forces you, White Peacemaker, to evaluate how you've been influenced by white supremacy and how you can find your identity as a Beloved person whom God made with European features. The most heartbreaking thing I hear from a White Peacemaker is, "I'm just White." No! You're not just White; you were intentionally made to live confidently in your skin by a good God. Every single person on this planet is a reflection of the image of God, *imago Dei*. What's not good is how this culture has codified your expression of the *imago Dei* and nullified mine. This is our work together, White Peacemaker: to reclaim humanity for both of us and create a counterculture that actively exposes and resists the violence of white supremacy culture.

This book argues that Jesus' invitation to the kingdom of God is good news for those of us suffering under the oppression of white supremacy—both you and me—if we have the courage to resist its various forms of violence with alternative practices of peace, like humility, prayer, loving those beyond our empathy, reconciliation, seeking justice, and generosity.

And while I know you may wonder, "Hold up, Osheta—when did Jesus talk specifically about racism in the Bible?," I want to caution you from using this as an out from engaging in anti-racism work. The short answer is Jesus did not explicitly speak of the kind of racial divisions we experience today, but what he did offer was infinitely more valuable. Jesus offered a new ethical framework for relationships that creates true peace, shalom, for all involved. His framework that has endured through the years and can be applied at any point in history, in any cultural context, is the Sermon on the Mount. As Glen Stassen and David Gushee encourage in *Kingdom*

*Ethics,* "Ours is a time of global encounter and cultural diversity, and that requires adaptability. 'Character ethics moves the focus from rules and acts to agents and their contexts.' Therefore, it is more aware of social context, the dynamics of history, and 'our need to respond to each situation's specific features.'"[3] What if we approached the Sermon on the Mount as a conversation about the ethics of this world versus the ethics of the kingdom? Then we can seek guidance and allow it to inform our anti-racism peacemaking.

The Sermon on the Mount is a faithful herald of the kingdom of God, and Jesus shows us how to live under his reign as peacemakers. Our calling is to be like him and run toward brokenness in this world. So, Dear White Peacemaker, I'm running toward you because I see how damaging white supremacy has been to your experiencing God's shalom. I'm hoping you'll run toward the stories of brokenness found in these pages, too. I'll share how I've missed the mark in my own attempt to practice anti-racism peacemaking and how I've been wounded by White people who just don't get it or don't want to get it. These are not indictments, my Beloved friend. They are indicators that the world needs us to show up. I live in the reality of white supremacy every single day, and so I'm inviting you in. James Baldwin says in an essay, "Dark Days," "To be black was to confront, and to be forced to alter, a condition forged in history. To be white was to be forced to digest a delusion called white supremacy. Indeed, without confronting the history that has either given white people an identity or divested them of it, it is hardly possible to any who thinks of himself as white to know what a black person is talking about at all."[4] I will not insult your intelligence or limit your capacity to create shalom by not trusting you with this truth—you need to become really comfortable acknowledging white supremacy's influence so that you can be effective in dismantling it. It is the only way we can mortify this sin and move forward together.

In these pages, we're going to look at Jesus' primary teaching, the Sermon on the Mount, to help us understand our anti-racism in light of two themes:

1. Jesus' kingdom ethics, beginning with his proclamation of the upside-down social order in the Beatitudes and continuing to sayings that challenge our imaginations for how to live into this peculiar way.

2. How those ethics help us actively dismantle white supremacy culture by understanding its various characteristics: perfectionism, a sense of urgency, defensiveness, valuing quantity over quality, worship of the written word, belief in only one right way, paternalism, either/or thinking, power hoarding, fear of open conflict, individualism, the belief that progress is bigger and more, a belief in objectivity, and claiming a right to comfort.

I want to tell you a little bit more about the weirdness of this book. It's not a systemic theology, it's a shalom story, so I'll cover some of the Sermon on the Mount not necessarily in the order that Jesus taught it in Matthew 5, but more as it flows with my story of becoming an anti-racism peacemaker. *Dear White Peacemakers* is about racial healing, and as we know from the best trauma therapists, healing is never linear.

Since this is a table set for White Peacemakers curated by a Black Peacemaker, we're going to use the Negro Spirituals as our guides. I love the Spirituals. They were the primary way enslaved peoples communicated their history and their hardships. Within the Spirituals' lyrics, my ancestors shared their subversive strategies of fleeing their enslavement and

resistance to the violence enacted on their bodies and minds
on an hourly basis even as they worked under the nose of
their White masters. We must be subversive and strategic in
our anti-racism, but we also must pay attention to our spiritual formation, so four Spirituals will lead us to the freedom
of the Beloved Community: "Wade in the Water," "There Is
a Balm in Gilead," "Down by the Riverside (Ain't Gonna
Study War No More)," and "Ain't Gonna Let Nobody Turn
Me Around."

Part 1 of this book is "Wade in the Water." Before we can
dismantle white supremacy, we must be troubled by all the
ways it has worked its way into our everyday lives. Comfort
and avoidance of conflict are characteristic of white supremacy culture that prevents us from looking like Jesus' sacrificial
love. We must engage with the problems of white supremacy
culture. We must acknowledge the harm it has done in you
and me, and we must be like the great number of disabled people sitting by the pool of Bethesda in John 5. The water was
known to have healing properties—especially when the waters
were stirring. Common knowledge suggested that the healing
came from the flutter of the wings of angels of the Lord. Jesus
came upon these people waiting for the water to be troubled
and asked one man in particular, "Do you want to be healed?"
Do you want to be healed of the ways white supremacy has
dehumanized you? Part 1 is about healing, healing from the
effects of white supremacy together.

It's also a call to leave the plantation of comfort and
privilege. Harriet Tubman taught enslaved people the lyrics
of "Wade in the Water" to teach them that when they leave
the plantation it's going to be hard. It's going to be terrifying,
especially as the hounds of the master come to bring them
back into their oppression, but when they come wade in the

water where the hunters can no longer detect them, they can make their way to freedom. Part 1 is a reminder to wade in the waters of your Belovedness because the hounds of white supremacy are ever at your heels. You must make your way to freedom. To long for freedom, we'll look at the culture of Jesus' kingdom as compared to the culture we live in that is steeped in white supremacy.

Part 2 is "There Is a Balm in Gilead." White supremacy culture is a culture of objectivity that de-emphasizes emotions and places a high value on facts, data, and the written word. However, anti-racism peacemaking is the work of solidarity and shared suffering—it's not perfect, it's not efficient, and this kind of healing takes incredible patience and vulnerability. Jesus begins the Sermon on the Mount announcing that those who have suffered are seen. White Peacemakers, you are called to be part of God's humanizing work of weeping with those in pain, but to do this you must be willing to see. Before we can work together we must grieve together. Part 2 will unpack some of the ways white supremacy has blinded you to the pain of communities of color and give you ideas of how to partner with God to weep with us in our suffering.

Part 3 is "Down by the Riverside." White supremacy is a system that relies on and perpetuates violence. It's just that plain and simple. In order to assure dominance and submission, White people in authority have not only been allowed but encouraged to use violence to maintain a social order in which White people are always protected, always believed, and will always thrive. The kingdom is a peacemaking, non-violent kingdom; in fact, Jesus says, "Those who live by the sword will die by the sword." The way of the kingdom is the way of nonviolent, direct, peacemaking action. It's just that plain and simple. In part 3 I will address the defensiveness that you may feel when you are called fragile and show you how this humble place is actually a gift.

Part 4 is "Ain't Gonna Let Nobody Turn Me Around." White supremacy culture is a power-hoarding, inflexible way that continually asks you to prove your worth. This can cause you so much distress. I've seen it. If I had a nickel for every time a White person asked me, "Well, what can I do?" I'd have enough for my own in-house Starbucks-level coffee bar—to which I'd invite you over to have a cup and we'd talk about how this incessant need to prove yourself shows me how vulnerable you are to the overwhelming outcome orientation of white supremacy. When you're overwhelmed, White Peacemaker, you are often tempted to overwork yourself or opt out of the work altogether, and it makes so much sense—you can't quantify your peacemaking, so why even try? White supremacy culture relies on apathy and discouragement. The kingdom of God, however, is a relational kingdom, one where small acts of grace and love have incredible impact. So part 4 is the most practical part of the book. It's where I'll offer you some insights on reclaiming the idea of white privilege as your unique calling to use what the enemy intends to harm you (the exposure of white privilege and how it affects you) for good (leveraging this privilege to create flourishing for others).

You will not get the hero's narrative from me: I used to be a hot mess and now I'm all put together. No, White Peacemaker, I'm still very much in process, doing the work, living the work, hoping God will take my small daily offerings of peace and create lasting shalom.

This book is a collection of peacemaking wins and losses from me and White Peacemakers I deeply respect. You'll walk alongside me as I take steps toward healing and make retreats after offenses. Some of the chapters will begin with a "Dear White Peacemakers" letter.

I've been writing letters for over two years now.

When I wrote my very first one and posted it online, it was in response to a nonprofit that seeks to end poverty in developing countries. I attended their gala where they used a Spiritual for their fundraising campaign but stripped it of its African American historical context. You'll hear more about how I had a conversation with one of their founders about my discomfort at that event, but when I wrote my first letter to White people calling you "Dear White Peacemakers," I couldn't get over how perfectly that incident reflected the problem at hand: good and well-meaning White people attempting to do the work of justice, maybe even racial justice, but causing unintentional harm.

My tentative offering to encourage White Peacemakers as they practice anti-racism peacemaking unexpectedly took off. Thousands of White people committed to anti-racism have read, shared, and written me back. I didn't know you were all out there looking for someone to help you along.

So, going forward, you will be my Dear White Peacemakers:

*Dear* because we belong to each other. The night Jesus was taken away, he prayed for the Father to unify us in the same way they were unified. This love is what theologians call "perichoresis." It's what is commonly known as the Trinity. It's an indwelling, interconnected, ever-trusting, overflowing love, and that's what Jesus prayed for us hours before being tortured, betrayed, humiliated, and nailed to a cross. That means I belong to you and you belong to me. This is a love letter first and foremost to my White siblings who want to be called *in* when you've felt like you've only been called *out* for your fragility, for your privilege, for your inability to fully understand what it's like for people of color. This book is your "olly olly oxen free!" Come out from hiding and come on in, my friend. I'm tired of playing this game where you're always on the losing end. We have much to talk about.

*White* because it's so important for us to know what experts identify as your "social location." Who you are in your body, in this moment, matters. It matters that God did not make a mistake in giving you your social location. If you identify as White, then you also need to know how to identify the unique ways you're vulnerable to white supremacy. This book will help you with that.

When I teach racism to mostly White, middle-aged, affluent people genuinely curious about anti-racism, I cover three things in our intro class:

1. I emphasize that "racism" can be thought of as what Paul describes in Ephesians 6:12: "For we wrestle not against flesh and blood, but against principalities, against powers, against the rulers of the darkness of this world, against spiritual wickedness in high places" (KJV). Racism is a "principality and power" that we must resist. It is a byproduct of a white supremacy culture. In the same way we build up stamina to resist pride or envy, we must build up stamina to resist racism. William Stringfellow, a lawyer, lay theologian, and White Peacemaker during the civil rights movement, said, "The realities to which the biblical term 'principalities and powers' refer are quite familiar to modern society, though they may be called by different names. What the Bible calls 'principalities and powers' are called in contemporary language 'ideologies,' 'institutions,' and 'images.'"[5] White supremacy is an ideology that fortifies institutions and is enshrined in narratives that celebrate people who look like you and dehumanize people who look like me.

2. Because we wrestle not against flesh and blood, then my response to White people in this work can only be radical empathy. Therefore, I never call White people racist. I always make the distinction that if you are White, you are not immune to the oppressive system of racism—it just affects you differently—and so my hope is that as you read this book and learn of how Whiteness has made it difficult for you and me to fully practice shalom, you'll know that I'm on your side. In some chapters, we'll talk about the traumas you experience in this work, because as one pastor says, "If we're not called to fight each other then we're called to fight for each other."

3. Racism must be dismantled because it is in direct opposition to the kingdom of God. Jesus is our King of Peace who brokered our shalom through sacrificial love in his life, death, and resurrection. Ephesians 2:14 says, "He himself is our peace, who has made the two groups one and has destroyed the barrier, the dividing wall of hostility." The cross of Jesus is where grit and grace met perfectly and the world turned upside down. Enemies were forgiven, outcasts brought into paradise, the foolishness of dying became the wisdom of a resurrected life, one that bears the wounds but heals even still.

Lastly, I call you *Peacemakers* because that's who we are. I chose to call you "White Peacemakers" and not just "White people" because I am rooting for you. I believe God has something incredible for you in this moment. I'm not playing around when I say that this work here is kingdom work. We are breaking down walls, building bridges to each other, and dismantling white supremacy brick by jagged brick. So, hey there, Peacemaker. I'm so glad you're here.

At the end of most chapters you'll find a breath prayer. When the pandemic started, I began showing up on Instagram Live every morning between six and eight to read a short

Scripture, check in with my followers, and pray. I wanted to do something short and subversive to resist the anxiety caused by a deadly respiratory disease, so I decided to end each time with a collective breath prayer exercise. The group started out with twenty people, and at the height of it two hundred women were showing up every morning to pray together. Every morning, I'd say, "Welcome to Morning Breath Prayers," and every morning I'd comment how we needed a better name because it assumed all of us were waking up and praying to the Lord with stinky breath, so somehow between jokes in the comments and me confessing my love for dragons, we became the Dragon Breath Prayer Warriors. So, each chapter has a breath prayer. A short, one-sentence prayer that is made of two parts: a name for God that is meaningful and a request from God for that moment.

I care about your spiritual formation, Peacemaker. I want you to know that you have the spiritual practices and techniques you need to ground you as you work. I'm not worried about you having enough calls to action or opportunities to do the work. I wonder, though, do you have the skills you need— are you living into the work? Are you being made whole as you dismantle white supremacy? Breath prayers are one short, realistic practice to help.

I'm also going to capitalize the word White when I refer to you. I do this for two reasons: my capitalizing White as I write this book reminds me of your intrinsic worth to God. You are a human being. You are Beloved. You as a White person are not intrinsically bad or a mistake. I capitalize to remind me to honor you in the same way I hope you'll honor me as a Black person. I also capitalize because I ascribe to the idea that capitalizing Black but not White is another form of normalizing Whiteness. When White is the standard, then there's really no need to denote it. White is not the standard. Human is the standard. Beloved is the standard. Made in the image of God is the standard. I capitalize because I want you to reckon with the loss of cultural identity. Historian Nell Irvin Painter writes, "White Americans have had the choice of being something vague, something unraced and separate from race. A capitalized 'White' challenges that freedom, by unmasking 'Whiteness' as an American racial identity as historically important as "Blackness"—which it certainly is."[6]

I want you to begin thinking of the constant lure toward neutrality and colorblindness as being as dangerous as the sin God warns Cain of, which is always "crouching at your door." Scales are falling from our eyes, remember? We must see and be comfortable acknowledging our social locations.

We'll cover so much, friends. My hope is this book will invite you into hundreds of different ways of anti-racism peacemaking.

So, come to the table, Beloved. Know that you belong here, and lemme top off your coffee for you.

As Alexis Rose says in the television series *Schitt's Creek*, "I love this journey for you."

Peace,
Osheta

# Wade in the Water

# 1

# God's Gonna Trouble the Water

*Fleeing White Supremacy*

I once heard a story about Harriet Tubman that I'm sure is exaggerated and therefore mythologized. Quite often in the retelling of their stories our favorite heroes move from ordinary people who were brave enough to show up in extraordinary circumstances to superhuman dissidents the likes of which we'll never be. This story is about one of Harriet Tubman's trips to lead a group of enslaved people to the North. After a few days of traveling, they heard hounds baying and in pursuit, so they moved their caravan to the river, where they hid for several days, slowly trudging in the water, taking rests when they could, keeping an ear out for the barking of the dogs and the galloping of the slave patrol horses. They were hungry, thirsty, sore, and cold. The mothers did their best to quietly comfort whiny children. The group was tense—anxious as they made their way to freedom, exhausted from the hard journey. "Wade in the Water," they knew, told them to stay in the water so as to confuse the bloodhounds used to track them—but singing something on the plantation while you harvest and process the cotton and actually living it are two very different things.

Wading is messy. Wading is dangerous. Wading is confusing. Wading often makes you long for the solid ground of the plantation—at least that's a discomfort you're used to. One man stopped abruptly and the procession behind him stuttered to a halt. Some of his fellow journeyers fell into the water, making a dangerously loud splash. Harriet whipped around and glared at the man. "Hush now," she hissed. The man, dripping with water and rage, walked up to Harriet and announced he was leaving the group. He was done. He would go back to the plantation and throw himself at the mercy of the master, and whatever fate would become him had to be better than this hard slog to the "promised land." Harriet looked around at the group and knew that if this man went back, if he got out of the water and alerted the men searching for them of his presence, the whole group, herself included, would be done for. The story goes on to say, Harriet pulled a gun from the pocket of her skirts, pointed it squarely at the man's forehead, and said, "You have a choice, then: die now or keep walking. We're getting to freedom and you will not stop us." Harriet cocked her weapon and waited. The others in the group began to whisper their pleas for him to stay—some appealed to his sense of self-preservation, "You don't want to die," some reminded him of the ways the overseers beat him mercilessly, some begged him to not cause a ruckus and get them all caught. Harriet stood quiet and resolved, revolver ready. The man looked around and realized that suffering together for the sake of freedom was far better than dying in that river, so he held his hands up, apologized to Harriet Tubman, his Moses from the oppression of the plantation, and got back in line, wading in the water—even though it cost him his comfort and even though he had very little hope for the journey.

Dear White Peacemaker, in a lot of ways, you're like the exhausted and discouraged man. You've looked around and seen how we cannot ignore race anymore. It's no longer enough to be polite, you've got to be proactive, and so you've left the plantation of white supremacy! You're making your way out of that mindset—however, when you run into trouble (when, not if), you're tempted to give up, to chalk up your zeal for freedom as a phase. Like the man, you want to turn back— you're unsure why you even left to begin with. He lacked vision for life without the oppression of white supremacy, and sometimes, White Peacemaker, you do too—even though it's keeping you sick, it's a sickness you're comfortable with.

I worry, friend, that you're building a legalistic practice of "read this, say this, protest here," which is always shame-laden and hustle-bound. Belovedness, however, undoes our striving and proving, and if there is one thing white supremacy reinforces, it is a scarcity mindset of identity and worth. This is partly why you're exhausted, my friend. You're constantly proving your worth and unsure how to measure your efficacy. Instead, the only thing you should be focused on is owning your Belovedness, proclaiming my Belovedness, and working to become the Beloved Community.

In part 1 of this book, we're going to look at one of the chief dangers of white supremacy culture: how it systematically and subtly strips you of your God-given Belovedness and its gracious lens of your identity—because before we can get to the kingdom ethics of the Sermon on the Mount, we need to wade in the water where we are baptized Belovedness.

**2**

# Your Name Is Not Racist, It's Beloved

One Friday, two years ago, I sat by a lake at sunset deeply troubled. Goldenrod, purple, and crimson rays reflected across the lake's still surface. For a split second I wondered if I should capture it with my phone. Maybe save it for a day when my life seemed anything but radiant and still so I could post it to social media with some calming quote, poem, or if on that day I wanted the world to believe I'm pious, a Scripture passage.

I wasn't still (or particularly pious even) by that Georgia lake, because violence was brewing in my belly. It was circling in my mind. Animating my fingers as they thrummed on my tree log bench. I wanted to unleash it. I wanted to contain it. I wanted it to empower me because I felt so incredibly powerless.

I was on a seven-day trip with a group of White people who wanted to know *why*.

Why is the church tackling such a divisive issue as race, one that surely brings more conflict than peace?

Why is our country so bound up in this cycle of uncivility?

Why are Black people so angry all the time?

Why is this even my problem? I'm White.

Why don't communities of color trust the police?

Why. Why. Why. Why.

That whole week I fielded questions and walked alongside them through civil rights museums and southern courthouses. We learned how almost everything in our world—education, housing, policing, media, laws, and even the church—has been influenced by the violence of white supremacy.

And the whole time I wondered, "When we get back home, will you still care? When you're no longer standing under concrete slabs with the names of lynched Black people, will you still care? When we're not standing in front of a wall of jarred dirt, all from places where the blood of innocent Black citizens seeped into the ground after White hands beat, shot, or stabbed them, will you still care?" We learned that sometimes, these extrajudicial executions happened on front lawns of churches with the pastor nursing a tall glass of lemonade while his parishioners bent their knees to the gods of scarcity and hate. I looked at this group of White Christian men and women and wondered, "How does this knowledge affect your commitment to Jesus, a man who suffered his own brutal and excruciating extrajudicial execution? Does it at all?"

Spending days gazing at our horrific past made me angry at White people in a way I never thought possible. All those pictures of White people committing various acts of violence toward people of color did the thing I feared it would—*I* began to hate *them*. White supremacy's violence was getting inside of me.

I wanted to serve them just a teaspoon of the gallons of internalized hate this world has force-fed me.

I wanted my anger to exact some form of vengeance—so very badly.

I wanted every White person on the trip to suffer—and while I couldn't enact on their pale bodies the kinds of things my ancestors endured, I could use the only power I had—I was their leader. Their teacher. The person entrusted with their anti-racism training for that week. And because this was a group of progressive-ish Christians: I could make them feel so incredibly bad. I could wield my moral authority as the Black leader in the group. I could manipulate them with shame and anger.

I knew how to do it, too. The next day we were going to have an extended check-in. I could prepare a discussion time that would make them feel the weight of the shame of their White skin. I could sneer "privilege" like an accusation and proclaim them "fragile" as if it were a death sentence. I would tell them my hard stories, my painful experiences with White people, and then expect them to atone for the collective sins of *all White people*. Repent for *their* aggressions, own *their* mistakes. White sin-eaters . . . that is what I could make them into. And they, wanting to be "woke," wanting to not seem like racists, wanting to be the ally and not the problem, would take it. They would take in my violence.

A fish leaped from the water and snapped at the fly hovering right above the surface, sinking back into the lake, her belly a little fuller. There's something nourishing about violence, I thought—even if just for a moment.

I was in danger of a kind of just war theory–approach to anti-racism that says I get to use violence in thought, word, and even deed toward White people to accomplish my end goal of a world free of violence to Black and Brown bodies. It did not sit well with me as I sat by the lake. This group trusted me to be a faithful shepherd primarily because of my commitment to Jesus the Good Shepherd.

In my heart, they were not my siblings, they were just beyond empathy because of their White skin—somehow on that justice journey, they became my enemy.

As the sun set and the moon came more clearly into view, I decided to sit with my violent impulses until the stars came out. "Only in darkness can you see the stars," said Dr. Martin Luther King in the last speech he would give before his assassination. I thought with a chuckle, "Where are the stars when the darkness is within you?"

I texted a friend before heading back to the group to call it a night and wrestle with my violence in my tent. "It's like the violence I've seen our people suffer has gotten on the inside of me," I wrote. "Pray for me. I want to love these White people, but I'm not sure I've got it in me anymore."

My friend, a gorgeous Black woman who specifically prayed for me to not be derailed from my calling to teach that group peacemaking alongside anti-racism, texted back, "I've got you, Sis." With a heart emoji and a star. She also sent a gif of Whitney Houston from the musical *Cinderella* because she loves me and knows fairy godmother Whitney makes everything better.

The last day of the trip was a Saturday morning, and we were all wrung out. Spent from being too close to each other in a fifteen-passenger van, pulling into campgrounds to set up after a day full of learning, processing, grieving, dialoguing about race in our country. The small joys we had were a comedy playlist from Spotify and meal breaks where we stretched our legs and made sandwiches from the coolers in the back of the van.

My small joys were a Frappuccino and white powdered donuts that I balanced in my hands while adjusting my hat that said "Nah. Rosa Parks 1955"—my own pre-trip passive aggressive purchase to fortify me for the journey. I remember the day I bought it, y'all . . . it's true, when it came, I danced around my house and ran to show it to my husband, a White man listening to The Roots while he worked on his sermon at our dining table.

"Look! Look! It's here!" I waved the heather gray baseball cap in the air and ceremoniously placed it on my head. "Isn't it the best?"

T. C. rested his headphones on his neck and squinted to read the writing on my hat.

"Nah. Rosa Parks 1955." He smirked and nodded. "Clever. So that's the hat you're going to wear on the trip?"

He knew I was worried about my hair over seven days of traveling, camping (especially in the inclement weather forecasted), and walking around in the South with all its curly hair–challenging humidity, so I told him I needed a really cute baseball cap to accessorize the puffy ponytail I was sure to have by day two.

"Yeah. It's perfect because it's exactly how I'm feeling about these White people. Nah. I'm not going to overextend myself on this trip. Nah . . . I'm not going to pull punches about how terrible racism is in our country and how they don't get to be complicit about it anymore. Nah . . . White people! Nah. I'm going to push them every single waking moment. We don't have time to play anymore, babes! Black children are dying over toy guns and loud music." I put the hat on my head and did my best Janet Jackson "What Have You Done for Me Lately" head wobble. Nah. This Black woman was done.

❀   ❀   ❀

I was adjusting my hat to block the sun when I noticed Aimee out of the corner of my eye. She was slumped against the side of the gas station, her phone clutched in her hand. She was more than exhausted, she was devastated. My first thought was, "Good. She looks in this moment how I feel every single day." I started to move toward the van when I remembered a line from a song I love that says we're all stardust, walking constellations on this Earthen land.

I looked at Aimee, and as clear as I have ever sensed God's conviction, I felt the Spirit say, "She is my Beloved and she doesn't feel like it. This week has made her question her Belovedness as a White person."

Stars in the darkness. "Here's where the stars are," I thought, remembering my prayer by the lake.

I walked over to Aimee and put my precious snacks on that hot concrete and wrapped my arms around her.

Aimee wrapped her arms around me almost instantaneously, melting into and clinging to me, as I cooed in her ear, "Shh . . . it's okay . . . You're going to be okay . . . We're going to be okay . . ."

My friend Sarah asks every morning, "God, how do you want to mother me?" and as I hugged Aimee I asked God a similar question. "Mother God, how can I care for your Beloved daughter today?"

*Just love her and allow yourself to be unguarded.*

So that's what I did. I hugged her for as long as she needed and let myself receive her White tears. I chose to love her by being present in her pain even though I'm told Black women who give their maternal instincts to White women are playing into the mammy caricature. A horrible narrative used to calcify White empathy for enslaved people says that all Black enslaved women were happy to serve White people. Our relentless compassion and forgiveness make us nothing more than large-bosomed, placating, enslaved women committed to the everlasting comfort of White people, often at our own expense. In the Jim Crow era this notion was used to support the political, economic, and social disenfranchisement of Black people.

I hugged Aimee even though I'm told to protect my Blackness at all costs because White people, especially White women, will always come for it.

But I could feel the anger, the disregard, the lack of empathy within me toward another human being, and its ferocity scared me. So, in that moment, I chose to disarm my violence and hug Aimee. I hugged her because I wanted to. I am not the mammy forced to put on a fake smile for White people, I was a Beloved daughter tasked to call in my sister from the cold of self-hatred. I *chose* to love her, and that made all the difference. I chose to put down my bitterness, put down my anxiety, and put down my fears to love her. This is the kind of love Jesus showed us on the cross, did he not? He made himself uncomfortable for the sake of others. He gave up his right to power-over dominion to model power-under love. This kind of downward mobility to grace enlarged my heart as I hugged Aimee. I choose to love her, a fellow star, and our little huddle by the side of a country convenience store became a constellation of peace that dismantled the violence of racism within me with grit and grace.

❀   ❀   ❀

It seems odd to begin a book on peacemaking and race on Belovedness. I know. You probably expected me to begin unpacking police brutality or give you a history lesson about Bacon's Rebellion in 1676 that instigated the social construct of race. I could start there, but it wouldn't help you one single bit, because white supremacy cannot be boiled down to a single event. It often hides in between the lines of data and to-do lists that distract us from the work of becoming human.

White supremacy, however, is a violation of our God-given identities as human beings . . . not human doings. We were made to reflect the generous, self-giving love of God. When God breathed into the first human, igniting his soul with divine love, God never expected us to prove our worth or fight for significance. We were already worthy. We were already significant. Out of a striving to prove ourselves to God, sin entered into the world, and it not only introduced an anxiety of what God believes about our inherent identities, but also fueled the flames of competition between image bearers. We've seen this play out generation after generation, and, Peacemaker, our current iteration is that of racism and the lie of white supremacy. When you really begin paying attention and realize that so much of what you've been taught about race relations has been tainted and skewed by white supremacy, I know it can feel like the ground is being pulled right out from under you. Belovedness is a sure ground on which you can stand.

And, listen, if there's one thing I'm so over talking about, it's Belovedness. It seems that it has become the Jesus juke of modern Christians.

Do you feel anxious about your calling? Know you are Beloved.

Ever wake up in the morning with a case of the grumpies? Remind yourself of your Belovedness and turn that frown upside down!

When was the last time you felt true joy? Can't remember? Well, look in the mirror, say "I'm Beloved" three times, and wink. Ahh, there you are, Beloved, in whom God is well pleased. Now take on the day, tiger!

Belovedness is not a foreign idea to us. When I first was introduced to the concept taught by priest and theologian Henri Nouwen in *Life of the Beloved*, it felt very tone-deaf and unrealistic for those of us on the margins or struggling with "real world problems." In the ways I've seen Belovedness applied to our spiritual formation, it's always individualistic. "God calls me Beloved." "I am Beloved." White supremacy culture is a highly individualistic culture, so no thank you. Why then do I base my anti-racism education on encouraging White people to own their Belovedness?

Because without Belovedness, all you have to build your identity on are the lies of white supremacy. When you are held up in a system as superior and right simply because of the color of your skin, then you must live up to a certain standard of excellence and you expect a certain level of comfort. Owning your Belovedness because it's evidence of a reality where God's unconditional grace and love are the standard and not some arbitrary social construct is an essential act of resistance to the dehumanization of white supremacy.

And if you don't ground your anti-racism work in your Belovedness, then you're in danger of being like Aimee— exposed to so many reminders of the violence caused by White people that you internalize hatred in your skin.

When I begin any anti-racism class, I begin with a lesson on Belovedness because I've seen so many White people reject

their Belovedness, thinking they are rejecting white supremacy. But all they're doing is practicing what Nouwen calls
"self-rejection":

> Yes, there is that voice, the voice that speaks from above
> and from within and that whispers softly or declares loud-
> ly: "You are my Beloved, on you my favor rests." It cer-
> tainly is not easy to hear that voice in a world filled with
> voices that shout: "You are no good, you are ugly; you are
> worthless; you are despicable, you are nobody—unless you
> can demonstrate the opposite."
>
> These negative voices are so loud and so persistent that
> it is easy to believe them. That's the great trap. It is the trap
> of self-rejection. Over the years I've come to realize that the
> greatest trap in our life is not success, popularity, or power,
> but self-rejection. . . .
>
> When we have come to believe in the voices that call
> us worthless and unlovable, then success, popularity, and
> power are easily perceived as attractive solutions. The real
> trap, however, is self-rejection. As soon as someone accus-
> es or criticizes me. As soon as I am rejected, left alone, or
> abandoned, I find myself thinking, "Well, that proves once
> again that I am a nobody." . . . My dark side says, "I'm no
> good. . . . I deserve to be pushed aside, forgotten, rejected
> and abandoned." . . .
>
> Self-rejection is the greatest enemy of spiritual life be-
> cause it contradicts the sacred voice that calls us the Be-
> loved. Being the Beloved constitutes the truth of our
> existence.[1]

We often stop at our understanding of Belovedness as that
internal adjustment to live a more peaceful and gentle life, but
Belovedness is a powerful weapon used by the Spirit for reconciliation. Nouwen goes on to say,

> The Spirit of God, the Spirit that calls us the Beloved, is the
> Spirit that unites and makes us whole. There is no clearer

way to discern the presence of God's Spirit than to identify the movements of unification, healing, restoration, and reconciliation. Wherever the Spirit works, decisions vanish and inner as well as outer unity manifests itself.[2]

What the world needs are more White Peacemakers, who know they are Beloved by a loving God and from that overflow seek the Belovedness of others. This is the part of Belovedness we often overlook. This is why I begin with Belovedness, because anti-racism is the work of reclaiming this essential part of our humanity.

After the justice trip down South, I began integrating Belovedness into my work with White Peacemakers as part of their anti-racism education. One of my students in my "Reconciling Love" course came up to me before class to share with me some of the work she'd already done around race and justice. As I was turning on the projector to make sure my slides worked, she said, "Well, the most important thing I learned is, 'I'm a racist. All White people are racist.'" I jumped down from the chair and said, "Well, hold on." Her big blue eyes widened.

"Don't say that about yourself. You are Beloved. That is who you are. Your name is not racist, it's Beloved."

That was the beginning of my practice in anti-racism classes to lead the students either in the first class or near the beginning of the course through a loving-kindness meditation to remind them of their Belovedness. This practice begins to disarm enmity within ourselves and each other.

I often wonder why Jesus began his ministry standing in line with the poor, the outcasts, the forgotten, the ones riddled with internalized hatred. I think about how he said he must be baptized by his cousin John the Baptist. Did you know that they should have been enemies? Both of their mothers were pregnant around the same time with fantastic stories of God's intervention to their pregnancies, and this was a common story beat for ancient Near East listeners: two women with miraculous pregnancies of strong leaders who were at odds with each other and then passed that legacy of division to their children—think Sarah and Hagar, the mothers of Isaac and Ishmael. Yet because their mothers chose peace there was peace between them and one baptized the other, facilitating the moment when we see all three persons of the Trinity (Father, Son, and Holy Spirit) present in a scene celebrating Belovedness. I reflect on the baptism itself: how Jesus waded out to the middle of the river Jordan, was held closely by his cousin, then came out of the water to hear the voice of God proclaiming delight and Belovedness—all this next to someone who should have been his enemy. In a lot of ways, we get to be like John and Jesus. There is an expectation of our enmity—what would happen if we resisted it with empathy and love?

We also must never forget that all of this happened before the official beginning of Jesus' ministry. Before he taught his disciples the ethics of the kingdom, he knew they must understand that the language of the kingdom of God is love and its citizens are called Beloved. So he went first.

Dear White Peacemaker, Jesus says that in this world we will have trouble, but to take heart, for he has overcome the world. He did this by first owning his Belovedness and then proclaiming it to every single person he met. His Belovedness empowered him to challenge societal hierarchies based on fear of the other, offer relief to those who have been oppressed, and eventually to sacrificially love on the cross. When you are grounded in something other than your works or results, when you are grounded in a truer, deeper, soul-healing confidence, you can continue to press on—even if it means death to all your comforts and control.

This is your calling when trouble comes as you practice anti-racism. White Peacemaker, own your Belovedness so that you can proclaim mine. Belovedness is like a flowing river of renewal and justice. It allows us to challenge systems and have difficult conversations. It moves us from individualism into community. Which is the second trouble we're going to tackle: the trouble of either/or thinking.

## *Breath prayer*

I no longer call you servants, because a servant does not know his master's business. Instead, I have called you friends, for everything that I learned from my Father I have made known to you.

—JOHN 15:15

First Beloved, Faithful Friend
*I N H A L E ,  E X H A L E*
Baptize me in Love

## 3

# Let's Forge a New Way

More than anything, this book is about shame resistance and resilience—me resisting the urge to shame you as a White person as you become aware of racism, and you becoming resilient to the internal shame that will creep in as you begin to understand white supremacy's massive influence in your everyday life.

When I got home from that trip to Georgia, I could not stop thinking about hugging Aimee. Why was I so resistant to hug her? What happened in that week that made it difficult for me to access empathy for the White people on that trip? Or more specifically, did I miss something? It was clear to me that in a week packed full of information, calls to action, and authentic sharing, I missed something important.

I took the whole week off to have extended time to work through all these questions from that trip.

We have a lake near my house with the best piers for con-
templating and an enclosed space for journaling. I walked
around it every day until I came to this realization: everything
I prepped for the week—the discussions, the books, the documentaries, the tours even—everything simplified dismantling
racism as a type of activism, activism that primarily serves as
a means of atonement for White people's complicity in the
sins of the past. Everything I prepped had an undercurrent of
shame and even anger. And while I knew it was appropriate for
the White participants to accept some responsibility and cul-
pability for the problem of racism in our country, the trip gave
little opportunity to offer an appropriate trauma response to
White people fully understanding the scope of white supremacy in our country. Guilt that is not fully tended to mutates
to shame, and shame is a dangerous dynamic in racial healing
work. Shame empowered me as a person of color to wield a
sword of moral authority.

Shame encouraged the group to internalize hate and helplessness. Shame is the barrier to your Belovedness, and it's one
you'll often accept because you hear teachings that say, "This
work isn't about you" and "Stop centering yourself." And
you take that to mean your emotions, your perspectives, your
honest feelings as you unlearn white supremacy don't matter—if not to other White people unlearning white supremacy
with you, then definitely not to the Black and Brown teachers
showing you the way.

How many times have you been told not to cry in front of
a Black person? That you're weaponizing your tears? I bet a
lot of times. You must understand how White discomfort has
played a part in perpetuating white supremacy culture. Over
the centuries as white supremacy matured and conditioned
some of your responses, you learned that if you cry, especially

if you're a White woman, then the Black person will be punished for making you uncomfortable. That punishment has ranged from calls for politeness all the way to calls for—and executions of—lynching. White tears are dangerous to Black and Brown people. What I've noticed when you receive this teaching is it can sound very either/or—either you accept that as a White person you're always wrong and never to be trusted or you're weaponizing your tears and pain. I have met so many White people who are honestly heartbroken over what they are learning and even embarrassed by something they've done who cry . . . to me, and I've welcomed those tears. I've had to set boundaries and encourage them to seek emotional support from White Peacemakers, too. It's not either/or, it's both/and. I think there needs to be a nuanced way we talk about White people's pain as they come to terms with racism that doesn't undermine their emotional health and their spiritual wholeness. One that allows for them to be appropriately vulnerable with the people of color in their lives. I know so many of you have worked hard to integrate Belovedness in your spiritual formation. I fear that the ways we teach White people to see the relational and emotional dynamics of white supremacy often elevates the feelings and experience of people of color over and above those of White people.

This trap of either/or thinking around the feelings of White people is one of the reasons I pushed the group so hard; I honestly couldn't care less how emotionally taxed they were—it felt wholly appropriate. Either they suffer or my people suffer. Retributive anger, though, is never a holy anger. Violating the *imago Dei* is never justified even if it's in service of attempting to restore the dignity of another, marginalized group. As Dr. King says, "The ends must be within the means." Oh, I got the ends I wanted—an emotionally weary group. But I'm a

peacemaker; wholeness and healing should be my goal. Shalom, the state of true peace and justice, should be my goal.
Because shalom is the active work of remaking broken relationships and systems, it requires us to be more creative in our
partnerships and more attentive to each other's needs. Shalom
allows us to find our equilibrium in the tensions often caused
by either/or thinking.

I didn't plan that trip with shalom in mind.

I know why it happened, too. I was afraid that too much
kindness, too much attention to the group's emotions, would
put me in danger of a philosophy of racial reconciliation that
is often taught within the church and that deeply hurt me: an
approach that makes dismantling racism an elective for the
believer, and if and when the believer chooses to participate
in it, the focus should be unity and oneness in Christ. This
approach celebrates a carefully approved short list of Black
leaders insofar as those leaders teach the gooey feel-good news
of Galatians 3:28: *There is neither Jew nor Gentile, neither
slave nor free, nor is there male and female, for you are all one
in Christ Jesus.*

This verse has been used as a bedrock for "racial reconciliation" panels, series, and MLK Sundays. It was also the
primary Scripture quoted back to me to justify why Christians shouldn't talk about race. Yet while the gracious heart of
racial reconciliation rooted in unity and oneness is a beautiful
aspirational goal for us, it is but one aspect of shalom—grace.
However, the reality I live with in this Brown body is that
no matter how unified in Spirit I feel to my White brothers
and sisters, at the end of the day, we live in a world deeply
beholden to white supremacist ideas, systems, beliefs, policies,
and postures that create comfort for them and struggle for me.
Nothing about that feels reconciliatory.

❀  ❀  ❀

I came to faith in a predominately White church in a predominately White community, and I loved the White people who brought me to faith so deeply. I started going to that church when I was about eight years old. They were committed to my discipleship and they showed me how to fall in love with Jesus. Through their faithfulness, I surely did. They showed up for me in beautiful, tangible ways. Yet it was very clear to me every Sunday that I was different from them. Even after so many years, I was one of the few, if not the only, Black youth in that church.

I grew up recognizing that I spent my whole week with my family, where we talked about our survival as Black people in this world.

Yet when I stepped into that church, I couldn't talk about race or my fears, because the driving narrative was that anytime I or someone else talked about race, we were being divisive. We should focus on our identity in Christ first, and we celebrate all the ways that we are more alike than we are different; talking about race actually causes more division.

We didn't talk about race unless it was within the context of "unity," "Dr. King's Dream," or his nonviolence. We didn't expose racism, because "we don't have a race problem . . . we have a sin problem." Lumping personal sin together with systemic racism communicates, "As long as *we as a church* don't have a hateful posture toward people of color—we're doing just fine." Or even more accurately, "As long as we have a *few Black members*, and a general politeness toward them, then we're a reconciled church." What's loving about that?

So being a young believer in a predominately White space, I always lived in this tension: most everyone I knew who loved

Jesus was White, but I needed to know that God didn't make a mistake in crafting me with brown skin and curly hair and wide lips. The church was never a place where I received this encouragement. In fact, it was quite the opposite. I learned to make myself safe and approachable to White people. I desired their friendship and approval so much that church became a place of stifling my Black identity with the hopes that "prayer warrior," "evangelist," and "Bible sword drill champion" would be enough. It wasn't.

Either I assimilated and stopped caring about the intersection of race and my faith or I risked becoming divisive.

This tension became a low hum in my background from eight years old into my teen years, until one instance really brought to a head my distrust for White Christians and, more specifically, White Christians' strategy that silence will create racial harmony.

The summer James Byrd Jr. was murdered, I was seventeen years old.

James was a forty-nine-year-old man in Jasper, Texas, a town just two-and-a-half hours away from my hometown in Texas.

One Sunday morning in June, James was walking home from his parents' house when three White men pulled up next to him. One of them, Shawn Berry, was an acquaintance of his, so when they offered him a ride home, James accepted. You guessed it—he did not make it home.

The three men, Lawrence Brewer, Shawn Berry, and John King, did the unspeakable, instead of taking him home. They took James to a field, where they beat him and treated his body like a common rest stop bathroom. They spray painted his face, urinated and defecated on his body. This alone would have been enough to traumatize a severely wounded James for the rest of his life, but that wasn't enough for the men. King was a member of a racist organization and needed to prove himself with the murder of a Black person, so they chained James to the back of their pickup truck and went on a horrific torture ride. Swerving the truck from right to left, they drug James three-and-a-half miles along a logging road. His skin and blood left a trail in over eighty-one places for officials to find, and even though he fought for his life until the very end, trying to hold his head up as it slammed against the road, when he hit the edge of a culvert his arm and head were severed from his body.

The men then continued to drag the remains of his torso all the way to the cemetery reserved for Black people in Jasper, where James was found the next day.

What happened to James Byrd was so gruesome and so horrible that in 2008, President Obama passed a hate crime prevention act named after him and another man who was also violently assaulted and killed.

I found out about James Byrd's death on the news.

Seventeen years old and stunned at this modern-day lynching, I looked over to my father sitting next to me watching the news coverage and studying the picture of James, and all I could think was, "He looks like Uncle Morris . . . he looks like Daddy's younger brother." My father, a man known for his stoicism, rested his hands on his head as tears formed in the corners of his eyes. Then I wondered, "Does he see his brother . . . or does he see himself?"

I honestly thought these kinds of things didn't happen anymore. Not in 1998, not in the age of colorblindness and melting-pot cartoons played for me on PBS about this great nation of tolerance. Not in a church that is admittedly mostly White but we have a few Blacks and "Mexicans" (the embarrassing shorthand I learned as a Texan for all people of Latino descent).

And these guys didn't look like Klansmen or White supremacists, they looked like regular Joes who grill on the weekends and drink beers on their porches and dance with their honeys under a starlit southern sky.

White people don't do these things anymore, right? And if they do, they do them under the covering of a hateful hood.

This was one of the first times I realized that being Black was not only a liability, it could get me killed. The color of my skin makes me an easy target to someone who never talks about the systemic reality of white supremacy and the dangerous implications of unexamined biases. I often wonder what would make a White person cauterize their empathy so completely that they would dismiss the emotional, spiritual, and physical pain of a person of color.

I think it's because the racial reconciliation movement of the 1980s and '90s that the American church bought wholesale emphasized a unity without sacrificial Christlike love. It never asked the White people in my church to experience discomfort for more than a couple of hours a year of preaching about race relations. It substituted mission trips to Africa for authentically caring about the Black members in their church. If there were stories of victory in overcoming racism, it was always in some other church or community and we'd wear their testimony like a secondhand frock so as to never be asked to take up our unique mantle of addressing the racism in our very pews. I once heard a Korean theologian describe this interpersonal-focused, systematic-downplaying form of racial reconciliation as "hug a Black friend."

But looking back, I didn't want hugs, I wanted justice. I wanted justice for James. I wanted justice for every time a White teacher refused to say my name on the first day of school because it's "too difficult." I wanted justice for the school secretary who put me in remedial English even though I tested into AP. I wanted justice for the anxiety I carried every time my brother got in his car—in addition to our mistrust of the local police, I knew my brother's unaddressed mental health issues caused him to blow up at a moment's notice and I worried that if he got pulled over at just the wrong time, he might offend the wrong officer and never come home again.

I wanted the White people who loved me to show they truly did by being willing to enter into my pain.

I spent the whole week after watching the news with my dad grieving James Byrd. I couldn't eat or sleep. I asked my mom to leave work early every day to pick me up from school because I was terrified of walking home by myself. I hugged my dad and older brother extra long that week. I didn't talk to a single White person—not even my friends. I couldn't get over the fact that James Byrd knew and trusted Shawn Berry— were any White people safe? Do all White people hide hatred behind their smiles? What might I possibly do that would unleash their desire to see me dragged and torn to pieces?

I spent that whole week anxious about going to church.

Something deep down inside told me that my church would not say a single thing about James Byrd's murder. I was hopeful, but naively so.

We talked about the discomfort of following Jesus all the time. How Jesus will ask us to be perfect as he is perfect. How God desires us to give cheerfully and generously because that tears down the idols of greed in our heart. How we fast from food, TV, and shopping so that we can show we have mastery over our bodies and wills, that we are not ruled by the tawdry, temporary things of this world.

I wanted to know what my White pastor would say in the face of such a horrendous death. What would he do? Could he lead the church to acknowledge that what happened to James wasn't a fluke but another flare-up of the chronic disease of white supremacy? Would he say a prayer for James's family and renounce the acts of those three Texas brothers?

He didn't say a single thing. No one said anything.

Not the pastor or my Sunday school teacher or my trusted mentors or the door greeters in the church saying "God is good, Osheta" as I passed by them to find my seat in the sanctuary. There were no moments of silence for James in the service, only the expectant pause as we waited for the appropriate response to proclaiming God's goodness . . . "all the time."

"God is good . . . all the time."

"God is good . . . all the time."

"God is good . . . all the time."

I remember mumbling that phrase over and over again that Sunday, as is the Pentecostal way of passing the peace, and every time I thought, "God is good for you because you're White. Was God good for James?"

Where was the sacrificial love of White people having an honest moment in our polished service to show love to the Black members in pain?

Where was the mastery of their anxiety of saying the wrong thing?

Where was their rejection of the idols they erected to the God of Comfort and where, Dear White Peacemaker, was their allegiance to Jesus, the one acquainted with rejection, the Wounded Healer, the Prince of Peace?

The cross is really beautiful in the sanitized glory of resurrection morning, but I was standing at Golgotha watching my hopes of a safe future in this body die a horrific death. And there were no witnesses to my pain and the systemic violence that caused it.

Our pastor got up after an extended worship set where we sang "You Are Awesome in This Place," and he preached (again) about living holiness.

And all I kept thinking was, "God, you are not awesome in this place, because I am grieving, and no one is paying attention. And God, if holiness means ignoring or over spiritualizing the suffering of others to preserve some measure of self-righteousness, then you won't get that from me!"

I was tired of being in a Christian context crafted for White people because we didn't have honest conversations about race.

And at that tender age of seventeen, because of the church's silence on race and racism, I built a wall to protect me from White people. Because of well-meaning White Christians who refused to talk about race and acknowledge the influence of white supremacy, I decided that it was not safe for me to grieve any type of racially charged death. But here's what happened in my heart, Peacemaker, that built the scaffolding for a lack of empathy for White people: I then believed that if there was to be any kind of racial healing in this country, then White people would not, and maybe even could not, be a significant part of bringing it to bear, because they simply couldn't care enough within the ease of their Whiteness. When given the power and ability they'd rather see Black men beaten and dragged to death behind a pickup truck than work together with people of color or care about our pain caused by white supremacy. They'd be unwilling to acknowledge that racism is not a personal posture problem, it's not an individualized sin-bent, but a pandemic that needs to be treated. White Peacemaker, you need to reach herd immunity to the virus of white supremacy, and you won't get there unless you acknowledge it and take steps to address it.

In that moment, White Christians were no longer the sweet, thoughtful, casserole-carrying mentors of my faith. They became my enemy. They, through their silence, hardened my heart and made it nearly impossible for me to have grace for them. How ironic that they supported a form of racial reconciliation built on a theology of grace that resulted in a dissolution of grace in my heart toward them. I spent the next fourteen years cautious of every single White person, waiting for them to harm me with their willful ignorance.

Enter anti-racism and its glorious, gritty expectations for White people to "do the work."

❀     ❀     ❀

Angela Y. Davis, leading activist and scholar, has said, "In a racist society, it is not enough to be non-racist, we must be anti-racist." Anti-racism came to me as I began to study the Hebraic concept of shalom.

In my first book, *Shalom Sistas*, I describe shalom as God's dream for the world as it should be: nothing broken, nothing missing, everything made whole. Shalom is the "it is good"–ness of the garden of Eden where humankind has everything we need to flourish: intimacy with God, invitation to tend and love the earth, the ability to create, and living unashamed in the bodies and skin we were given from a good God.

Shalom is the deep, abiding peace we experience when we know we're right in the palm of God's hands and shalom is the fire in our belly to defend those on the margins. Shalom is the culture of the kingdom of God, and Jesus, through his life and ministry, taught us how to express this culture in a world of great violence and division.

Part of my shalom journey included coming to terms with the hatred I internalized as a Black woman.

I often spent many days in the White spaces I inhabited wishing I were White, hoping my curly hair would "behave" in the southern humidity, avoiding slang so I didn't sound like I was from the ghetto, and laughing at racist jokes to let the White people know that I was safe and not overly sensitive about race. "I would never play the Black card—I'm not like the other Black friends, I'm a cool Black friend!"

During what I called my Forty Days of Peace, I was getting ready for a bath and brushing my hair while thinking about something my friend Amena said to me: "Girl, there's no one way to be Black. You're Black. God made you Black and that's proof enough for you to own it."

Black enough. God made me Black and that's enough.

If shalom is flourishing, if shalom is the proclamation that "it is good"—even to this brown skin—then I was a hypocritical peacemaker if I didn't learn to love it.

I filled the bathtub and began my first of many brown skin blessings.

"May you, Osheta, find peace in this brown skin." I prayed as I lathered the loofah, shaved my legs, rinsed, and wrapped the fluffy towel around my beautiful brown body.

Something happened, though, as I began advocating for this brown skin to be loved in this world: I started writing and thinking about racial reconciliation from a place of seeking peace, of wanting to create shalom for myself and others who look like me.

Honestly, I cared first for me and mine, and if White people came along for the journey—cool. I was focused on disrupting the systems of racial oppression—which meant the oppressors were not necessarily my allies, but obstacles and maybe even my opponents to getting the job done. White people served only one function—to do the work of anti-racism so as to reduce harm, anything more than that was, as we say in New Orleans, "lagniappe," a little extra but not expected. I was not interested in trusting White people with my heart again.

Now, I feel it's important, White Peacemaker, that you hear me when I say that my observation that the work of racial reconciliation can range between two ends of a spectrum—grace-based unity with a de-emphasis on action, and grit-fueled mobilization to hustle for anti-racism—is my experience, and mine and mine alone.

Actually, let's just get this out of the way before we go forward: I don't speak for all Black people, and the pivots you'll see me take in my journey to racial healing are mine. Some Black people will hold the same convictions I do or share experiences similar to mine, but we're not a monolith—as Amena says, there's not one way to be Black.

What I did notice as I began reconceptualizing my racial reconciliation work as less focused on grace for each other in order to live in unity (a position, as I said, that made me feel incredibly neglected) to one more focused on disrupting unjust systems is that I really loved the gritty, honest, in-your-face power it gave me. I loved to tell White people to "do the work" and show them their blind spots without being close enough for them to actually step on my toes as they fumbled around in the dark, straining to perceive their surroundings, hoping for healing.

This power unchecked by Christ's love and example of shalom for all people had me seething by the lakes in Georgia and Saint Paul. I thought this question and then frantically put it in my notes app on my phone: "Lord, there has to be some other way to do this work? I have to find integrity as an anti-racist and a peacemaker committed to my shalom and the shalom of others."

❀    ❀    ❀

The either/or thinking of white supremacy culture influenced my anti-racism work as I struggled on both sides of the spectrum:

Offering too much grace to White people that did not require them to change or grow.

Operating with too much grit toward White people, expecting them to work for change but not offering any space of healing or empathy.

It was time for me to forge a third way.

❀    ❀    ❀

Jesus had this really annoying way of teaching, called third way. When offered two binary choices, Jesus often offered a third, completely out of the box, creative option. When asked if his followers should pay taxes, an attempt to catch Jesus either supporting the violent Roman Empire or committing treason by telling his followers to not pay taxes, Jesus offered a third option. He held up a coin and said, "Give back to Caesar what is Caesar's and to God what is God's." They were amazed at this response because it made sense but was infinitely harder to accomplish because it required separating your identity from money and trusting in a God you cannot see. Give your money to Caesar with an open hand and give yourself to God with an open heart.

This third way perspective that Jesus forged is one that reminds his followers of their true citizenship: to the kingdom

of God, and as ambassadors living under an earthly government, we have an obligation to render to the state whatever
material and personal services are required for the common
good of society.

We must obey the just laws of the state. At the same time, as
citizens of the kingdom of God, if laws of the state or expectations of our government threaten our true allegiance, then we
must resist ("give to God what is God's").

❀   ❀   ❀

I was once asked, "What are your favorite words of Jesus?"
and I said, "'You have heard it said . . .' because I know Jesus
is going to wreck me with a third-way teaching that will both
challenge me and set me free."

Matthew 5:38-42 is an example of a third-way ethic, and
my decision to call the way I engage in anti-racism work
"anti-racism peacemaking" is deeply rooted in this passage.
I read it shortly after I wrote my prayer in my notes app. I
wanted to resist the violence of pride and bitterness in me and
address the violence of silence and atrophy in my White brothers and sisters.

> You have heard that it was said, "Eye for eye, and tooth
> for tooth." But I tell you, do not resist an evil person. If
> anyone slaps you on the right cheek, turn to them the other
> cheek also. And if anyone wants to sue you and take your
> shirt, hand over your coat as well. If anyone forces you to
> go one mile, go with them two miles. Give to the one who
> asks you, and do not turn away from the one who wants to
> borrow from you.

One of the most common misconceptions about this teaching from Jesus is that it renders a person weak. It would place

me, a Black woman doing the work of anti-racism, in danger of being harmed by others. When I started to think of my anti-racism approach as living into this nonviolent way, I was told that "turning the other cheek" was unwise. My ancestors had turned the other cheek for centuries; it was time to rise up and resist. The right to defend oneself is such a cherished value for so many Americans, but what do we do with a savior who healed on his way to the cross when he justifiably could have defended himself? When I look at the historical and cultural context in which Jesus lived and taught, I see that this saying was just as offensive then as it is now. Jesus' people lived under the occupation of a brutal military empire. In the midst of this, Jesus taught his disciples a way that is both for their survival and a subversive resistance to maintain their God-given dignity.

As a Black woman, a Black Peacemaker, this was crucial. Jesus was speaking to a group who would have been equally scandalized by his call for them to turn the other cheek. They had their backs against the wall, too, yet kingdom ethics don't budge. We are ambassadors of the peaceable kingdom. We are the subscribers of a way of living that looks like the lion lying down with the lamb, swords turning into plowshares, and losing our lives in order to find them.

Biblical scholar Walter Wink views Jesus' teaching here in Matthew as a "third way" that rejects both violent opposition and passivity. Wink writes, "Jesus abhors both passivity and violence as responses to evil."[1] While Americans like to romanticize revolution because of our history, even practically it isn't wise to send civilians like Jesus' disciples to violently resist Rome's professional military. Instead, Jesus taught his disciples to resist nonviolently as an act of subversion, maintaining dignity, and an attempt to wake up the oppressor to their sin. Wink continues,

> There are among his hearers people who were subjected to these very indignities, forced to stifle their inner outrage at the dehumanizing treatment meted out to them by the hierarchical system of caste and class, race and gender, age and status, and as a result of imperial occupation.
>
> Why then does he counsel these already humiliated people to turn the other cheek? Because this action robs the oppressor of the power to humiliate. The person who turns the other cheek is saying, in effect, "Try again. Your first blow failed to achieve its intended effect. I deny you the power to humiliate me. I am a human being just like you. Your status does not alter that fact. You cannot demean me." . . .
>
> The oppressor has been forced, against his will, to regard this subordinate as an equal human being. The powerful person has been stripped of his power to dehumanize the other.[2]

I will not allow white supremacy to turn me into a bitter and afraid person towards White people. However, I will not stay silent on or explain away issues of systemic racism to pacify White anxiety. I will forge a third way that gives unto Caesar what is Caesar's and God what is God's.

The Sermon on the Mount is Jesus' third-way ethic for how we should live with one another and is why I've had to figure out a third way to practice anti-racism: one that offers grace and encourages grit simultaneously.

Our problem with racism in this country is we can easily forget it is an ancient conflict, one that was forged when European settlers violently removed Indigenous Peoples from their lands and, in 1619, brought the first enslaved African people to the shores of Virginia.

If I think about racial reconciliation as a type of conflict, then it helps me process my responses in the fight/flight/ freeze framework.

What I've noticed is that racial reconciliation as I experienced it in the church was a form of freezing or fleeing—they were not actively engaging in the issue at hand, kinda like when my husband and I are fighting over shoveling the walkway and all we do is talk about snow and shoveling and laziness and how I'm sick and tired of slipping down the porch steps. We talk about all the things on the periphery of the issue because one or both of us are afraid to deal with the real thing: we've both been injured shoveling and we're afraid of it happening again. Also, we're angry the other one hasn't realized it and come up with a better plan (like pay one of our sprightly and able-bodied teenage boys to do it more consistently). This is what racial reconciliation felt like for me—talking about all the periphery things but not getting to the root of the issue. Without getting to the real issue, everything done for the sake of unity is impotent and short-lived.

Anti-racism as it's been fleshed out in works like *How to Be an Antiracist* and *White Fragility* is a fight response because built into its DNA is a clear opponent—racism. Practitioners of anti-racism know what they are against, they are fueled by their disgust of systemic racism, and they are well equipped to "do the work." Anti-racism's biggest obstacle is long-term commitment; what sustains that kind of energy is almost always tragedy, trauma, or heartbreak. I attended a rally the day after George Floyd was murdered and I looked around, marveling at the diversity of people committed to speaking truth to power. We walked around and chanted George's name. I stood next to a young White family with a toddler in his stroller and behind his sweet little mask he screamed,

"Black Lives Matter!" I saw young adults handing out water bottles and cars with encouraging messages hanging from the windows. It was an electric space. But I wondered, "Does violence to Black bodies have to be the conduit necessary for White allyship?" I asked my husband on the way home, "Do you think half those people at the rally today will still be interested in anti-racism in six months?"

He shrugged.

I went on. "I mean, with a global pandemic and a divisive election, do you think they'll know what to do in between tragedies?"

T. C. placed his hand on mine and said, "For some this will be different, but for most they'll be passionate for a while and then ambivalent until the next thing happens."

The problem with building your peacemaking on what you're against and not what you're for is that you're always prepared for a fight and always looking for an enemy.

But that's the thing: neither response is truly peacemaking.

This is a book written to White Peacemakers by a Black Peacemaker who has reckoned with the Beatitudes of Jesus, especially the invitation to peacemaking in Matthew 5:9, "Blessed are the peacemakers, for they will be called children of God," and found both paradigms of anti-racism work lacking in their ability to holistically dismantle racism.

Both responses are a means of racial uprising peacekeeping:

Avoid discomfort by casting a vision for unity and being really sweet, all the while sweetness doesn't create real change for those suffering, *or* manage your anxiety by picking up your sword and get to hacking at racist systems, people, politicians, and pastors who are complicit to white supremacy. Peacekeeping responses almost always have some unintended emotionally, spiritually, or even physically violent results.

Peacemaking, however, is a nonviolent third-way response rooted in three things:

The kingdom of God's exposure of the kingdoms of this world.

The honoring of the image of God in all people.

The forging of the community of God that creates eternal flourishing.

Love is the reason we offer each other grace and dream of reconciliation, but love is also the reason we relentlessly pursue justice and equity. Both . . . with grit and grace.

When I ground my anti-racism work with the word *peacemaking*, it reminds me to make love and the kingdom of God my North Star, and not simply make White people come to terms with racism and feel appropriate remorse for its effects.

I went back to the Saint Paul lake to journal, and this time I came home with my notebook filled with ideas of how to practice anti-racism with a peacemaking perspective. I then began studying the work of Dr. Martin Luther King more closely, and everything came into clear vision. I no longer needed to choose one side of the spectrum—white supremacy culture robs us of our creativity and the ability to follow the lead of the Spirit when we are trapped in either/or thinking. No, there was precedent in Scripture and in history of a community that operated with grit and grace—the Beloved Community.

# *Breath prayer*

———

How beautiful on the mountains
are the feet of those who bring good news,
who proclaim peace,
who bring good tidings,
who proclaim salvation,
who say to Zion,
"Your God reigns!"

—ISAIAH 52:7


Prince of Peace
INHALE, EXHALE
I will follow you

**4**

# Oh Lord, She Put Tomatoes in the Gumbo

I really do wish you were sitting at my kitchen table today, because I know just the thing I'd make for you: gumbo. But you should know, I put tomatoes in my gumbo. I've heard it's a faux pas. I don't care. They mean too much to me. But to most Cajun cooks, it's unthinkable to ruin your carefully, thoughtfully, patiently browned roux with tomatoes.

An authentic roux, the thickening agent for your gumbo, takes forever to get a perfect caramel brown. All the chalky, stick-to-your-tongue flavor of the flour changes as the butter and heat stretch the molecules to absorb all the richness inherent to butter until your roux becomes savory, complex, absolute perfection. A well-made roux can handle myriad ingredients.

Protecting the integrity of the roux is important because when your roux is ready, it's so glorious, you think you've seen God. You in fact understand the theological idea of the Already but Not Yet, you have already created something gorgeous with this roux, but it's not yet the thing for which it was created—your gumbo.

In a lot of ways, you and I, White Peacemaker, are living into the Already and Not Yet—we are already Beloved by Jesus, already empowered by the Spirit to create peace all around us, already catching glimpses of the kingdom of God all around us, but still in the Not Yet. We still see division, hatred, anxiety, death, and destruction because the kingdom of God is near but not fully here.

See . . . see what happens when you make a good roux— transcendence and theological truth.

But, still, I put tomatoes in my gumbo.

I know, I know, I'm told by native New Orleanians when you make a stunning roux you want everything else to be its very best. They are coming to Roux's party so they must, as my Aunt Tammy says, "come correct." Garlic and the Louisiana Trinity: bell peppers, celery, onions—as fresh as they can be—chopped and reporting for duty.

Cajun sausage sliced into generous coins of spicy, fatty goodness.

Chicken boiled ahead of time is added to the pot to cook with the spicy roux until it becomes full flavored and ready to be shredded.

And of course, the shrimp—plump and snappy. Even though gumbo is a salt-of-the-earth, grounded kind of dish, the shrimp will make you long for the expanse of the sea with every bite.

Into all of this you combine your super-super-secret seasoning mix, which differs from one cook to another. Maybe by the end of this book, I'll tell you what's in mine, but we're still getting to know each other. Instead of my seasoning mix recipe, come in and sit down at the table and I'll tell you why I put tomatoes in my gumbo and why I will never, ever stop.

Tomatoes are part of my gumbo because one evening in Boston a White woman named Aubrey made a pot for me when I was in the midst of a postpartum depression spiral. Aubrey was from Portland and studying architecture at Harvard. Although she'd never visited New Orleans before, she was smart (obviously, I mean . . . Harvard!) and she was adventurous (she spent a summer building wells in Haiti) and she was trying so hard to fully invest in her new multicultural church. So when the associate pastor of our church shared from the pulpit that our baby girl was born and to sign up to bring a meal—she signed up and wrote in the comments section, "I'll bring a pot of gumbo." When I checked the meal train website to see what my dinner plans were for the day and saw that a White woman I'd never met was bringing me gumbo—y'all . . . I was suspicious. The first time I had gumbo, it was made by Black women at my wedding and it was amazing—those southern aunties set the gumbo bar incredibly high. But I hadn't showered in five days and was plagued with thoughts of hopelessness by the hour, so I decided I had spicier sausage to chop and let it go.

Aubrey showed up at my house with a Dutch oven full of gumbo. Her Korean boyfriend wanted to help too, so he brought a pot of rice, and when I lifted the lid of the Dutch oven, I was skeptical—tomatoes in gumbo? Child, no. Why?

Even still, I was sad and soup is the food our soul craves when the world feels unsafe, so I set the pots down, hugged Aubrey and said, "Thank you."

It was one of the best gumbos I've ever tasted.

Now, would I have added more seasoning? Yes. I'm Black. The family myth is the first time I had scrambled eggs as a toddler, Mama took away the spoon as it was halfway to my mouth because she forgot to put Lawry's seasoning on my eggs.

Would I maybe not have added kale to the gumbo? Um, yes . . . I did mention Aubrey was adventurous, right?

But that gumbo with bits and pieces of petite diced tomatoes floating in that caramel broth meant more to me than an obligation to a new mom fulfilled—her thoughtfulness to make something that would bring me comfort, her skipping study group to show up on a cold New England November evening, her hug and whispered prayer for Jesus to be close to me when she didn't know I was in the throes of suicidal ideation, were all acts of sacrificial love. In that moment, I felt loved. I caught a glimpse of God's love for me and it filled me with hope. This act of love that came from a White woman to me, a Black woman, is what I think about when I hear MLK's vision of the Beloved Community.

Aubrey, a Beloved, cared for Osheta, a Beloved, and the sting of loss and death were driven away by our little expression of the Beloved Community, if only for a night.

❋    ❋    ❋

During the civil rights movement, the Beloved Community was the vision Dr. King set before Whites and Blacks alike as to why to even show up for racial equality. Why study, why practice "social dramas" of peace, why spend money and take time off work to drive to southern towns still under the oppression of white supremacy to invite them into collective freedom? Why march for the dignity of Black lives, why be beaten and gassed and chased down by dogs, why do any of it? Because Jesus, the Author and Perfecter of our Faith, the First Beloved, was calling us into a new way to be human, a new society of hope, the Beloved Community.

Dr. Martin Luther King describes the Beloved Community this way:

> But the end is reconciliation; the end is redemption; the end is the creation of the beloved community. It is this type of spirit and this type of love that can transform opposers into friends. The type of love that I stress here is not *eros*, a sort of esthetic or romantic love; not *philia*, a sort of reciprocal love between personal friends; but it is *agape* which is understanding goodwill for all men. It is an overflowing love which seeks nothing in return. It is the love of God working in the lives of men. This is the love that may well be the salvation of our civilization.[1]

In his book *The Beloved Community*, Charles Marsh, professor of religious studies at the University of Virginia, describes King's vision this way: "King's concept of love was surely not the platitudinous, 'all you need is love'; it was rather the passion to make human life and social existence a parable of God's love for the world. It was *agape*: the outrageous venture of loving the other without conditions—a risk and a costly sacrifice."[2]

Agape. Agape love is the language of the Beloved Community. It empowers us to actively resist division and violence—in thought, deed, and action toward each other and our enemies. It's the picture of Jesus on the cross and holding his scarred hands before Thomas after the resurrection. Agape is what drove the early Christians to adopt babies thrown away by the Roman Empire and to care for the dying during a plague while knowing they too would probably contract the disease and die. Agape love is what propelled Jonathan Daniels, a White twenty-six-year-old man who left seminary and joined the civil rights movement, to cover the teenage body of Ruby Sales when a White supremacist shot at them from the porch of an Alabama store.

Agape love is our calling, and it's the only force strong enough to dismantle racism and mortify white supremacy.

Yet it's much easier to be afraid of each other, to blame each other, to not believe each other when we say we're in pain—both person of color and White person alike. It's easier because the principalities and powers have thoughtfully woven xenophobia, fear of the other, into this world. When we actively resist these forces, we're anti-racist peacemakers, Beloved children of the God of the universe, disciples of Jesus, cross-bearing members of the Beloved Community, and against such love the gates of hell will never prevail.

I put tomatoes in my gumbo to remind myself that the Beloved Community is as peculiar as a Cajun gumbo with tomatoes, but given the chance it could be quite nourishing.

❀   ❀   ❀

One of the first traditions I initiated in the summer of 2005 when we evacuated New Orleans because of Hurricane Katrina and moved to Boston was to make red beans and rice on Mondays, partly because it reminds me of the city I love, but also because soaking the beans, chopping the veggies, making the cornbread all force me to slow down and pray for shalom as I cook.

In my first book, *Shalom Sistas,* I describe shalom as the "breadth, depth, climate, and smell of the kingdom of God."[3] Shalom is God's dream of flourishing for the world, and you and I are peacemakers when we seek God's shalom in our everyday lives.

Gumbo has a similar meaning for me, except gumbo, with its many recipes as diverse and varied as the people who dream them up, is a picture of us living out shalom in the nitty-gritty of life, from all our social locations, honoring all our stories, preferences, experiences, and cultures.

Every gumbo recipe tells a story.

Gumbo represents the Beloved Community in all our diversity, all our complexity, and all our spiciness.

It's unity in action. Gumbo is resistance in a bowl topped by a scoopful of rice.

And this is what the enemy is trying to take down.

In Ephesians 2, Paul tells us that Jesus who "is our peace" came to create one new humanity. He made "two groups one and has destroyed the barrier, the dividing wall of hostility, by setting aside in his flesh the law with its commands and regulations. His purpose was to create in himself one new humanity out of the two, thus making peace, and in one body to reconcile both of them to God through the cross, by which he put to death their hostility" (vv. 14-16).

The call to be an anti-racism peacemaker is not easy, because the shalom of God does not come easy. This kind of peace that lasts was shown to us in Jesus' life, ministry, death, and resurrection, and then we as peacemakers are called to live it out. Anything that does not require us to sacrifice for each other is another form of peacekeeping, not peacemaking. I'm interested in dismantling white supremacy in order to build up something better for you and for me. I'm interested in the peacemaking North Star of the Beloved Community. This is our third way of anti-racism—not the cheap grace of the racial reconciliation movement and not the callous grit of anti-racism work apart from Jesus, but the Beloved Community that holds us accountable to be in right relatedness to each other and create an environment where we can all thrive.

The whole of Jesus' ministry was to establish a community so convinced of their Belovedness to God that they proclaim the Belovedness of others. Belovedness is a massive act of owning and accepting your humanness as a gift from a God who deeply loves you. As we adjust our thinking of this work as rehumanizing those who have been dehumanized, Belovedness is essential in our anti-racism peacemaking. Which is why nonviolence in thought, word, and deed is a pillar in my anti-racism work. If I believe you are Beloved, I will not intentionally hurt you. I will not say, do, or allow myself to think of you, White Peacemaker, as anything less than Beloved. When I encourage you, I must hold grace and grit together—grace to remember your core identity, grit to call you to live into a braver, bolder expression of it. I will never use coercion, manipulation, or attack. I will appeal to your Belovedness and trust the Spirit of Love to work in your heart. Now, have I been disappointed in this approach? Sure. But have I made lifelong friends and won over skeptics simply by building my peacemaking ethic on Proverbs 15:1, "A gentle answer turns away wrath, but a harsh word stirs up anger"? Absolutely.

You see, if you, White person, are coming to this work already bracing for attack, already preparing to be shamed, already expecting to become the scapegoat for the valid anger of the oppressed from centuries of racial injustice—then, I would imagine, it is nearly impossible for you to feel unified or loved in this work.

Some may say that's not the point—you, White person, should feel terrible, should accept our anger as necessary recompense for your ancestors' actions, should never be comforted or cared for as you create new neurological pathways away from white supremacy and toward shalom.

I don't think this is what Jesus had in mind when he couldn't breathe, nailed to a cross, with droplets of his blood pooling on the ground around him. In fact, I know that Belovedness was an aspect of the joy set before him because he offered forgiveness and grace, paradise and compassion, vulnerability and authenticity to those around him.

When Jesus couldn't breathe, he loved. Jesus, who left the first Beloved Community of Father, Son, and Holy Spirit, came to create the Beloved Community of the misfits and the marginalized of this world, and he proclaimed our Belovedness all the way to the cross.

Our Jesus, who gasped for his last breath, never lost sight of the mission: to bring us back to God's dream of shalom—loved fully by the Father so that we can love his creation fearlessly. These are the hallmarks of the kingdom of God: Love God, love self, love others, love the world.

Therefore, this is the way of the Beloved Community:

Claim your Belovedness: love God, love self.

Then proclaim it: love others, love the world.

Henri Nouwen says this holy cycle is necessary to becoming the Beloved. "If it is true that we not only are the Beloved, but also have to *become* the Beloved; if it is true that we not only *are* children of God, but also have to become *children* of God; if it is true that we not only *are* brothers and sisters . . . if all that is true, how then can we get a grip on this process of becoming? If the spiritual life is not simply a way of being, but also a way of becoming, what then is the nature of this becoming?"[4]

This process of becoming happens when we seek to create the Beloved Community, especially when we're partnering together to dismantle the violence of racism.

This is why I've chosen an approach that centers nonviolence. Nonviolence is the best way we can communicate our Belovedness to each other.

The Student Nonviolent Coordinating Committee (SNCC) was the primary way students joined the civil rights movement and learned how to practice its nonviolent technique. In 1962, at a staff meeting they reaffirmed their commitment to nonviolence by describing it this way, "Love [is] the central motif of nonviolence," the "force by which God binds man to himself and man to man."[5] Marsh, in *The Beloved Community*, describes how these students wanted to create a community that is a "circle of trust, a band of sisters and brothers, gathered around the possibilities of agapeic love, the beloved community."[6]

I put tomatoes in my gumbo to remind me of the possibilities of the agapeic love of the Beloved Community that chooses nonviolence in the face of incredible violence in this world.

Daily I tell myself this when I choose to engage with anti-racism peacemaking work from a nonviolent, peacemaking posture:

I, a Black Peacemaker, am Beloved and you, a White Peacemaker, are Beloved, and we belong to each other.

This is what we build our anti-racism peacemaking on, White Peacemaker. This is our why. Everything else will disappoint and overwhelm, but the love of God owned and reflected is the living water we need along the journey.

The last time I made this gumbo recipe with tomatoes in it was during the racial healing pilgrimage I went on with Aimee. Students of SOMA, a nine-month discipleship program in Minneapolis, had invited me to lead them in some classes on racism and peacemaking and then lead a week-long trip to visit specific landmarks in the civil rights movement. We left Minneapolis on a Saturday morning and drove down South, camping along the way and attempting to dialogue about the experiences of the day. We visited the National Civil Rights Museum in Birmingham and the courthouse where the Dred Scott case was decided. The day we were supposed to walk across the Edmund Pettus Bridge in Selma, Alabama, we were met with a torrential rainstorm and, y'all . . . I love camping, but I was not having it. I was not interested in setting up camp in the rain. I knew if we did, I would be distracted and frustrated the next day mostly because my hair would be so wild and dried out. When you're camping you don't really have time to deep condition, blow-dry, flat-iron, and lay your edges down. (If that last one is lost on you, White Peacemaker, when we meet, ask me about it, and I'll tell you. Or you can You-Tube it. Either way, edges mean everything to Black women.) I was craving something more than peanut butter sandwiches and fast food. I wanted gumbo and I wanted to make it for my friends.

I pulled my phone out while we were a good hour from the drenched campsites and found the most perfect Airbnb. Nestled in the woods behind a Wetumpka suburb sits a cabin that looks like a treehouse with an expansive deck and floor-to-ceiling windows. The bathroom has a galvanized bucket for a sink and the decor is lumberjack chic. It was perfect to make two large batches of gumbo: one gluten- and meat-free, the other with everything including the tomatoes.

After a quick trip to Walmart, I had everything I needed. The group dropped me and a few others off at the house to clean up and rest, while everyone else drove on to walk the Edmund Pettus Bridge in the drizzle. I turned on my Spirituals playlist, breathed a happy sigh because I was finally at the stove, and began chopping.

I was worried because a man named John who was born and raised in Louisana was on the trip and said, "I'm curious about your gumbo. It's been a while since I've had a good pot of gumbo."

"Lawd," I prayed silently, "go before me and prepare this man's heart." My gumbo was going to be different, I knew. This Texas-proud, New Orleans–transplant, New England–loving, Minnesota-settled cook combines everything I love in my gumbo—it was surely not going to be authentic enough for John. "He's gonna hate my gumbo. Especially because I put tomatoes in it," I muttered while I chopped the peppers.

But I cooked on, tomatoes and all. I also decided to skip the group debrief and just be for the night. I felt in my bones that we needed a night off from talking about dismantling racism and to just try to be a multiracial, Jesus-loving group of learners. This group of fifteen included three Black people (me, a Black male co-leader, and a Black SOMA student). I was concerned about them; I also knew it was a painful trip for nearly everyone. I processed with one woman, as she simply could not comprehend the violent story about a Black woman gang-raped by White men in the Deep South that she'd read about on a placard. I listened and tried to answer the many questions of a skeptical man as he asked some variation of "Why?" and "Is it really that bad?" for almost an hour. I needed us to take time to become the Beloved Community, so as I prayed, I chopped and stirred the roux nonstop, hoping that table fellowship would help.

Jesus was known for this unconventional approach to teaching the kingdom of God—table fellowship. He had meals with people who were ignored, rejected, and reviled for a host of reasons: socioeconomic status, sinful choices, politics, gender. People judged him for his table companions. One of these companions, Levi the tax collector, I think of when I pray for you, White Peacemaker. Walking by a lake with a crowd hanging on his every word, watching his every action, Jesus said to Levi, "Follow me." Tax collectors were something like our modern-day equivalent to a mob boss. They worked on behalf of the Roman Empire to collect taxes, but they often extorted their own people in the process, oftentimes resorting to violence or manipulation to do their jobs. And Jesus turns to a man like this and says, "You are more than a tax collector, you are Beloved who is caught up in a system of oppression—come, let's have a meal together and let me set you free."

I think what I wanted to do for my group was what Jesus did for Levi, to invite them to the table and say:

You, White Peacemaker, you are not just White, you are not the stories of oppressors and the master's whip, you are not the greed that ended Reconstruction after the Civil War, you are not Jim Crow terrorism, or prejudiced neighbors upholding the red-line housing exclusion laws; you are not the War on Drugs, or the school-to-prison pipeline, you are not police brutality with White knees on Black necks, you are not billy clubs and tear gas, you are not the silent pastors and theologians who use Scripture to justify sins against Black and Brown people—you, White person, are Beloved, a fellow Peacemaker who is caught up in a system of white supremacy.

Come, let's have a meal together and let us reason together and find a way to set each other free.

We sat around various tables in the cabin with bowls of gumbo and rice in our laps, cupped in our hands, precariously balanced on the edge of the live-edge wood island. I prayed for our meal and we ate.

We didn't talk about racism explicitly—no one mentioned a civil rights hero or lamented the pain of enslaved people, but I saw the violence of white supremacy dismantled all around me with ever slurp and laugh and request to pass this pot or the cornbread or (my favorite) the seasoning mix I put in a little sugar bowl at the center of the table. We passed the peace that night and I was grateful.

We were sitting at the table of the Beloved Community and I got to serve my White brothers and sisters whom I was worried had been crushed under the weight of that week.

The table fellowship with one another is one practical way we can resist white supremacy.

The table of the Beloved is one way we break the chains of oppression for both people of color and White people.

I think this is why the kingdom of God is likened to a great banquet, and it's the picture of our movement as we go forward as anti-racism peacemakers, as we seek to build the Beloved Community. Let us come together and be free. Let us come together and be nourished. Let us come together and offer unconditional positive regard because we have been unconditionally loved by God. Let us avoid the traps of either/or and violence. Let us become the Beloved Community, moving forward together with grit and grace.

❀   ❀   ❀

So: Come to this table of the Beloved Community, White Peacemakers.

Come because you are Beloved and there's a place setting with your name written on it.

Come because you are strong and because you are weak.

Come because you are awake and you are still dreaming.

Come because you are enough and you are not afraid to ask for more.

Come not just because you have something to offer but because you have a great responsibility.

Come, the table is set with grace and mercy, promise and passion, hope and expectation, love and loyalty.

Come because he loved us first and come because his kindness is the fire that keeps the candelabras burning.

Come and meet our Prince of Peace, and

when you get here, please, pass the gumbo.

Tomatoes and all.

## *Breath prayer*

Because there is one loaf, we, who are many, are one body, for we all share the one loaf.

—1 CORINTHIANS 10:17

Bread of Life

*INHALE, EXHALE*

Nourish us for the journey

# 5

# Nah.

## An Eviction Notice from the Beloved Community

Satan,

Lucifer. Beelzebub. Great Accuser.

Your disgusting squatter ways have been noticed. We come into a room where you've been, and the stink of hatred fills our nostrils, making us retch. You let your nasty pets of greed and blood-lust crap all over the place, and I'm not even sure where to begin cleaning up. I know some good old words of my testimony and the blood of the Lamb is a fantastic start.

Satan, you've got to get up out. We're constantly stepping over and into the debris of doubt—doubt of the God who made us good and doubt in the goodness of each other. Well, I'm sure you're tired of hearing this, but I never tire of saying it: "Not today, Satan. Not today."

I love my White brothers and sisters too much to let you have them. They are glorious.

I love this Brown body and this Africanity soul too much and I know it is glorious.

Regardless of what your chief lie of white supremacy says.

Here in the Beloved Community: Christ and his love is supreme.

Your weapon of white supremacy has been nullified. Dull. Impotent. You should be really embarrassed. You brought a knife to a gun fight.

It's time for the Peacemakers to rise up because, as my friend Kaitlin says, "Glory is happening right now." And we've got no more time for your shenanigans.

You must have been pissed off when God stepped back from making this beautiful world and said, "It is good." Listen, if I'd made it my life's goal to destroy and debase, then yeah, I'd be pissed too when God shows off and creates glory. And that's what it is, Satan, you hate this glory oh so much. Our reflection of God's glory—wow it's brilliant and blinds you and makes you feel small. In fact, you were there when Glory was crucified, but, dude, you were also there when Glory was resurrected, and—listen up—you will see this glory continue to fill the earth. You have no hold here anymore. You are evicted.

Pack your stuff. Turn in your key. Move out.

We've got work to do in this place you've jacked up. We've got cleaning and candle lighting and roof repairing. We've got to do the hard work of putting together furniture—tables and chairs where we'll sit and share communion, beds for the exhausted, Adirondack chairs for the porch to sit and watch the sunset, grateful for another day to be human together.

We've got bathtubs to disinfect so we can be washed of your divisive influence.

We live here now. You're not moving us. So, you move along.

And yet, I know you won't. You're prideful like that. You're stupid like that. Don't you know you've already been displaced? Don't you know that we are the homeowners, this is our land, this is our territory, this is ours to protect from you?

The kingdom of God is moving in. We're bringing with us grace that exposes your violence, love that confounds your anger, joy that resists your despair.

So, here's the deal: We're going to keep reminding you that you don't belong here. We're going to keep making you uncomfortable with our dogged resilience and our unwavering hope. We're going to keep reminding each other that we're on a mission to kick you out. When you slink around and try to make us fight with each other, we're going to be ready. We're going to say, "Satan, get the hell out!" and we're going to fight for each other and not against.

We live by the sword of the Spirit, and you's about to get cut down.

> Effective immediately and in perpetuity,
> Osheta Moore
> On behalf of all the Peacemakers who
> are done with your nonsense

# PART II

# There Is a Balm in Gilead

It's my face man
I didn't do nothing serious man
please
please
please I can't breathe
please man
please somebody
please man
I can't breathe
I can't breathe
Please
[inaudible]
man can't breathe, my face
just get up
I can't breathe
please [inaudible]
I can't breathe sh*t
I will
I can't move
mama
mama
I can't
my knee
my nuts
I'm through
I'm through
I'm claustrophobic
my stomach hurt
my neck hurts
everything hurts
some water or something
please
please

I can't breathe officer
don't kill me
they gon' kill me man
come on man
I cannot breathe
I cannot breathe
they gon' kill me
they gon' kill me
I can't breathe
I can't breathe
please sir
please
please
please I can't breathe

George Floyd's last words, May 25, 2020

Now when Jesus saw the crowds, he went up on a mountainside and
sat down. His disciples came to him, and he began to teach them.

—MATTHEW 5:1-2

# To Heal the Sin-Sick Soul

*Rejecting White Apathy*

"You're going to need a stole," T. C., my husband, said while rubbing my back. It had been another long day of grieving, protesting, and processing George Floyd's murder for both of us; we were taking turns rubbing each other's back. It was my turn. Somehow my turns were longer and more frequent because my husband is a very, very good man.

I turned and shook my head. "Don't you have one I can borrow?"

"Well . . . I do, but I think it's time you have your own. The invitation requested all clergy, pastors, and faith leaders wear something from their faith tradition, and you are definitely a pastor. You've been one for a while, now you need a stole."

Having not been raised in a tradition that put stock in religious garb and to-dos, I resisted again. "I'm sure I can dig out a Christian-y T-shirt and wear that. Do I really need a *stole*?"

T. C. shrugged. "Need? No . . . but I think it's important, it's kind of like you are owning your calling to lead and love people. Right now, with all that's going on, you've been showing up. Take some of the money you've been given from your online community and pick out a stole."

I thought for a moment and had an idea. "Can I get one in yellow?!" My favorite color. I swear, I once bought a brand-new vacuum cleaner just because it was a gorgeous mustard yellow with a gray accent that's simply . . . perfection. I hate housework, but that didn't stop me—it was yellow!

"Yes," T. C. said. He motioned for me to turn around and resumed rubbing my shoulders. "I'm sure they'll have a stole for you, in yellow."

❀     ❀     ❀

They did not.

I stood in the religious supply store in my neighborhood, taking deep breaths through my Hufflepuff face mask, staring at their very limited, very expensive selection and wondered if maybe I should just dig out my "Afewbreadcrumb and fish" T-shirt to wear to the Black clergy–led march for peace. They required religious leaders to wear something identifying, and my husband was convinced it was time for me to have a stole, but I didn't like a single one of them. Not at all.

I held a pink one with purple and gold threads that I could live with for a few hours, but it was too long for my 5-foot 3-inch frame. Several had specific offices assigned to them, like deacon, or were for special occasions like confirmation, and I was like, "No, thank you, I do not need God or his servants throwing me the side eye while we march for George Floyd simply because I wore the wrong kind of stole to a freaking peace rally." Even though my theology says God sees me as wholly Beloved, I often struggle to truly believe it. I work so hard to earn God's approval, although I think God throws more side-eye at *that* than at any silly high church faux pas I could ever commit.

I was about to text T. C. that maybe I would just borrow one of his generic non-religious interloper stoles when my eye caught the Agnus Dei symbol on a purple stole slightly pushed toward the back of the shelf.

The Agnus Dei is an important piece of iconography in the church. It is a lamb with a halo bearing a cross or banner. This is a symbol of Christ, the Lamb of God who takes away the sins of the world, and this symbol of his sacrificial love is often found in artwork and stained glass windows. It's also the symbol I wanted for a tattoo when I decided to live my life as a peacemaker. I wanted a reminder to be someone who looks at the sins of the world that cause so much chaos and asks God, "What, if anything, can I do to bring peace?"

I pulled the stole out and rubbed my fingers along the thin gold thread. Despite my misgivings, I knew that owning a stole and wearing it was a specific proclamation—about my Belovedness and my commitment to Jesus and his way. A stole is not just a physical representation of leadership in a faith context—which made me feel a little anxious in that religious supply store—but an opportunity for me to embody Matthew 11:28-30: "Come to me, all you who are weary and burdened, and I will give you rest. Take my yoke upon you and learn from me, for I am gentle and humble in heart, and you will find rest for your souls. For my yoke is easy and my burden is light."

As ministers place a stole over their shoulders, they're reminded of the animals paired together on the farm—one stronger and has seen many harvests, the other weaker but committed to the work at hand.

This is how I felt when I watched the 8 minutes and 46 seconds of the video of George Floyd's murder just weeks after seeing Ahmaud Arbery be chased and shot at close range with a shotgun. I needed to take on Jesus' yoke, as my heart was broken and I felt wholly incapable to do the work of anti-racism. I also didn't want to do this work alone.

❄    ❄    ❄

I stood in a crowd with pastors from all walks of life, waiting for instructions. Pastor Stacey Smith, a Black woman pastor of a 130-year-old historically Black church, was one of the organizers, and she grabbed the microphone.

"This is a peaceful and silent march, friends. We are coming together to demand justice and be a witness to the suffering in our community. This is a Black clergy–led march"—the crowd erupted with applause, and I looked around at all the White pastors, most wearing masks, their eyes alight with passion.

"This is Black-led," she continued when the crowd died down, "which means, my White brothers and sisters, we're going to ask you to hang back and let all the Black faith leaders line up and begin the march, then we invite you to join in behind us, and then our collective congregations and community will follow. This is a silent march, so I encourage you to pray or reflect as we make our way to the Target parking lot. It's closed down due to rioting in this neighborhood, but we have the National Guard out here and we've been promised that they will protect and serve us." Again the crowd celebrated. We wanted to believe the best of law enforcement officials; we wanted them to do their jobs justly and safely.

I turned to my husband, a White pastor wearing his colorful rainbow stole, and said, "I've got to go, babes." He chuckled and said, "You're leaving me?" I shrugged while joining my Black co-laborers. "Yeah, I'm Black"—I pointed to my stole and smiled behind my face mask—"and I'm a peacemaker."

Walking in that crowd, I kept praying for those White pastors behind me who in their own way were sacrificially loving us Black leaders. I prayed for them to have stamina for the work of anti-racism, for them to know their Belovedness first and foremost and how they specifically fit into the work of dismantling white supremacy. I prayed for their families and friends who didn't get why they're so radical and I prayed for their hearts to stay tender like clay even when exposed to the heat of pride, fear, frustration.

Silent. Peaceful. Purposeful. We marched in unity.

After a week of standing in crowds with so many White people passionate about creating real change in our country so that every Black and Brown person feels safe, this silent walk among my Black brothers and sisters, supported by my White siblings, and all of us leading our communities toward peace, I felt something I hadn't felt in a while—hope. In all the heartbreak, their peacemaking presence gave me comfort.

❀　❀　❀

For many of my White brothers and sisters, these videos of the murders of Ahmaud and George, seemingly back-to-back, awakened in our country a desire to do the work. But anti-racism isn't a weekend project like cleaning the basement or hanging twinkle lights over your deck. Anti-racism is a deeply emotional and challenging undertaking. If you do not build up practices of inner shalom, you'll put expectations on the outcome of your work that will turn your peacemaking into peacekeeping.

The old Spiritual "There Is a Balm in Gilead" speaks to our inner pain and reminds us that there is healing for it. It's a cry from Jeremiah, the weeping prophet, the one who noticed that Jerusalem was inundated with sinful practices and adopting a culture of violence. He noticed how the culture undermined God's dream for true shalom, with manufactured peace, "saying 'Peace, peace,' when there is no peace" (Jeremiah 6:14 NRSV). And so he cries out in Jeremiah 8:22, "Is there no balm in Gilead? Is there no physician there?"

If you listen closely, White Peacemaker, this is what BIPOC have been crying out. With every hashtag and every YouTube video, we're crying out for healing from the trauma of white supremacy. With every letter to the pastor and Instagram post, we're reminding you of the chronic pain we live with. With every conversation and memo, we're asking you, "What are you going to do about it?"

Racial healing is never easy, White Peacemaker. But we get to be the ones who proclaim there is a balm in Gilead. The healing comes when we answer Jesus' question, saying, "Yes, I do want to be healed" and then he puts his hands over our eyes and we see. We see and we are moved to share suffering. We're changing the white supremacist narratives that you don't have to care and I'm wise to not trust you.

The healing comes when we have proximity to each other's pain—when you hurt, I hurt; it's as if we share one throbbing nerve ending.

Healing will never come if you succumb to white apathy, the condition where, when you encounter the pain and suffering caused by white supremacy, you ignore, explain away, reject, or give in to overwhelm. White apathy is the antithesis of anti-racism peacemaking.

In his teaching "White Apathy and the Crucifixion," Jesuit priest Brian Engelhart says,

> When we are apathetic to the plight of our BIPOC brothers and sisters, we buy into the system that tells us that we are superior, that it is better to keep what we have than to risk losing it for the benefit of another, or that minorities wouldn't be suffering so much if they were more like White people. As antiracists, this attitude is unacceptable but easy to fall into for those socialized in a racist culture, so we must remain on our guard.[1]

In this part we're going to look at white apathy and all the ways it short-circuits our collective healing. There is a balm in Gilead, yes! This spiritual's origin story is lost, like many rich pieces of African American history, but right after Lincoln signed the Emancipation Proclamation, writings from Black ministers quoted the lyrics of this healing, hopeful song that freed enslaved people sang to remind them that all that suffering was not in vain—Jesus, the balm in Gilead, sees. White Peacemaker, there is healing available, but first you have to notice your pain and mine. You must be like Jesus who, as he sat down on the mount before he taught, looked and saw. He saw the diversity of people drawn to him: sick, poor, rejected, outcast, and hurting. He noticed and he brought the good news that he had seen them, he knew their pain, and if we embrace his kingdom ethics, we can be a part of binding up wounds, healing fractured relationships, and speaking truth to the powers that oppress us.

# Where Does It Hurt?

Blessed are the poor in spirit, for they shall see God.
—MATTHEW 5:3

Dear White Peacemakers,

Right after George Floyd was murdered, I noticed so many White people posting about the books they were reading and the people they were following. A woman shared how one specific anti-racism teacher was really encouraging her, so I decided to check out the teacher's most recent Instagram story. For five minutes she yelled at White people. There's no other way to describe it. It was not a rant, it was a carefully thought-out takedown of white supremacy (which I loved) wrapped in language like "If you don't see this then you're selfish and you need to get right with your God" (which I didn't love). She called White women Karens and Beckys. She told her followers that she was offering them tough love and if they didn't like it, then they weren't ready for the work. I watched with a sort of train-wreck curiosity. I wondered if I should turn it off—I knew the rage in my heart needed only a spark of her fiery anger to become a destructive flame. I experienced how close I came to dehumanizing White people just a year earlier, so I closed the app and sat still. I couldn't stop thinking about the comments rolling in from White followers during her live video. "Thank you for speaking truth!" "This is just what I needed!" "I receive your correction." "I'm a Becky and I accept that."

This Black leader has a prophetic gift to call out the ugliness of white supremacy in the starkest language she could find, and I respect her for that. However, I think there's a danger in conditioning White audiences to receive our correction with a side of humiliation.

That's how I felt for those White people—humiliated. Not a single thing in that video spoke to their humanity or the very real pain they might be experiencing as they leave behind racist ideas and frameworks.

I went over to my account and did a little experiment for four weeks. Once a week, I posted a heart check-in for White Peacemakers, asking some variation of a question I learned from a podcast interview with civil rights activist and teacher Ruby Sales: "Where does it hurt?" Every week the comments filled with White Peacemakers thanking me for the chance to share their heart and request prayer. All of them treated that space as a gift; no one took advantage. I think there's a fear that if we as Black leaders give White people an inch, they will take a mile right across our backs. It's a well-founded fear; we've been trampled over time and time again. But sacrificial love for me, peacemaking for me, is a holistic work of hope.

I choose to trust the good in you, and if you let me down, I'll lean into the goodness of God to sustain me. This is the only way I can practice anti-racism and live into my peacemaking values with integrity.

My friend recently told me she needed to take a break from my social during that season. "You're just too nice," she said. "I need you to yell at me." The question I wanted to ask her but couldn't because we were meeting in a group was, "Why do you need to be yelled at?" This is an expectation I've encountered in so many White Peacemakers, a desire for my Black anger, a need for me to put them in their place. Do you know that when you ask me to do this you're asking me to dehumanize myself? Do you know when you ask me this you are taking away my agency to choose to love you in the ways God is asking me to? When you ask me to get angry, to be "real," I need you to honestly ask yourself whether it is because you want to learn and be challenged or because you want an acceptable "angry Black woman" in your pocket, your own little social justice warrior Beyoncé. Are you afraid if you don't have the sting of my anger, the ringing in your ears of my clapbacks, that you'll be in danger of giving up on this work? I will not be your daily dose of anti-racism flagellation. I will love you with my words and wield kindness as a tool of repentance. Yes, it's true that kindness makes us uncomfortable, but that's the nature of living with grace, is it not? We all are undeserving, yet while we were yet sinners, Christ died for us. While you are still undoing your complicity to white supremacy, I will lay down my retributive anger and take up a holy desire to see you made whole. Let me check in on you. Let me listen to you. Let me stay fully human as I humanize you in this work. Only then can we move forward together, wholeheartedly and healthy.

We can never forget that oppressive systems oppress everyone involved. I will remember that you are poor in spirit too, and I'll treat you as such.

Sorry but not sorry,
Osheta

❀     ❀     ❀

Anti-racism work is traumatic. Being a White Peacemaker causes you an emotional pain you're not used to as you grapple with ideas and change your behavior. Being a Black Peacemaker who will walk alongside you requires me to prepare for disappointment and frustration. We are both coming to this work with the daunting task of living like Jesus even though everything about this world made it possible for him to be crucified.

I once heard a pastor say, "It feels like we're stuck in the shadow of the plantation. We should learn how to step out from it and into the light of Jesus Christ." I was having coffee with him and we were talking about me potentially speaking at his very large church, so I bit my lip and nodded noncommittally. Yes to the being stuck part, yes to the moving into the light of Jesus Christ part, but I don't think it's helpful to forget its shadow. I think we cannot truly live in the light without a visceral reminder of the shadow of the plantation and a proximity to those still suffering from its influence. I don't want allies who only know Jesus, meek and mild. I want allies who see Jesus on the cross and who rail against the empire that put him there.

In order for that to happen, we must acknowledge the specific poverty of spirit we're vulnerable to and invite God to fully redeem us.

If you're reading this in a U.S. context, we are living in the shadow of the plantation. We are contending with the extreme violence of the transatlantic slave trade and chattel slavery.

The plantation is where white supremacy's methods of dehumanization were codified and condoned: including but not limited to dismissing Black enslaved people's ability to experience pain to justify extreme work conditions or using them for medical studies without anesthesia or pain medication. Black bodies were used as entertainment in gang rapes and manhunts. Masters were instructed to separate Black enslaved people from their children and families and breed them to make more slaves. Overseers harshly punished Black bodies for all kinds of infractions. The violence of the plantation is unfortunately knitted in our relational DNA.

It is trauma for me as a Black woman to process the plantation with White people. But you know what, White Peacemaker, it's trauma for you, too. Racial trauma is what both Aimee and I were responding to—I by the lake and Aimee by the convenience store.

What I'm curious about now, friend, is what we do with this trauma. Can we become aware of it, listen to it, and then learn appropriate trauma responses? Otherwise we will fall into a hopeless cycle described by Richard Rohr, "If you don't transform your suffering, you will transmit it."[1]

During our group trip to Georgia, one thing I kept thinking as we walked around the Legacy Museum was, "What must it have been like to be a White child during the Jim Crow South with all your trusted adults committing incredible acts of violence toward Black people in the name of law, order, God, and country?" Near a wall of soil collected from the sites of lynchings all across the country is a postcard of Black bodies dangling from a tree with White men smiling smugly, and right in the front are their children. Children. Young boys and girls, none of them looking older than thirteen.

Resmaa Menakem, a Minneapolis-based therapist, has a framework I really love when approaching anti-racism work. He calls himself a somatic abolitionist. He thinks of anti-racism work as setting our bodies free of the trauma impressed onto us because of white supremacy. For people of color, or people of cultures as he defines us, he says we deal with HIPP: historical, intergenerational, persistent institutional, and personal trauma. I didn't realize this, but sitting by that Georgia lake, I was experiencing vicarious trauma from my ancestors through their stories and experiences I'd encountered while visiting museums. I was experiencing persistent institutional trauma being in a framework that centered the needs of efficiency and cost over the time required to emotionally process all that we learned about racism. I was experiencing personal trauma in every conversation I had, group discussion I led, and resource I taught because while the peacemakers on that trip were so eager to learn, they were still White and were dealing with the trip's trauma as White people. They were experiencing "white body trauma."

Menakem's framework extends to White people by addressing your trauma as not the same as that of a person of culture. Because White people have always been the standard of humanity, framing your trauma as equal to mine actually prevents us from moving into racial equity. For Black and Brown people to become fully human and treated with the dignity God designed for each and every human, which God intends as the standard of humanity, you as a White person will have to sacrifice some benefits you've received because of your White skin and will have to actively resist the system of white supremacy that has reinforced your inherent worth.

This work requires you to, as writer and research professor Brené Brown, says, "rumble with the truth."[2] Rumbling, to me, is such an internal, deep-seated work. When the ground begins to shake, yes there are external effects, but something deep in the core of the earth is happening. Tectonic plates are shifting. White body trauma addresses those tectonic plates. Menakem encourages White people to do this work of addressing it in community with other White people. I have given this advice so many times: White people, you have to be at the forefront of these conversations. You have to ask each other, "What does it mean to be White?" "How has that affected people of color?" "Where does it hurt?" "What can we do together to protect and love our siblings of color?" When you do this, you are building a culture of peacemaking with buy-in from the very people who recognize that white supremacy has placed you in a position to be poor in spirit.

❀　　❀　　❀

When hundreds of people gathered around Jesus to hear what would be the Sermon on the Mount, the crowd was full of traumatized people. Tax collectors, hyper-religious leaders, prostitutes, Gentiles, and every person deemed "outsider." When faced with systemic brokenness, Jesus offered the wholeness of his kingdom. Jesus came not with a list of how to be your best self and achieve success, but with a new vision of humanness, and that begins with acknowledging our collective vulnerability.

Jesus, knowing that their trauma was not wholly their fault but the result of systems of oppression working exactly as they had been designed, didn't begin his great sermon with to-dos; he began it with truth. The kingdom of God is a kingdom of blessing those who have often been ignored, reviled, or rejected by society. The culture of Rome was influenced by exceptionalism, profit, power, and expansion. It valued innovation and protected its reputation at all costs. Even though today we benefit from technological advancements from the Roman Empire such as modern plumbing, air conditioning, and clean water, to name a few, Rome was also known for its horrific punishments and tortures. The value of a human life was so insignificant that oftentimes, if a master was accused of a crime, instead of taking his rightful punishment, he would send a slave in his place. The crowd gathered around Jesus understood the trauma associated with living in a Roman supremacy society. So Jesus began with the Beatitudes. "Blessed," Jesus says to those who feel anything but. Blessed, or favored, or as I have begun translating when I read the Beatitudes, Beloved, is Jesus offering compassion: "I see you and you are not alone." Each beatitude takes on a common picture of Roman thriving: wealth, prominence, strength, cunning, and comfort and turns it on its head. In the kingdom we acknowledge our poverty of spirit, in the kingdom we allow space to grieve, in the kingdom we are driven to humility, in the kingdom our passion for true justice is unrelenting, in the kingdom we choose gentleness over harm, in the kingdom we are honest and courageous, in the kingdom we sacrifice for what matters; through the Beatitudes and the sayings on the Sermon on the Mount, Jesus gives us the good news that the kingdom of God has come near and will change every oppressive paradigm, if only we'll let it.

❀     ❀     ❀

Maybe you feel deeply inadequate to have a conversation about race. I see you, White person for whom race has always felt like a zero-sum game. I see you not knowing how to engage. I've heard you express that you know something is wrong in this world and that you're invited to help fix it but you are also keenly aware of your shortcomings. The ways you've been taught about race, the social construct that says White people are superior to all people of color, oftentimes singling out Black people as the most inferior, have left you with some nagging questions: Is something inherently wrong with you, simply because you're White? Isn't the whole point of engaging with racism to stop judging people's worth by the color of their skin? Is it okay for you to think something feels unfair when only White people have to "do the work"?

Please don't stop asking questions, and please don't stop caring. You care because God made you human. Fully. One hundred percent. Caring is what makes you human. To choose to opt out is to choose to ignore the very thing Jesus left heaven to attain, the very thing that adds beauty to our everyday lives: authentic, fleshy, in-real-time human connection. I'm sorry if in the ways you've processed this issue you've felt less than and not deserving of the benefit of the doubt. I'm sorry for the ways white supremacy has dehumanized you.

I've seen you, White friend, bumping against the topic time and time again.

In the twenty years I've been in ministry and the ten years I've devoted to helping White people process racism in America, I've known White people who started on this journey fully energized to "do the work," and after weeks of reading, calling out, and study, they've reached their limit—they are burned out and over talking about racism, and so they speak of diversity and inclusion but their friend group remains mostly

White. They talk about the hard things of life like marriages on the brink, alcoholism, and impending financial ruin, but racial restoration and healing? No, that's a thing they do with their church during Black History Month with a safe Sunday gathering and a community breakfast where they watch Dr. King's "I Have a Dream" speech.

They avoid the pain because they are human.

I've known a descendant of slave owners whose schooling and first houses were paid for with trusts that accrued wealth generation after generation from the sale of cotton in the 1800s. She called while sitting on her wraparound porch with her syrupy Alabama drawl and asked, "Why should I be ashamed for something my great-great-granddaddy did?"

She is confused because she is human.

I've sat with an interracial couple in premarital counseling, the Black woman angry with her fiancé for not "getting it." When she's neglected or mistrusted while they are out and about, he blames the incompetence of the worker and she blames racism. When he cannot admit it or, even worse, when he says she's playing the "race card," the betrayal is almost too much to bear. The ring itches and she turns it over, and over, and over again—can she marry this colorblind man? she asks me.

He is resistant because he is human.

I've held a mama of Brown boys after another unarmed Black teen was shot, and she weeps and she just doesn't know what to do next. Nothing in her life as a White woman has prepared her to adequately protect or provide for her children. She wants to bleed and suffer for them, yet she knows if she is pulled over by an officer she'd get a tip of the hat, a condescending warning, and a ticket she'll have to pay for with her Sephora budget, not seventeen bullets in her torso.

She grieves because she is human.

It doesn't feel difficult to imagine that all these negative experiences with race and racism would paralyze our White brothers and sisters on this journey. It frustrates me every time a White ally becomes apathetic because someone lacked empathy when giving that ally her first anti-racism education.

This book reflects the bedrock ethic of my anti-racism work: we are doing the work of rehumanizing those who have been systemically and relentlessly dehumanized by white supremacy. Which is basically every single person who lifts a fist and chants, "No justice, no peace" or kneels and prays, "Lord have mercy."

We should remember that the work of dismantling racism is not only recognizing, repenting of, and repairing the damage done after four hundred years of oppression of Black and Brown people. Yes to all the above, and this work is a deeply interpersonal one that requires grace, nuance, kindness, and empathy. This is the work of healing a fractured relationship. It is the fleshy, in-real-time, upside-down work of peacemaking. We can do this together, if we open ourselves to one another, allowing each other to see our pain, share our trauma, and invite Jesus to be our balm in Gilead.

As an Aboriginal activist group in Queensland in the 1970s put it, "If you have come here to help me you are wasting your time, but if you have come because your liberation is bound up with mine, then let us work together."[3] Let us agree to be boldly, lovingly honest. Let us be fully human, fully empathic, and fully committed to our collective shalom.

When Jesus began the Sermon on the Mount by acknowledging the pain, the trauma, and the ways his listeners suffered, he in effect said, "The kingdom is yours." I imagine there was a collective sigh. Today, I read the Beatitudes as an anti-racism peacemaker in a white supremacist culture, not unlike Rome, and it's such a relief. It frees me to be honest with you that this white supremacist society has caused untold pain throughout generations, and it frees me to be patient with you, for in this white supremacist society you have not been given permission to feel. Together, let's step into the rare, free air of the kingdom of God. Let us breathe in the blessing of being seen and invited in by Jesus as he teaches us the Sermon on the Mount.

## *Breath prayer*

———

For this reason he had to be made like them, fully human in every way, in order that he might become a merciful and faithful high priest in service to God, and that he might make atonement for the sins of the people. Because he himself suffered when he was tempted, he is able to help those who are being tempted.

—HEBREWS 2:17-18

Jesus, Faithful Confidant

*INHALE,  EXHALE*

Help me

# 8

# I'm Sorry and I'm Listening

Blessed are those who mourn, for they will be comforted.

—MATTHEW 5:4

Dear White Peacemakers,

I sat on my deck on the phone with my friend Emily, whom you'll read more about later in this book, and said one of the truest things I've ever said about racism: "Seeing what happens to Black and Brown people in this country because we have not adequately dismantled racism just makes me sad, perpetually sad." I asked if she would sit with me on the phone and let me cry for a bit. She said yes, and then a teen came to the sliding door and waved me inside to help with a distance-learning issue. I told her I didn't have time to lament together in that moment, maybe let's schedule a time to sit shiva, the Jewish practice of offering your presence for seven days after the death of a loved one. She said okay. I never got around to taking that time, but later that week she sent me seven letters, with a note on them that said "Seven letters for seven days of lament." Each day spoke to my heart and led me toward healing:

Day 1: Let Yourself Feel

Day 2: The God Who Cries

Day 3: Why Do The Wicked Prosper

Day 4: You Were Made For This and You Are Enough

Day 5: Sit with Your Creator

Day 6: Hold on to Eternity

Day 7: What Comes Next

She used her words and presence to mourn for me even when I didn't have the energy or presence of mind to make time to process my grief. I think this is what Jesus is promising to those of us with perpetually broken hearts.

Pass the tissues,
Osheta

Three months after my Mama died suddenly from a massive heart attack, I had the worst flu of my entire life. I also had to board a plane to speak at a women's retreat for my friend Katherine. There are very few speaking requests I accept automatically, but women's retreats are one of them. So when Katherine, one of my favorite people in the world, asked if I would come minister to the women of her church for two days in the beautiful wilderness of Michigan, I said yes—even though my body felt heavy and my throat was killing me.

"Katherine, I'm coming but I want you to know I'm really sick, like I might need to not come to the fellowship time tonight."

Katherine, one of the best pastors I know, texted back, "If you don't feel well enough to fly here, it's totally okay. We'll book you for next year and figure out something else for this weekend."

I had just helped my family with funeral expenses for Mama, who didn't have anything set aside, so I really needed the money, and honestly, I needed to get out of Saint Paul for a few days.

"No, I'm coming. I'm not running a fever. I just need the night to rest."

I flew into Chicago and finally met Katherine, an online friend, in real life. We talked about everything from her favorite band to how my family was settling into Minnesota.

"How are you since your mom's passing?" Katherine asked as she pulled into a Panera to get me soup and a green smoothie.

I shrugged. "Some days I forget she's gone, but then something happens and it triggers my grief all over again. Like the other day, my dog did something really ridiculous and I would have called Mama to tell her, since she loved dogs, but I realized I couldn't. I spent the rest of the day in bed crying with that stupid dog nestled up against me."

Katherine ordered and I found a place by the fireplace to warm up—the chills were setting in. When we sat at our table with my smoothie, she tilted her head to the right side and studied me for a moment. Katherine is my mystical pea in a pod; she reads people and energy so effortlessly. I can use flowery, emotional language with her and at the same time know that I can bring an intensely logical idea to her, either way she'll read between the emotions and the spiritual lines and offer rich insight.

She was reading me.

"Do you think your body is grieving your mother?" she asked.

I had written on my social media weeks before that I didn't know how to live in this world without Mama, my first home in it. How do I be a real human girl when the real human woman who made me is gone?

The server brought my chicken noodle soup and Katherine's salad. I avoided her eyes. I didn't need to be read anymore.

She waited. I stirred my soup. She took a sip of her water. I stared at the fireplace.

This evasion of grief probably took two minutes tops, but it felt like an hour.

"Yeah. I'm grieving. I haven't really let myself grieve Mama. I mean, I was at home for the memorial and I flipped into big sister mode. Then I got back here and there's so much to do with the church, so I flipped into pastor mode. And I've got teens constantly in need, so my baseline is mama mode. I don't think I've let myself just be a grieving daughter."

Katherine steadied her eyes on me. "And your body's telling you to stop and listen. To let it grieve."

❀   ❀   ❀

To be Black in America is to be constantly grieving.

When Africans were taken from their land and put on cramped boats, over two million of them died in the journey, called "the Middle Passage," from West Africa to the Americas.

Nearly two thousand Black Americans were terrorized and lynched during Reconstruction, a number that would surge to an estimated sixty-five hundred during the Jim Crow era.

In 2020 alone, 226 Black people were killed by police.

Black women are four times more likely to die in childbirth than White women.

Black people have been tested and subjected to horrific medical studies because of a myth that Black people don't feel pain the way others do.

Black people have died from COVID-19 at a disproportionally higher rate.

There is a great deal for us to grieve.

In her article "The Relentlessness of Black Grief," Marissa Evans says,

> The grief we feel today also echoes back through time, to our ancestors, enslaved people who mourned long before I existed, and to those who endured the indignities of the Jim Crow era. Our traumas are handed down through the generations and intensify with each new death and realization that American systems were never designed to work in our favor. We know, too, what the inequities mean for our future. Our pain comes not just from those we've already lost, but from those we stand to lose over time. A specific sadness emerges when you realize that someone may be denied the chance to be their ancestors' wildest dreams.
>
> We've had to overcome insurmountable losses for the sake of self-preservation. And while resiliency has long been crucial to our emotional survival, enduring is not easy.[1]

And yet, White Peacemaker, usually when this kind of information is shared, it's explained away and sometimes there's a defensiveness, and I think I know why—you don't know how to hold our grief.

When Kobe Bryant was killed in a helicopter accident, many White people posted about his past mistakes, and I thought, "Oh, they don't know how to respond to Black grief."

When there was protesting in my city that in some places turned to rioting (mostly instigated by people coming into the city and not the protestors themselves), I heard stories about friends whose property was damaged or questions like, "Why do Black people always tear up their neighborhoods?" And I thought, "Oh, they don't know how to identify Black grief."

When I posted an eight-minute video crying over the death of Philando Castile, someone messaged me and told me I was overreacting because I didn't personally know Philando or his family. And I thought, "You don't know how to honor Black grief."

To be Black in America is to never be allowed to fully grieve.

What you're seeing in this moment, White Peacemaker, is not just a great racial reckoning, it is an invitation to grieve. To listen to our collective bodies, to hold, see, and share in grief. To mourn with us, as we mourn.

Jesus was described as a man of sorrows, acquainted with the deepest grief (Isaiah 53:3 KJV), and in his teaching on the Sermon on the Mount that those who mourn will be comforted, Jesus is teaching us that to unlock the kind of trust and vulnerability necessary to bring true peace, we must grieve and grieve together. You, as a White person, must learn how to enter into the great, unrelenting pain of people of color that has been caused by white supremacy. In entering in when you don't have to, when you could choose to ignore, you are walking in the way of Jesus. Get acquainted with our grief, mourn with us, and build a bridge with your compassion.

To be a peacemaker is to be someone who learns how to grieve.

There's a picture I keep on my phone that I've looked at several times when I'm writing.

It's a picture I took at a prayer vigil for the nine Black brothers and sisters who died on June 17, 2015, when Dylann Roof, a White supremacist, attended Bible study at Mother Emanuel Church, a historic Black church, and at the end of Bible study during the prayer time opened fire, killing:

Cynthia Graham Hurd

Rev. Sharonda Coleman-Singleton

Tywanza Sanders

Ethel Lee Lance

Susie J. Jackson

Rev. DePayne Middleton Doctor

Rev. Daniel Lee Simmons Sr.

Myra Thompson

Rev. Clementa Pinckney

At the vigil, these two women held on to each other—one Black, the other White, both lamenting, both singing about how they pray for each other and how much they need each other.

I have no idea what hard road and harder conversations they had to come to this place of shared empathy and passion for racial justice. They remind me of the Scripture that says, "For the joy set before him [Jesus] endured the cross" (Hebrews 12:2).

I imagine the joy set between these two peacemakers was so beautiful, so worthy that they endured the work of dismantling white supremacy together. That day, I watched them weep together, both sets of shoulders heaving and working out their pain and I thought, "That White Peacemaker has done some hard work learning how to grieve."

That night I wondered, What would that Black woman have wanted to hear her White friend say in the hours after a racial tragedy? What would I want to hear? And I went home and wrote this to White Peacemakers:

I almost wrote this post when there were riots in Ferguson and I almost wrote this post when protestors were holding up signs that read "I can't breathe" in response to Eric Garner's murder by a police officer in New York City. This post was very nearly published when Black women stood in the street topless, a prophetic picture of both the African American woman's vulnerability in this broken world and her strength in the face of brutality. Then I saw Dejerria Becton, a Black fifteen-year-old, wrestled and held to the ground by a White police officer, so I wept and sat at my computer with these words. And now, nine brothers and sisters lost their lives to racism in Charleston last night and I cannot ignore the need to write this post anymore.

In the next few hours there will be even more coverage of the shooting of nine people at a historic African American church in Charleston, South Carolina. Soon news outlets and bloggers will begin speculating about the motive of Dylann Roof, the accused shooter, and we'll be tempted to assign blame and make assumptions. These are the critical hours that set the trajectory of this new conversation on racism in America. These are also the hours our helplessness rises to the surface and we'll use our words to alleviate it.

Two weeks ago, in the hours and days after the McKinney pool party where Dejerria Becton was assaulted, I read some of the most hateful words used to shore up defensiveness. I saw people blame the teens. Memes were made that called a vulnerable young woman rude, disrespectful, and deserving of the treatment she received. I can't fathom how it's appropriate to blame her for her mistreatment in a day when there is a collective gasp of disgust when someone suggests that a drunken girl raped at a party brought that onto herself.

Our words matter. Right now, they matter, oh so much.

*Let no corrupting talk come out of your mouths, but only such as is good for building up, as fits the occasion, that it may give grace to those who hear (Ephesians 4:29 ESV).*

You see, there is a deep pain in the African American community today. Last night, when my White husband told me what happened in Charleston, I sat still. Unmoving. Heat pounding. Tears burning in my eyes and lump in my throat. I saw those nine lives taken. I saw welcoming the newcomer, offering him refreshments, inviting him to cast his cares on Jesus. I heard the loading of the gun, the yells, the running. I saw the pools of blood on the church floor. I'm a pastor's wife. My church meets in downtown LA, and we invite everyone—those with mental illness, people who are homeless, folks who live in lofts—to meet Jesus, learn of his great love, and leave with a new sense of their immeasurable worth. This is the life we're called to—loving the stranger well because we've been wholly loved by God. So I saw what happened as a pastor's wife who worries about her husband's safety.

Then I saw it as a Black woman. I imagined my initial confusion when a White man who's never attended shows up, but then Holy Spirit–anointed love brings me to invite him in. I imagined the questions I'd have—"Who? How? What can we offer him?" I imagined the brief moment of hope, maybe gladness that the Lord has brought us a new person to pray for. I imagined the fear-soaked confusion. The terror of running for my life. The desperate last thoughts for my family, my babies, my church.

At this moment, this painful imagining is happening for Black people across this country. The pain we're feeling right now is akin to the loss of a child because whenever Black lives are treated as worthless, whenever our story is marked yet again with violence, whenever we're forced to remember the brutality our grandparents endured when they stood for freedom and dignity—it feels like Dr. King's dream is a hope deferred and our hearts are sickened. As a White person, you may have heard Dr. King's "I Have A Dream" speech and thought, "Yes, that's a nice sentiment." That "nice sentiment" is a defining dream for the African American community. We don't want to be angry anymore. We're tired of being afraid. We're tired of these headlines. We want to have peace. We dream of unity too.

But sadly, race and division and the rending of the *imago Dei* are Satan's favorite weapons, so I'm not sure we'll ever completely get past this. Lord help us, something like this may happen again. Maybe not next month or the month after, but racism is still infecting the system of our country. I fear the disease will flare up again and again.

So, what then? Is there nothing we can do? No. No, not at all. It's time to claim these hours as our stand for peace and stretch out our hands for solidarity.

*God blesses those who work for peace, for they will be called the children of God (Matthew 5:9 NLT).*

Reading the news stories and getting the details of this shooting is painful in and of itself, but one thing makes our pain even greater. When in these dark hours as we mourn the loss of the nine lives of the Charleston martyrs, our suffering is used as a means to push your agenda, whatever it may be.

So today, I offer two responses that promote peace, lay a foundation for unity, and point to the love of Jesus as displayed on the cross.

*I'm sorry.*

And

*I'm listening.*

*I'm sorry* because we're called to be peacemakers. We are the ones on the front line of violence with the sword of the Spirit—his words that bring life.

We're called to be the ones to cry out, "Immeasurable worth!" when image bearers are devalued.

We're the voices of justice.

We're the ones who draw in the sand and level the playing field.

As peacemakers, we're tasked with identifying with our Prince of Peace who overcame our bloodthirsty enemy by shedding his own blood—selflessness and love flows from the cross and lays out our chosen path, humility. *"I'm sorry"* tames the anger. *"I'm sorry"* respects the pain. *"I'm sorry"* positions you as a friend and not adversary.

*"I'm listening"* because we're called to be reconcilers. Like Jesus reconciled us to the Father—it's a painful process. A denying process. A humiliating process. But a kingdom process, nonetheless. *"I'm listening"* says, "Yes, I have an opinion, and yes, I have strong feelings, and yes, this makes me feel more than a little helpless, but I'm going to press into this specific pain and listen."

Last week after I watched the video from the McKinney pool party, I called my White friend to process. As the phone rang, I crafted intelligent analysis and a bullet point list of angles to talk about the issue, but the most profound moment of that call was when I broke down and cried for almost five minutes. She sat and listened as I wept for the lost dream. I didn't have words for my grief and neither did she, but she healed me in her silence. Her willingness to sit shiva with me mitigated the loss and cleared out the anxiety. *"I'm listening"* is all you need to say right now. *"I'm listening"* disrupts the enemy's plan to pit pride against pain. He's delighted with every defensive word, every zinger post, every grandstanding status; they perpetuate us versus them. Right now, kingdom people, our Prince of Peace is asking us to rally behind him with few words, compassionate hearts, listening ears.

*My dear brothers and sisters, take note of this: Everyone should be quick to listen, slow to speak and slow to become angry (James 1:19).*

I'm kneeling at the cross today, wetting the ground with my tears for the suffering of Emanuel African Methodist Episcopal Church. I'm full of sorrow for Dylann Roof. And right now, I need to hear *I'm sorry and I'm listening.*

I suspect I'm not the only one.

Will you let your words be few and your love be great today as we process the shooting at Mother Emanuel? Will you practice shalom by putting aside your agenda and taking up the call of the cross to die to yourself? Will you hold ground for healing where violence trampled our hope? The choice is yours, kingdom person.

And if you can't say *"I'm sorry"* or *"I'm listening"*; if you can't understand the need to enter this conversation, then may I gently ask you not to speak? Stay away. Go before the Lord and ask him to touch your lips with coals so that you may use your words wisely. These are critical hours, people. Defining hours. Let's push back the darkness, one peacemaking response at a time.

❀   ❀   ❀

Katherine was standing at the back of the room after I gave three talks about shalom seeking and everyday peacemaking. Quiet music played and she waited patiently, almost serenely, with a small bottle of anointing oil in her hands. One by one the women went back to her for prayer. I watched Katherine with admiration—she's the pastor I want to be someday. I wanted to go to her to receive prayer, but I also didn't want to get too close to her with my sicky germs and speaker breath. But the Lord prompted me to go when I noticed the last woman had received prayer. Katherine smiled, rubbed the oil between her hands, and prayed, "Lord, heal Osheta and let her listen to her body. Give her space to grieve. Let her know she is not alone."

Then she just stood with her hands fragrant from the oil on either side of my head. I knew she was holding space with me. Standing before God with me in my sickness and my sadness.

White Peacemakers, when you mourn with us, you're allowing yourself to be anointed by the Spirit and to hold space. This is holy work. This is the work of Jesus, our Wounded Healer.

# *Breath prayer*

How long, LORD, must I call for help,
but you do not listen?
Or cry out to you, "Violence!"
but you do not save?
Why do you make me look at injustice?
Why do you tolerate wrongdoing?
Destruction and violence are before me;
there is strife, and conflict abounds.
Therefore the law is paralyzed,
and justice never prevails.
The wicked hem in the righteous,
so that justice is perverted.

—HABAKKUK 1:2-4

Wounded Healer

*I N H A L E ,    E X H A L E*

Help

# 9

# Last Words

I can't breathe
—George Floyd, May 25, 2020

I wasn't reaching for it
—Philando Castile, July 6, 2016

You promised you wouldn't kill me
—Natasha McKenna, February 8, 2015

I can't breathe
—Freddie Gray, April 19, 2015

They tasing me
—Walter Scott, April 4, 2015

I didn't even do nothing
—Samuel DuBose, July 19, 2015

I can't breathe
—Eric Garner, July 17, 2014

I don't have a gun. Stop shooting
—Michael Brown, August 9, 2014

Please don't let me die
—Kimani Gray, March 9, 2013

Why are you following me for?
—Trayvon Martin, February 26, 2012

Why did you shoot me?
—Kendrec McDade, March 24, 2012

I love you too
—Sean Bell, November 25, 2006

It is finished
—Jesus Christ, King of the Jews

# 10

# If I Don't Make It Home Safely

Dear White Peacemakers,

It took me forever to talk my sons into going on the youth retreat. For weeks, I did the not-so-subtle nagging mom thing where I'd bring it up when I had them as a captive audience in the car and put the brochure on the fridge—a place I knew they'd see it. It took me calling in a favor to my friend who worked with the youth and promising they'd get out of their chores if only they'd go—give it a try. I wasn't pushing them for the spiritual aspect of it—they're pastors' kids. They've seen the seams of retreat planning. They know busy and normal people make all the fun happen, and more than a few times they've seen their mom and dad stumble in after a retreat weekend, exhausted and over people, so we do the least spiritual thing we can think of—get into comfy pj's and watch ridiculous reality TV. I did it for the hopes of them finding community.

We had just moved from Los Angeles to Saint Paul and they didn't know very many people, so I thought the retreat would be a good icebreaker for them. They finally agreed. The day I dropped them off at the church, my oldest looked around and said, "Oh my gosh, Mom, they're so White!" It was true, the group was so White. These youth were White suburban kids and the leadership team was mostly White, but I worked for the church and got a really sweet scholarship for my boys, so what was I supposed to do? "No, look, see there's Deklan, he's biracial like you!" They turned to each other and shared a look. I knew what that look meant—"Oh great, so everyone is going to assume we're all going to be best friends because we're all biracial," my oldest, Tyson, said. This is what happens to my kids often, and today I enacted a microaggression—assuming all biracial kids should or want to be friends with each other. "Sorry, guys." I said. "Listen, try and give it a chance—you don't have to hang with Deklan if you don't want to. You don't even have to make friends if you don't want to, just be open to having a really fun weekend, okay?"

Tyson, who was sixteen at the time, shrugged, pulled his duffle bag from the back seat, and opened the door. "I doubt it, Mom, but since I don't—ahem—have to clean the kitchen for two weeks, I'm game."

He and his brother ambled to the group and checked in. Before I drove off, I got a text from thirteen-year-old T. J.

"Thanks for trying, Mom. See you on Sunday."

They had a wonderful time. On the drive home, T. J. leaned in between the driver's and passenger's seat to tell us all about his cohort leader, and Tyson gushed about some weird skit they created. I was laughing and thanking God for their good weekend, until Tyson noticed the police lights behind us. "Yo, Mom . . . is that for you?" I wasn't speeding, our registration was current, both taillights worked properly—in fact, I'd taken the newer of our two vehicles to pick them up because I'd noticed one of the brake lights was out in our older minivan. I had no idea why I was getting pulled over. "No, let me change lanes to see." I changed lanes and the police officer followed me, then turned on her sirens.

"Oh my god, Mom, isn't this the city where Philando Castile was shot?" Tyson exclaimed as I began to pull over.

"Shh . . . that was nowhere near here." I turned the loud music we were yelling over all the way down to zero, no distractions, no confirming biases . . . we were just a mother and her two sons driving home on a Sunday afternoon.

The officer, a White woman with curly brown hair, exited her car, stopped, and put her hand on her holster.

"Mom . . . Mom . . . she's going to pull her gun." Tyson pulled his phone out.

T. J. leaned back, quiet, fidgeting.

She was just pulling her pants up and adjusting her top. She resumed walking toward my car.

"Get still, guys, and stay quiet," I whispered, trying to steady my voice. These kids needed their mom to remain in control. "T. J., can you take Tyson's phone and keep recording? Keep it down by your side, though, or she'll tell you to turn it off. Tyson, can you pull my registration and my license out quickly and set them on the dash where the officer will see my hands when I reach to grab them?"

Both boys obeyed. I could hear their shuddering breaths as I rolled the window down.

"Hello, Officer," I said as she came up to my window.

"Ma'am, are these your children?" she asked.

I looked to them, confused, and then back to the officer. "Yes."

She stepped to the back window where T. J. was and demanded, "Roll the window down."

Why wasn't she asking for my paperwork? What was her obsession with my kids and the car?

Confused, I asked, "Excuse me?"

"I SAID . . . Roll . . . the . . . window . . . DOWN!" she yelled. I wanted to assume it was because of the highway traffic behind her, but I knew I'd annoyed her by not obeying immediately.

I rolled the back window down and she stuck her head in the car.

"Oh . . . ," she chuckled lightly as she muttered to herself, "he *is* buckled in."

The officer walked up to my window.

"Ma'am, why didn't you pull over immediately when I began pursuing you?"

"I didn't know you wanted me to pull over. I wasn't doing anything wrong—"

"Well, it's wrong to not comply with an officer attempting to stop you," she interrupted.

"You're . . . you're right." I threw my hands up in exasperation, and both of my boys took a sharp intake of breath. I'd scared them by moving quickly.

"Ma'am, I need to see some ID. I saw your boy leaning up and wanted to make sure he was buckled in, but you're being difficult so I need to make sure everything's okay."

She ran my driver's license. Everything was okay. She came back to lecture us about safe car riding.

"This is a warning, ma'am. Have more deference with police. We're just out here to keep you safe." She ambled back to her squad car and drove away.

We were silent the whole drive home.

T. J. got out of the car first. "I'm glad we got home safe, Mom," he said before he closed the door.

Tyson shook his head. "Tell me again how not all White police officers hate Black people?" He got out and slammed the door. Hard. I didn't blame him. I wanted to slam doors and break things and scream.

Two years later that same kid tweeted about George Floyd's murder: "For the first time in a while I watched a video of a Black man getting killed by a police officer, I didn't cry. I sigh because this happens so often I can't help but be desensitized. The police aren't helping the Black community, they're inflicting fear . . .

Killing our sisters, brothers, mothers, fathers, cousins, nephews, nieces, aunties, uncles. The police don't protect Black people, they hunt them, then justify their deaths with a badge. I'm disgusted, America. How can you throw away our lives, after we built you?"

❀    ❀    ❀

There's one story of police brutality that I can't shake. On August 24, 2019, twenty-three-year-old Elijah McClain was walking home wearing a ski mask. He did that sometimes because his extremities got cold, but I guess to someone predisposed to thinking Black men are dangerous, he looked like he was up to no good. Hands flailing and head bobbing, he more danced than walked, but someone saw him, assumed he was on something, and called the police. I mean, could you blame them—ski mask, brown skin, moving to his own beat—offensive. Even though the caller said he didn't believe Elijah was armed or posing danger to anyone, one has to wonder—why the phone call at all? Why the speculation and observation?

Elijah was a gentle young man who, when approached by the police, resisted because he wasn't doing anything wrong, and when the encounter escalated and three officers held him to the ground, one using the now-illegal carotid control hold on Elijah, effectively cutting off the blood supply to his brain, Elijah spoke kind words, true words, respectful words:

> I can't breathe. I have my ID right here. My name is Elijah McClain. That's my house. I was just going home. I'm an introvert. I'm just different. That's all. I'm so sorry. I have no gun. I don't do that stuff. I don't do any fighting. Why are you attacking me? I don't even kill flies! I don't eat meat! But I don't judge people, I don't judge people who do eat meat. Forgive me. All I was trying to do was become better. I will do it. I will do anything. Sacrifice my identity, I'll do it. You all are phenomenal. You are beautiful and I love you. Try to forgive me. I'm a mood Gemini. I'm sorry. I'm so sorry. Ow, that really hurt! You are all very strong. Teamwork makes the dream work. Oh, I'm sorry, I wasn't trying to do that. I just can't breathe correctly.

They didn't release him. They threatened to have their K-9 bite him, and when the paramedics arrived they didn't ask for care for his neck or relief for his asthma attack. No, they suggested he was high, and Elijah received an injection of ketamine, sending him into cardiac arrest. Seven days later Elijah was declared brain dead.

Elijah did everything right. He was a Beloved child who even as he was being callously attacked proclaimed the goodness of the officers. Elijah loved animals and taught himself to play the violin and guitar. During his lunch breaks he'd go play music for the animals at the shelter. Elijah was a healer, a massage therapist who treated his patients with care. Elijah was a peacemaker.

And they killed him.

I am a peacemaker. I try to do everything right. I believe in my heart that White people with biases are not evil, just deeply beholden to fear. I pray for them. I pray for police officers who become power-drunk. I prayed for that officer who stopped me. But the reality is, I'm Black. I am never impervious to the potential of police brutality. It could happen to me. Even if I am proclaiming Belovedness and de-escalating and trying to remain respectful. There's nothing I can do that can protect me from white supremacy.

❀   ❀   ❀

So, White Peacemaker. I have a favor to ask of you. If I don't make it home one day. If I get pulled over by the wrong cop on the wrong day and I don't get home safely. If my body is wrangled to the sidewalk and I die gasping for breath, begging for my inhaler. If I get shot in my driver's seat with no one to witness and no one to protect me. If I get taken in and processed and then something mysterious happens to me. Can you please speak up and cry out for my justice? Will you not wait for the details as if I did something so bad it would warrant that kind of mistreatment? Will you hold the police officer and department accountable ?

Then will you love my biracial kids for me?

You in your White skin can help heal their trauma and prevent them from internalizing hatred for White people. Will you pray for them and send my husband messages checking in on them? Will you remember the day of my death and remind them that their mother loved them something fierce and that because you love me, you'll care for them? I worry all these images of White people enacting such violence on Black people will cause long-term damage, and every day I try to do my best to mitigate it—I tell them stories of White Peacemakers showing up and doing good. I invite them to learn about their Irish and Jewish identities so they love their whole selves. But it's hard. If something happens to me, I worry their dad will be too grief-stricken to do this work alone.

And don't come out the gate with all the Jesus talk. Ask Jesus to comfort them, but don't expect them to be incredibly receptive to him in the first few months after my death. They'll know I went down loving because of my commitment to cross-like sacrificial love. They'll know I chose nonviolence. And they'll understand but they'll resent God for it—I'm hoping only for a little while. They'll know that I would have appealed to the officer's Belovedness. I've been practicing the Lord's Prayer several times a day for years just so it's like second nature if I'm ever in danger, so I'll be ready to choose peace when I'm confronted with violence. So you're going to have to be smart when you talk to them about Jesus. You're going to have to be patient and kind. You're going to have to follow their lead, and honestly, White Peacemaker, that's the best thing for them to see, a White person hold vigil and practice humility, because agape love is never a coercive love.

So, if I don't make it home safely, will you do what you can to seek shalom for my family?

❀     ❀     ❀

Every day I get in my car, pray for safety, and trust God that I'll run my errands in peace and make it home okay.

I know there are more than a few officers who are kind and good, who see the systemic nature of racism and try their best to truly serve their communities. I've been pulled over for speeding before and the officer was a young man who couldn't have been sweeter. He noticed I was anxious and said, "I just wanted to check to make sure you're okay—you were going fifteen over the speed limit." When I confessed I was speeding because I was late to a work meeting, he laughed and told me, "Well, don't get a ticket and have to use your hard-earned money on a fine—use it for something nice for yourself."

He sent me on my way with a warning and a recommendation of a good restaurant near my home.

Some days, however, the errands-in-peace part doesn't happen—I get profiled by a store employee or yelled at by a White man in the Starbucks drive-through lane. Even still, I've always made it home and for that I'm grateful.

But if one day I don't, White Peacemaker, I'm counting on you.

Love,
Osheta

# 11

# We Raise Our Hands

Today, Lord, we raise our hands. These holy hands made holy to do the holy work of reconciliation in this sin-stained world. I raise my hands and ask God to redeem the violence, redeem the suffering, redeem the heartbreak in our countries. I raise my hands to thank you because you have overcome, and to ask him to come, be present, and bring peace. With our hands in the air we pray, "By your wounds we are healed, Lord. Usher in healing for the suffering caused by white supremacy."

Today, we raise our hands, because perfect love casts out all fear and because Abba Father sees the suffering of his children. We raise our hands to bear witness to our brothers and sisters who have faced isolation, neglect, mistrust, and violence. We raise our hands because our love for them is restless. I can't do anything tangible with these hands but raise them high. Lord, we are restless for change and anxious for hope. We are witnesses of injustice. We are the women at the foot of the cross—empower us to stay through the torment so that we can be present to bind up wounds and then see resurrection.

We raise our hands to God who out of his great love for his children heard their cries and carved a path toward justice when there seemed to be no way. Make a way in our world, Lord. Make a way and drown the Enemy of your peace in your waves of Justice.

Today, we raise our hands because of the truth that Jesus identified with the poor, broken, marginalized, and ignored. We raise our hands because Jesus is our Truth and he will make us free, free from shame and free from insecurity. We raise our hands because it is so true that he will empower us to beat our swords into plowshares and our spears into pruning hooks—we need only identify ourselves as willing truth-tellers. So we lift our hands to receive the necessary tools of this heavenly alchemy: a humble heart, listening ears, love-spun courage, and most of all, open palms that refuse to cling to bitterness, hate, or fear.

Today we raise our hands in surrender. I can't do this work on my own. We can't even pray for reconciliation on our own—we need the Holy Spirit to come and take our jumbled, incoherent words and turn them into something powerful. Lord, place a terrible fear in the heart of the Enemy, and advance your kingdom of Peace where Violence has made its camp.

We are but one gathering of your people with a heart for the many who are sweltering in the racially charged climate of our countries—nevertheless, we raise our hands.

We raise our hands in surrender.

We raise our hands in protest.

We raise our hands in holy anger.

We raise our hands in solidarity, as one people who reject the wall of hostility and want to build bridges of community.

We raise our hands because we are the Beloved Community.

Amen.

# PART III

# Down by the Riverside

# 12

# Ain't Gonna Study War No More

## *Disarming White Fragility*

On any given Halloween night, you'd find me cuddled up on the couch with a big bowl of chili watching *The Village* in that year's chosen Halloween-themed pajama set. But I lost a bet to my snarking teens, so the first Halloween post-lockdown, I was running through the cornfields while an actor chased me with a prop chainsaw.

To be clear, Peacemaker, my Halloween aesthetic is cozy-plot-twist creepy not Mama-peed-her-pants terrifying.

But nothing has been the same since the lockdown—holiday plans included. In Minnesota between October and November, there's a general sense of resolve that winter truly is coming so we'd better do every single outdoor thing we can think of. With the pandemic in full swing and outdoor gatherings deemed the safest to prevent the spread, so many of us in the North attempted to squeeze in every last chance to see our friends around our firepits. One of my friend's husbands built her a tarp gazebo around their firepit in her backyard just to extend outdoor gatherings past the first big snow.

My children were feeling the Minnesota winter anxiety too, and they desperately wanted to see their friends, so I did the unthinkable. I suggested we plan a big trip to a haunted hayride event. Well, friends, the parenting cardinal rule—never bring up an idea to your children unless you're one hundred percent invested in doing it—still holds true. My kids could talk about nothing else or imagine any other way to celebrate Halloween. I thought I had an out when one by one their friends ended up not being able to come, but the day of the hayride, as T. C. and I tried to come up with every reason why we shouldn't go, we got this series of texts on the family thread:

Mom and Dad, when are we leaving for the farm? (truck emoji + ghost emoji)

YEAH (scary face emoji) I was on the website last night. It looks SCARY (dead face emoji). Mom are you going to be ok?

She'll be fine.

No she won't.

$10 says Mom will scream.

Ty, I'll see your $10 and raise you $20 she'll pee *and* scream!

Stop betting on how big a wimp your mom is!

Ha! You have to say that because she's your wife.

Deal

Deal

Y'all stop it! I'll be fine. $20 and two weeks of chores says I won't do any of that.

Various memes and gifs came through to intimidate or taunt me. Teenagers are a special kind of ruthless.

I muted them and got ready. The gauntlet was thrown down and I was up for the challenge.

Peacemaker. I was not.

Within twenty minutes, I screamed, hid my face in my blanket scarf, and yes, at the very end I was chased through the forest by an actor with a chainsaw. And I peed.

It was humiliating. It was also one of my favorite nights since the start of the pandemic. The vulnerability of doing something scary together bonded us anew. I once heard on a podcast about the science of fear that if a couple goes to a haunted house on their first date, they end up feeling closer to each other than if they did something boring or predictable like dinner and a movie.

It was interesting to see each of my kids' fear responses too.

When triggered by one of the actors, one of my kids used humor—she just talked right back to them, even commenting on how cold they must be in their thin costumes and wondering, "Is your throat gonna be okay after all this screaming in people's face?"

Another kid just stayed silent, stoic even. Later I asked, "Weren't you even just a little bit afraid?" He shrugged, "Yeah, I mean I was more startled and thrown off than truly afraid, but they're in it for the reaction so I just didn't give it to them."

My oldest child's strategy was to just get through it as fast as he could. During the hayride portion of the trip he was constantly moving from one side of the wagon to the other to avoid encountering an actor. When they forced us off the wagon and made us walk through the haunted forest, he just walked as fast as he could, nearly leaving our group behind altogether.

Good Lord, my husband and I must be old and fragile because we clung to each other, screamed, jumped, prayed, and yes, y'all, in my case, peed.

Dear White Peacemaker, I wonder, what if you began thinking of the emotions you feel as you undo white supremacy's influence in your thinking and your actions as a type of fear response?

You may be familiar with the idea of white fragility. In an interview on her website, Robin D'Angelo, a sociologist who has been studying race and multicultural education, describes white fragility this way:

> In a nutshell, it's the defensive reactions so many white people have when our racial worldviews, positions, or advantages are questioned or challenged. For a lot of white people, just suggesting that being white has meaning will trigger a deep, defensive response. And that defensiveness serves to maintain both our comfort and our positions in a racially inequitable society from which we benefit.[1]

I like this definition a lot, and in these chapters we're going to disarm white fragility. However, D'Angelo and I part in thinking in this one way: you know I don't call anyone racist. I think for too many of you, you have worked hard to heal from toxic self-identities: fat, stupid, ugly, poor, lazy, not enough, too much. I began this book with an exploration of Belovedness and practices to help you settle into your Belovedness because I believe that only when you know you are Beloved—simply because you are human—only from that grounded place can you do anti-racism. If you believe you are a racist or you take on all the emotional, historical, and societal baggage that comes with that word, then you're prone to unhelpful thought patterns like "I'm the worst" and "What's the point, I can't change anything on my own" and "I can't believe my White pastor, friends, family members are still so stuck in racist thinking, thank God I'm not like them." None of these help you to be a peacemaker.

When I think about your fragility in anti-racism, I choose to think of it as a fear response. Are you like my daughter who uses humor or bravado to deflect? Are you like my middle boy who gets quiet, retreats, and stonewalls? Are you like my oldest who ignores his anxious energy by barreling ahead, running from the trigger?

White Peacemakers, it may be helpful to acknowledge that when you begin exploring racism and even when you get into the nitty-gritty of it, you may be moving outside your "window of tolerance." Therapist Aundi Kolber, author of *Try Softer*, says, "The space between hyper- and hypoarousal, which might be thought of as the 'just right' amount of intensity, is the range in which we can experience emotions, sensations, and experiences without feeling physiologically overwhelmed. . . . Each of us has a window of tolerance, whether we find we are constantly pushing against the edges of it or not. When we are in our window, the brain stays integrated with the prefrontal cortex, which allows us to pay compassionate attention to ourselves . . . this is where we want to be."[2]

White fragility is a natural and understandable reaction you may have to talking about race and confessing your complicity to racism. Anti-racism is a practice of pushing against the edges of your window of tolerance. It's good and necessary to do so because unless you are actively working to dismantle white supremacy in your mind, heart, and actions, then it's unlikely we'll see the types of systemic change necessary to see lasting generational racial healing.

One of my peacemaking practices is to tell a better story about people who are just beyond my capacity for empathy. So when a White person doesn't respond well to correction, challenge, or change, I often say to that person, "It is less likely you're exhibiting fragility because you simply don't care," (I know there are many White people in this world who don't care—I'm not naive—but you're sitting at my table, so I'm choosing to believe you care). "Rather, your fragility is bubbling up because you are afraid and you don't have experience with trying and failing in this work."

White supremacy culture is a defensive culture—it has to be. The architects of Whiteness and gatekeepers of White spaces know how arbitrary it is to endow superiority to one group simply because of their ethnicity. So you're taught, from a very young age, various defensive techniques that masquerade as self-righteousness, politeness, or godliness, or even (a false) humility. Then when you begin unpacking Whiteness and realize some very core things are in danger, those defensive mechanisms come to protect you.

Jesus, however, teaches that those who try to save their lives will lose them and that those who live by the sword will die by the sword. Anti-racism peacemaking is an invitation to interrogate your defenses, know your fear responses, and respond with nonviolence. White Peacemaker, my prayer is you'll do this nonviolent work within yourself, first by calling yourself a Beloved and then by acknowledging your fragility. Fragility needs to be an idea that's neutralized. We all have our fragilities (mine include working out and incontinence at haunted hayrides).

There's a Spiritual for us as we begin disarming our defenses: "Down by the Riverside." The lyrics take us to a riverside where we lay down our swords and shields and study war no more. What would it be like to know, White Peacemaker, that you have the emotional tools and reserve to attend to all the uncomfortable feelings that anti-racism brings up? You see, of all the most grounded and generous White Peacemakers I've encountered, they have all done one thing: they have, through therapy, dialogue, spiritual direction, meditation, and study, embraced self-compassion and cultivated self-awareness. They have practices that center them and they have loving account-ability. They've laid down the swords and shields that belong to their inner critic and inner skeptic. They're not thinking of anti-racism as a battle; they are anti-racism peacemakers who engage with curiosity and mercy.

"Down by the Riverside" is a come-to-Jesus, repentant, moving-forward spiritual. Written post–Civil War, its origin story is a mystery, but some historians think it was a song for the soldiers coming back from war promising that now that the war was over and they were home, they would be peaceable men. I, however, believe that story is an example of Black cultural appropriation. White soldiers sang the songs they heard the slaves sing as a way to heal from their time at war. However, this song originated with enslaved people, who experienced untold dehumanization nearly every day. I believe the song that begins at a riverside baptism and moves through various moments in the life of a disciple walking with Jesus, the Prince of Peace, is a declaration of freedom from the violence of the plantation once they are freed.

So let's go down by the riverside together, White Peacemaker, and let Jesus' teachings about meekness, purity of heart, and mercy help you reframe white fragility. It does not have to be a dangerous idea and understanding it will allow you to build into your anti-racism humility, compassion, and attentiveness.

## 13

# Who Told You You Had to Do This Alone?

Blessed are the meek, for they will inherit the earth.
—MATTHEW 5:5

Dear White Peacemakers,

I know you. You hear Black leaders like me say things like "Do the work" and "This work isn't about you," and in the back of your mind you wonder, "What does that look like for me? I mean . . . where do I begin? I want to learn. I want to engage. But this is all so very new to me. I want to look like Jesus and overturn the tables of racial oppression, but I'm afraid of saying the wrong thing . . . I mean . . . I'm just a White person?"

You love Jesus with your whole heart but when you think about his ministry of reconciliation, you feel overwhelmed. I

get that! I'm a Black woman, married to a White man, raising biracial children. I've gone to workshops and trainings on
multiculturalism. We chose to live in the city for the diversity
and we intentionally build relationships with people from different social locations. I'm someone who loves Martin Luther
King, James Baldwin, Maya Angelou, and John Perkins, and I
still wonder about the logistics of dismantling white supremacy culture. Just literally the other day, I was wondering if I
had committed a microaggression against a Chinese American
friend. This is not for the faint of heart, Beloved. And still, I
believe in you. I know how you feel sometimes. The calls for
action are varied and sometimes opposing:

*Do your work, White people*
*Pray for unity, people of God*
*Defund the Police*
*Black Lives Matter*
*Blue Lives Matter*
*All Lives Matter to God*
*Show up*
*Stop centering yourself*
*Silence is complicity*
*Speaking up is exerting your privilege*
*If your pastor isn't preaching about race, then you should
leave*
*If your church isn't talking about race, then stay and use
your voice*
*Use this hashtag*
*Stop using that hashtag*

If there is one question I get with some regularity, it is,
"What the heck am I supposed to do?"

Sometimes it's asked with a passive shrug of the shoulders
and a small voice.

Sometimes it's asked with great enthusiasm and manic energy.

I want you to know I get it. All of these calls to action are so frustrating and oftentimes seemingly in conflict with each other. Because anti-racism educators bring their personalities, their theologies, and their histories to this work, you need to step back from all the calls to action for a moment. Quiet yourself to help you discern what to do next, work through your confusion in community, and then reject white supremacy's pull toward inaction or, even worse, transferring that anxious energy into a defensive tactic of comparing two teachers' pedagogies against each other.

Let me caution you, though—white supremacy is not an easy problem to fix. It has influenced everything that makes up Western life: media, education, housing, nonprofit organizations, finances, churches, history books, healthcare, city planning, even food. There is not one thing in our society that has not been tainted by white supremacy. It's going to take a long-haul, sustainable strategy of undoing and rebuilding. There are no quick fixes here. If you want to dismantle white supremacy, you're going to need to get comfortable with trying and failing. You'll need to have tough skin and a tender heart. You'll need to know that the small, intentional acts of humility, of you sacrificially loving your Black and Brown neighbor enough to reject a system that has made you comfortable, will be the work of your life. It's okay. You can do this. You are not alone. Even though I know everything in you feels like you've got to fix it all and fix it now. That's white supremacy's influence for ya.

White supremacy culture values quantity over quality. Efficacy is the standard by which something's worth is measured. You can see its influence in questions like: Does it accomplish the job in record time, with the least amount of effort and the biggest profit? Wow . . . as I type that, I think, well it's obvious why chattel slavery became indispensable to a young America. It was effective. It's why after the Thirteenth Amendment was passed, outlawing slavery except as punishment for a crime, thousands of recently enslaved men were criminalized for not having a job or loitering in public places. They were put in prison and forced to work to keep the southern economy afloat. But I always quote this from pastor Bruxy Cavey: "Love is the most inefficient thing we'll do." If you want to do this work, you're going to have to accept that it's not going to be easy, nor will you see the results you want, and you may even feel like you're taking two steps forward and three steps back. You'll need humility, dear one. So let's unpack that.

Love,
Osheta

❀    ❀    ❀

Jesus had some nerve, y'all. Right out of the gate in Matthew he begins teaching about the upside-down kingdom of God by saying everyone who is currently ignored, undervalued, or assumed forgotten by God is actually seen and favored by him—blessed.

Then he goes on to cast this huge, startlingly beautiful vision of the world made right and somehow expect everyone—even the ones in the crowd who were just fine with things the way they have always been—to be like, "Cool, cool, Jesus. When do we start? When do we start suffering for this kingdom you talk about?"

I can't help but imagine when Jesus looked at the crowd of people learning the new culture of the kingdom of God that some of them felt a similar frustration as you. Which is why I'm glad the Sermon on the Mount came at the beginning of his ministry and not the end. Jesus fully intended to walk alongside his disciples and model the kingdom way.

Jesus was teaching this whole new way to be human and live in this world, but like the best of teachers, he knew he had to do it with his followers. He had to not only be the example but empower them to try (and fail) in their discipleship. Jill Biden, the forty-sixth First Lady of the United States, had this quote from Benjamin Franklin stitched into the lining of the coat she wore to the inauguration festivities that I think reflects Jesus' teaching style beautifully: "Tell me and I forget. Teach me and I remember. Involve me and I learn."

One of my favorite hymns about Jesus calls him "meek and mild." It's a prayer of Jesus seeing us in our truest, most vulnerable states because he himself knows vulnerability; he understood that the kingdom of God will come only when we collectively embrace downward mobility, and so he went first.

> Who, being in very nature God,
>     did not consider equality with God
>         something to be used to his own advantage;
> rather, he made himself nothing
>     by taking the very nature of a servant,
>     being made in human likeness.
> And being found in appearance as a man,
>     he humbled himself
>     by becoming obedient to death—
>         even death on a cross! (Philippians 2:6-11)

I wonder if when Paul wrote these words about Jesus, he had the Beatitude from the Sermon on the Mount, in Matthew 5:5, in mind: "Blessed are the meek, for they will inherit the earth." The Hebrew word Jesus uses in Matthew 5:5 for meekness can be translated to "humility." It evokes the picture of someone who has surrendered to God and is so acutely aware of their poverty in spirit (and status) that they resist pride. They look to God, not others, for their validation and sustenance.

In this beatitude, Jesus is beginning to speak to the character ethics of the kingdom—when we follow behind Him, we will embrace meekness.

Listen. Did I try all kinds of Bible reading gymnastics to get around that word, *meek*? Yes, y'all. I did. I even went through this stupid phase when I would say, "My meek is on fleek," as if to say, my meekness is so impressive it's the greatest meekness you've ever seen. Which, Lord, don't let my teens read that. Meekness is humility in action. Sometimes "do the work" looks like laying down your pride, checking your ego, and relinquishing your fame for the sake of the Beloved Community.

Humility is one of those concepts that invites us to hold certain tensions: to be confident in our Belovedness and comfortable with owning our Brokenness.

This push and pull is incredibly important in your antiracism formation.

The question, "What the heck am I supposed to do?" in both inflections, resignation or zeal, reminds me of something I've learned from Dan Kent, author, counselor, and pastor, who wrote in his book *Confident Humility* that when we attempt to cultivate humility, we can easily fall into two ditches: the Ditch of Bigness and the Ditch of Smallness.[1]

If we're overzealous for "the work," we're in danger of falling into the Ditch of Bigness because we're trying too hard to avoid being shamed for our inaction.

If we're resigned that we can't do anything meaningful to address racism, then we're in danger of falling into the Ditch of Smallness because we just don't want to be accused of being prideful or taking up too much space.

Jesus' invitation to a life of meekness mitigates this temptation and shows us a third path, one that allows us to be mindful of the ditches but allows us to walk confidently toward our peacemaking.

We often don't want to embrace humility, because when we hear the word *meek*, we assume "weak," and if there is anything white supremacy culture resists, it is any semblance of weakness.

However, Jesus himself embraced meekness and invited us into it. The yoke of Jesus, White Peacemaker, may be the very thing that will settle and ground you in humility as you do this work. Maybe instead of asking "What the heck am I supposed to do?" you could ask, "Jesus, are you going to do this with me?"

❀   ❀   ❀

In Matthew, Jesus gives his overwhelmed, overtaxed, overstimulated disciples an invitation that has been words of true comfort for thousands of years:

> Come to me, all you who are weary and burdened, and I will give you rest. Take my yoke upon you and learn from me, for I am gentle and humble in heart, and you will find rest for your souls. For my yoke is easy and my burden is light. (Matthew 11:28-30)

For his audience, well accustomed to the everyday work of animal care, the yoke image offered them both comfort and a challenge.

Two animals were often paired together on the farm—one stronger, resilient, wiser, and had seen many harvests; the other newer, still fragile, its muscles not yet tried, unsure of how exactly to hold its neck and carry the weight. The farmer would pair them together so the younger animal would learn from the older. He'd pair them together so the older one could challenge the younger but also pick up the slack when it failed. They'd be paired until they began working in unity, harvesting together, partnering with the farmer to tend to the land.

This is a picture for you, White Peacemaker. To be paired both with an older anti-racism teacher and with Jesus, our ultimate anti-racism peacemaker. It's a calling to you to remember that you are not alone and you are needed to harvest the field.

The promise from Jesus of a light burden is not an ease or a vacation from the work. The light burden is the ease of not having to do the work by yourself.

I stood in four different crowds of protestors after George Floyd was murdered and was amazed at the intensity of passion in the air. The spirit of the air was one of justice and justice now. I've read reports that say in order to see the kind of sea change we want in race relations we'll need at least fifteen years, quite possibly two to three generations.

Two to three generations.

That means our great-grandchildren will live in the world we're dreaming now—if only we keep our heads down, stay yoked together, and don't let up. We as peacemakers have turned our swords into plowshares and now it's time to put them to work.

Humility makes it possible for us to stay committed. White Peacemakers, I've learned from priest Sullivan McCormick that there are two kinds of meekness you can cultivate now to build the strength, resilience, and wisdom you need to reduce the harm caused by white supremacy culture.

Moral humility and intellectual humility.

Moral humility is a posture that says you need God. You do not have the moral high ground, you will not use your goodness or good intentions to explain away unintended harm, and you will accept accountability as you work because you know that you are only human. You will make mistakes. This doesn't mean you're a terrible person or that you are a hopeless racist. This means you are a White person unlearning white supremacy. It's hard, but part of white supremacy culture is an assumption that the White person is never questioned and never challenged. It's the cultural equivalent to "The customer's always right." So, taking on the yoke of meekness means you're willing to make mistakes and you're willing to acknowledge your failings with self-compassion and grace—we'll talk about how to do this in the next couple of chapters.

Intellectual humility is curiosity. Simply put, if you, a White person, want to be a peacemaker, then you have to be curious. Curiosity is the birthplace of connection. If you are unwilling to acknowledge what you don't know or even to acknowledge that you may have received bad information, possibly information that you've built a whole belief system around, then you will be unable to participate in the liberation of suffering.

Let me say that again: your lack of curiosity can keep others in bondage.

Having an intellectual humility about racism in our country will take you to places you never thought you'd go. You will start to learn about the history of our country. You'll see loopholes. You'll see cowardice. You'll rethink quoting your favorite theologian when you learn of their participation in the transatlantic slave trade. You will be wrecked. It's okay. It's expected that you'll feel angry, protective, and even betrayed. You have been living in the ignorant bliss of Whiteness. But I'm so glad you're here now.

Once you've learned a few things, even led a few small groups, white supremacy culture will cause you to want to take the lead on these conversations—be careful. You must temper this newfound expertise with intellectual humility. Be willing to let people of color lead and teach you from our experiences, and always point others to resources created by people of color. In that, you are modeling intellectual humility.

I have to balance this yoke too, White Peacemakers. Moral humility for me looks like not taking the moral high ground simply because I'm part of a marginalized group. My ancestors' and my suffering does not give me the right to treat you like you're an idiot or a burden. Intellectual humility for me looks like acknowledging the areas where I need to learn from other people of color and people in marginalized groups. It also means that I do my best to stay present in conversations with White people. I try not to assume I know what you're going to say and I try really hard to not judge. Remember, I'm yoked with you—we've got to figure out how to do this together. Maybe I'll disagree with you and have to correct you, but I'll always listen to you because as I listen, I'm learning to love you a little bit more.

There's this one story about Jesus and a young man I often think about when I consider the call to White Peacemakers to embrace meekness. So there's this young man, he's called a rich young ruler, and he comes to Jesus and asks him what good thing he needs to do to gain eternal life ("What the heck can I do?"), and Jesus replies by asking him, "Don't you know the laws and the commandments already?" Jesus, the thorough teacher that he is, goes down the list of all the commandments, and the young ruler tells him that he's already done all that. So Jesus ups the ante and tells him to give all his belongings to the poor and come follow him. The young ruler goes away grieving. Scripture says "because he owned much property." The rich young ruler was unwilling to embrace downward mobility, giving up status and wealth that he (or his family) amassed to follow Jesus, an itinerant teacher from a janky town with a father who was a tradesman and a mother who had scandal follow her because of his conception. This is your calling, White Peacemaker: to embrace downward mobility, to choose moral and intellectual humility, to give up all semblance of having it all figured out, and to follow gentle Jesus, meek and mild.

So I have one question for you, White Peacemaker:

Will you take on the yoke of anti-racism peacemaking?

## *Breath prayer*

────

Therefore, as God's chosen people, holy and dearly loved, clothe yourselves with compassion, kindness, humility, gentleness and patience.

—COLOSSIANS 3:12

Compassionate Teacher

*I N H A L E ,　E X H A L E*

I choose humility

# 14

# Your Love Is Not Fragile

Blessed are the pure in heart, for they will see God.
—MATTHEW 5:8

Dear White Peacemakers,

I want to have a heart-to-heart about, well . . . your heart. I have taught anti-racism in many predominately White contexts, and when I get to the class on microaggressions—small, everyday ways White people often unintentionally harm people of color—I can tell you with one hundred percent certainty that I'll hear some variation of this phrase: "Well . . . if you knew my heart you'd know I'm not a racist." Sometimes it's "I have a good heart, I love all people." The most compelling of the heart-centric responses is "The Lord knows my heart and he knows that I'd never do a single racist thing."

Okay.

So, yes. I see your heart, and yes I believe with all of mine that you have really good intentions. But peacemaking is not about intentions. That's peacekeeping. Peacekeeping functions to preserve the status quo, and nothing prevents change more than an argument about intention when what is needed is a discussion about impact.

Peacemaking is the active, tangible, in-real-life practice of making peace. When a person of color in your life tells you that you've done something that has caused racial harm and you reply, "If you knew my heart," it doesn't invite that person to ask more questions. It shuts the conversation down because if we keep pressing, our only option is to somehow suggest that you don't have a good heart.

Jesus never calls us to have good hearts. He does, however, call us to have pure ones.

Wholeheartedly,
Osheta

❀     ❀     ❀

I sat in the coffee shop nervous as all get-out. Drumming my pen on the table, I watched the door for the man I was supposed to meet. This was my first time having this kind of conversation, you see. I, a Black woman, was confronting a White man about a racial microaggression that happened at his nonprofit's annual gala. I'd confronted White people I knew well and could lean into our shared affection for each other, but a straight-up stranger—no.

The work the nonprofit does is truly Christlike: they raise money for struggling communities overseas through what they call "adventures": running, hiking, cycling. As a nature lover, bicycle optimist, and hearty encourager of runners (from the sidelines, mind you—need an encouraging poster board sign, I'm your girl), I loved everything about the night.

Their theme was "Overcome!" Overcoming poverty, overcoming oppression, overcoming apathy. YES! My little do-gooder justice-y heart warmed. I opened up the giving app and was ready to support them, until they ended their program with the song "We Shall Overcome."

A group of children from Thailand sang this iconic civil rights anthem and then a White woman who was clearly trained in the gospel style ad-libbed the evening to a close. Then the wife of one of the founders, another White woman, led a prayer and invitation to partner with their organization. That was it. She left the stage, people got back to their cheesecakes and coffees, and I looked around to see if any of the other people of color in the room noticed what I did.

No attribution to the Black preacher whose hymn inspired a version crafted by Black activists in the 1940s in response to Jim Crow terrorism. No honoring of the history of this song of great cultural importance for Black people in America during the civil rights movement. No connection between justice-seeking overseas with our ongoing march toward freedom here. It became clear to me, these White people cared more about the suffering of Brown people overseas than right in their backyard or in the audience of their fundraising gala.

I left the gala really disappointed. How could someone with such a clear understanding of oppression and systemic brokenness have such a blind spot around race as to use a song so dear to the Black community, invite someone who wasn't Black to sing it in the very same style, and not even honor the Black and Brown attendees in the room by at least highlighting how the missions of anti-racism activism and overseas economic poverty activism parallel each other. It felt disrespectful. To make matters worse, these types of events are mostly attended by White Peacemakers. I was deeply concerned about the example they were setting—it felt like an invitation to a saltwater love affair for White well-meaning Christians who want to appease their altruistic anxieties.

That night I texted the friends who'd invited me to the gala. They're members of the church my husband and I pastor together, we love them dearly, and I was afraid of triangulating them in my conflict. However, they got it, and because they are good friends with the founders, they offered to help set up a meeting so I could ask some questions. I genuinely wanted to understand the oversight.

I was finished with my polar bear white mocha when Patrick showed up with a big smile and offered to buy me a coffee.

I showed him my nearly empty mug and he said, "Could you do a second round?"

And here's a pro-tip, Peacemaker: always take the coffee, hot cocoa, or tea. Always, even if you don't drink it, because the warmth of the cup will fortify you for the conversation and it's good to help you pause and think. If they say something offensive and bat-poop crazy, you just sip and pray for the Holy Spirit to hold your earrings.

He bought the second round and I knew he was a peacemaker from the very beginning.

"Osheta, right off, I want you to know I respect you, and I know that you as a Black woman didn't need to take this time. I don't know exactly what happened that night that troubled you, but I'm willing to listen, but I want you to know that even if we don't fully agree at the end of this, I'm grateful for this conversation."

*Well . . . Holy Spirit, I'mma hold on to my earrings for now. I think we're going to be okay.*

I explained to him my experience of the gala and even how his event gave me significant pause in participating in any of their upcoming fundraisers.

He listened. He pushed back when he didn't understand. He asked clarifying questions. He told me he was the adoptive father of Black children and he was trying. He said, just because he had proximity to Black people and had learned from Black leaders didn't mean he was without blind spots.

He apologized for the harm and thanked me for the meeting.

He demonstrated a pure heart.

I told him that someday I'd love to do a hike for his organization. He nodded enthusiastically and told me about several ones coming up.

I just nodded and finished off my moose tracks mocha. Because I have a pure heart for hiking for Jesus, and unrealistic intentions.

❀    ❀    ❀

Purity of heart sounds pretty self-explanatory. Yet, as with anything Jesus teaches, we have heard it said one way, and he is pushing us even further.

When you think of purity of heart, have you thought of it in this way:

*My heart is pure because I am holy. My holiness is defined by this action or lack thereof.*

*I demonstrate purity of heart by living a righteous life. My righteousness is expressed in certain practices and rituals. My purity is confirmed by these tests of faithfulness to God.*

These are all transactional ideas: *if* I do this, *then* God calls me pure.

To Jesus, the life of a disciple is not transactional, it's transformative.

As we commit to living our lives in the sacrificial peacemaking example of Jesus, our hearts are changed.

Purity in this passage from Matthew 5 is not a blot test on our souls to see if there's any residue from the world that makes us too unclean for God; no, purity in this passage is Jesus' invitation to check the motives and the desires of your heart: pure hearts desire to know and love God, therefore it's easier to see God at work in and through your life. When your motives are anything else, then it can be easy to feel conflicted, discouraged, and distracted.

In this case then, Peacemaker, purity, holiness, and righteousness to Jesus are not transactional words, they are covenantal words.

Covenant to God and covenant to your fellow image bearer.

What if we thought of our commitment to anti-racism as one of the criteria of our covenant to God?

I think this is why so many White Peacemakers I know get deflated when they're held accountable for the impact of their actions. They believe the purity of their hearts is enough—they've done enough, they've read enough, they've proven their core goodness in some way, and so they could never be in danger of committing racial harm.

But James 4:8 resists that moral exceptionalism mindset you've inherited from white supremacy.

"Come near to God and he will come near to you. Wash your hands, you sinners, and purify your hearts, you double-minded."

It seems like purity of heart is directly connected to action. For the anti-racism peacemaker, the kind of action James 4 is calling us to is recognizing God's invitation to create shalom, repenting of how we've rejected or missed opportunities, and recommitting to the way of Jesus. I think this is another one of those times when both/and, third-way approaches are needed.

"Blessed are the pure in heart, for they will see God" is also a beautiful reframing of our lives as Christians to allow Jesus into our interior lives so that we can do the reorienting work of James 4 without shame or fear. We see God and know we're not alone in this so we can be gracious to ourselves when stepping into the gritty work of repentance.

Oftentimes, Peacemaker, I think you worry you're not good enough at making peace or faithful enough in our anti-racism work, and so when you're challenged, your insecurity comes to the surface. All the lies you've believed about yourself and all the frustrations you've had since you began become exposed. You have two choices, engage them and become resilient, or ignore them and become dependent on external validation for your anti-racism.

What if you accepted that you'll make mistakes, and that's okay? Yes, the stakes are high. Yes, you need to fight for change. Yes, you need to do the work. But also, you're human and were never meant to carry the full weight of an evil system on your shoulders. You were never meant to fix it in one fell swoop. You were never expected to be perfect. Just present, friend. Just be present and let Jesus forgive you and send you back into the world to dismantle white supremacy with "Go and sin no more" ringing sweetly, gently in your ears.

I deeply believe that you have a good heart, Peacemaker. You wouldn't be reading a book about anti-racism and peacemaking if you didn't have pure intentions, but because you don't have a lived experience as a person of color, because you don't process everyday interactions through layers of racism, you will make mistakes. It's okay. Lean into the correction and know that while your mistakes will have consequences, no matter what is required for repair, a few things remain: your inherent worth, your Belovedness, and your capacity to grow and do better next time.

The conversation from the person of color about your actions is a gift. It's an invitation to purify your heart in the kiln of sacrificial love.

White Peacemakers, your love is not fragile. Allow the love of God to ground you in your Belovedness, and allow that love to inform how you receive guidance from the people of color in your life. We don't bring up race to be divisive, we bring up race to grow in intimacy. That's what living in covenant with each other is all about: authentically correcting and courageously connecting.

And while I may never run to raise money with Patrick's nonprofit because running makes me cry and puke, sometimes simultaneously—not a good look for my fundraising website—I will run alongside him and every other White Peacemaker who is humble enough to have a conversation and committed enough to learn along the way. We used to sing a song that asks God to "break my heart for what breaks yours." God is brokenhearted by our self-righteousness and our self-preservation that often comes up when we have hard conversations about race. But my prayer is that we not lose heart and that we choose the posture of the pure of heart, brokenhearted and brave because we are Beloved.

# *Breath prayer*

———

Search me, God, and know my heart;
test me and know my anxious thoughts.
See if there is any offensive way in me,
and lead me in the way everlasting.

—PSALM 139:23-24

Search me, O God
*INHALE, EXHALE*
Lead me to peace

## 15

# Yes, You Can Touch My Hair

Blessed are the merciful, for they will be shown mercy.

—MATTHEW 5:7

Dear White Peacemakers,

You can touch my hair.

Yes, go ahead, you can touch my hair. But before you do, I want to know why. Why do you want to run your hands through my curls, along my braids, and in my locs? Is it intrigue? Are you fascinated by something new, something foreign, and you want to say, "I've done it!" Then, no. I resist your doctrine of discovery. Keep your hands to yourself, hold them together in a prayer of repentance, for you are in danger of seeing me not as a person, but as a prop in your quest for knowledge. Dominance is ever close to you, White Peacemaker—stay vigilant.

But if you're curious—truly curious about God's creativity, about how I wear this crown so elegantly—then yes, you can touch my hair. But when you do so, I want you to look me in the eyes and honor my humanity. When you do so, I want you to whisper, "It's so beautiful; you are so beautiful." I want praises to God on your lips and I want you to thank me for allowing you to touch a piece of heaven on this earth.

Yes, you may touch my hair, but then are you willing to hold my hands, turn them palm up, and kiss the callouses and creases? Kiss them for the years of service they've offered, holding others up while letting myself down.

You may touch my hair, but then are you willing to kiss my feet and wash them with your tears? Lament and weep for how they've shuffled through this violent world, taking me to places I do not want to go, but have no other choice—places where I'll be rejected, overlooked, mistreated, misunderstood, undermined, stepped on and stepped over. Are you willing to kiss them because they are beautiful and bring the gospel of peace to you, White Peacemaker?

I bring this good news—you can be set free from the culture of white supremacy that turns you into a consumer of bodies when we were made to celebrate them. Made to care for them. Made to praise God for them. Made to protect them. Maybe and sometimes especially we protect bodies with our own.

So yes, White Peacemaker . . . you may touch my hair, but first have you counted the costs?

Leaning in,
Osheta

"Oh my gosh, Osheta! I'm so glad I ran in to you. This is so God!" exclaimed my friend Helen. With an infectious passion for the oppressed that I've grown to love, she told me about a seven-year-old Black girl in Tulsa who was expelled from school for having dreadlocks.

"That's . . . horrible! Don't you think?" she asked.

I nodded, not quite sure why it was "so God" she ran into me and how I, a Black woman who regularly relaxes her hair, could help, but . . . like a good social justice Christian, I nodded and echoed her horror.

"Today in class," she continued, "I had this idea to encourage her with pictures and messages from professional, African American women wearing dreads and I need your help because obviously . . . I can only do so much." She pointed to her fine chestnut hair.

Then the other shoe dropped—she expected me to help her as a White Peacemaker do something for a Black little girl because I am a Black woman. Even though at the time I was wearing my hair chemically straightened and pressed. I stood in the greeting card aisle while she shared her generous heart to surround the little girl with virtual support in the days to come. The girl and her family were fighting the school and Helen thought it would be cool if we could start a hashtag or social media campaign.

Stunned at the reminder that yes, she sees me as a Black woman and yes, she expected me to care about that story, I nodded and even laughed at her little joke about her hair, but inside I wondered, *Does she see me or my hair?* We tossed around some ideas and I told her to send me a link to the news story—I'd see what I could do. We hugged and gave each other knowing smiles, smiles that said, "You go, Social Justice Girl, let's smash the white supremacy and patriarchy," and I rushed away feeling like a fraud.

I walked away from that chance meeting simultaneously angry about white supremacy culture and how it perpetuates the lie that anything Afro-centric is "unprofessional" and unacceptable. I was hell-bent to restore a girl's self-esteem, because I've been that girl. In grade school, I once washed my hair the night before a field trip and my mama didn't have time in the morning to do it, so she sent me to school with it in a bun that eventually began to frizz throughout the day, leaving it curly. A group of girls teased me mercilessly. At one point one of them acted like she was sneezing and threw hair gel on me. And I want to stop in the telling of this story for a second, White Peacemaker, because I haven't yet described that group of girls, but did you assume they were White? They weren't. They were Black. I couldn't understand why they did this to me—beyond preteens' special brand of meanness—but the more I understand how white supremacy has infected our beauty industry, the more I realize these girls had internalized a kind of hatred for Black hair that corroded their empathy. When they could have helped me on a bad hair day, they teased and transferred their insecurity to me.

I ended up not working on the project with Helen—Black hair and all its complexities was something I was still working through, and I did not, or maybe could not, trust Helen with it yet.

This is one of the things I'm most frustrated about when trying to dismantle white supremacy in multicultural set-tings—wanting to do good things with White people but not knowing if they understand all the dynamics and implications of working together. For you, White Peacemaker, Black hair is maybe beautiful, fascinating, and even brave. For me, it's personal, it's historical, and it's part of my identity.

❀    ❀    ❀

When I went to see *Black Panther* with my husband, I fully expected to fall in love with Chadwick Boseman. I told T. C., "Listen, I'mma dream about that man tonight and you can't be mad about it." I did not expect to leave that theater just slayed by the power and beauty of Danai Gurira, Lupita Nyong'o, and Letitia Wright. I already knew Auntie Angela Bassett would take me straight to church with her regal voice and flawless skin. The hair of every woman in *Black Panther* moved me to tears. The joke about Danai Gurira's character Okoye hating her wig had me nodding with recognition— sometimes wigs are incredibly itchy. If my itchy scalp keeps me distracted in a staff meeting, imagine during espionage and a bar fight—which is why, when Okoye threw that wig at a man she was beating up, I just about came apart. It was glorious.

The diversity of Black hair in African hairstyles in *Black Panther* was also healing. For centuries, African communities have created hairstyles that are uniquely their own. I often lament one of the greatest evils of white supremacy: the systematic stripping away of the God-given African culture from the slaves, so much so that I have no idea what tribe my ancestors came from. I have no idea if the matriarchs in my line wore their hair in braids or knots. Maybe they kept their heads shaved bald, their melanin glowing under the African sun.

My hair—even when I wear extensions—is not just dead cells on my head. It is an expression of me. It contributes to part of my identity—as a creative woman who loves beauty, as a brave woman who likes to try new things, as a woman who expresses her femininity in traditional ways with braids flowing down my back, as a confident woman when I put my crocheted locs up into a high bun—it feels a little like a crown, and I love it.

My hair connects me to other Black women. When I see a woman in Target with hair just so healthy, so moisturized, so shiny, I will literally walk up to her and ask, "What do you use?" Once at a coffee shop a Black woman sat at a table catty-corner to my daughter and me. Trinity's curls were popping that day. There is no other way to describe them. They were full and breath-taking. "Excuse me, little sis," said the woman with a short Halle Berry pixie cut, "whatever you're doing to take care of your hair, keep it up." Trinity smiled and blushed—she had just begun wearing a silk bonnet to bed regularly to prevent frizzing and tangling. When I go to my stylist for a wash, deep condition, and braid, I am comforted by her camaraderie, and her touch makes me feel a little more human. Tanya, another Black woman, washes my hair and massages my scalp. She combs my hair with that no-nonsense Black mama strength that says, "Child, if you're still tender-headed at forty then there's nothing I can do for you." She braids my hair with such precision and surety—she's a mathematician and a magician and an artist. All Black women are miracles. I feel seen when she steps back and smiles and says, "Girl, you better go out tonight—you look too good!"

My hairstyles have ranged from pressed to blow-dried to wigs and scarfs when I don't have time or want to make a statement.

I love Black hair.

I do not love White fixation on Black hair. Invasive questions, calling attention to it at inappropriate times, and unwanted touches all reveal to me that White people don't understand the history of their touch. In particular, they don't know that White women were the primary inspectors and purchasers of slaves. White women did not have much in terms of power or economic freedom apart from the slaves they owned. Slaves were often a part of a woman's dowry and slaves were a large part of inheritances. White women would dress up in their finest and go to slave auctions—touching, prodding, sizing up, and determining the worth of Black humans. They'd buy slaves and bring them home to work. Some bought female slaves for the express purpose of getting and keeping them pregnant—every single child the enslaved woman had was another addition to the White woman's wealth.

In her book *They Were Her Property: White Women as Slave Owners in the American South*, historian Stephanie E. Jones-Rogers dispels the myth of the fawning and helpless White southern woman. Women were often integral parts in the economic structures of slavery. Part of the reason the Civil War happened was because the women refused to imagine a future without slavery. They were invested, and they participated in enacting significant trauma to Black bodies. Jones-Rogers writes,

> When we listen to what enslaved people had to say about White women and slave mastery, we find that they articulated quite clearly their belief that slave-owning women governed their slaves in the same ways that White men did; sometimes they were more effective at slave management or they used more brutal methods of discipline than their husbands did.[1]

When you, White Peacemaker, touch a Black woman's hair without her permission, you are participating in reenacting this historical trauma on possible descendants of enslaved people.

❁   ❁   ❁

I can tell where White Peacemakers are on their journey by
how they interact with Black hair. It's true. The most common
encounter I have with White women that brings their fragility
to the surface is when I've changed my hair and they, without permission, reach to touch it. It's amazing how quickly
the conversation turns and I find myself comforting them
because they simply wanted to give me a compliment. I thank
them for the compliment (even though it wasn't one at all,
really) and they smile through their tears of shame and I walk
away. For years, I've just let White people touch my hair and
be fascinated and give this back-handed compliment. Until
I was on vacation at a family camp in Northern California
and a White woman I did not know came up behind me in
the campground dining hall and began petting my long, curly
extensions. "Is this your hair, or . . ."

I turned to her, put down my plate, and said, "Yes. Would
you mind not touching my hair without asking?"

Her cheeks began to redden and she took a small step back.
"Oh . . . oh . . . I didn't mean any—"

I cut her off before her shame prevented me from inviting
her to change. "It's okay. I really love my hair. I just want you
to know it's not appropriate to touch a Black woman's hair. If
you're curious, I can tell you all about it and then I don't mind
if you want to touch it. Do you want to know more?"

Her granddaughter came up beside her, and she turned to
her and said, "My, the pancakes sure look good, don't they?
Let's make you a plate and get back to our table." She was not
interested, but I walked away from that encounter with a newfound confidence. I can be direct and loving to White People in
a way that doesn't undermine my physical boundaries.

I've had the same thing happened to me so many times, but now I've got my script and if something happens and I can't correct and teach in the same moment, I'll find the next opportunity to explain and educate.

When a White woman touches my hair, I explain what she's done and that I understand why she's interested. Then I explain why she shouldn't touch a Black woman's hair without permission. Almost every encounter has ended with some tears, an apology, and a promise to do better. Recently this happened and the White woman said to me, "Thank you for teaching me about White women and slavery and how impactful unwanted touch is to a Black woman—I had no idea."

Sometimes, White Peacemaker, I've learned the best way for me to respond to your fragility is with honesty, clarity, and mercy.

❊   ❊   ❊

Mercy is the act of withholding judgment. It's a conscious decision to view the other person with kindness and compassion. White Peacemaker, the way I approach encounters with my hair is just one of the ways I've decided to embrace mercy in my anti-racism peacemaking. The merciful view of you is that you're so influenced by white supremacy culture that you do not realize when you have offended, and so I choose to invite you into your liberation. I will process with you, listen to you, and encourage you. I have experienced the mercy of God and mercy when I enact a microaggression to other people of color—how in the world could I withhold mercy from you?

Jesus teaches about mercy in the Sermon on the Mount, and as with every other teaching, he lives it out for his followers. In

Matthew, Jesus came upon two blind men who heard that he was close, and they cried out, "Lord, Son of David, have mercy on us!" The crowds following Jesus told the men to hush, stop bothering the Messiah, figure out your healing on your own. But that didn't stop them, they cried out even more for Jesus to heal them, to give them their sight. Jesus looked upon the men and, the story says, he had compassion. When they asked for mercy it was because they had internalized shame for their condition; every ailment was considered a curse from God. They were asking Jesus to not judge them, to just look upon them and take away the curse. Lack of sight made it impossible for these men to care for themselves, and they were always being a burden to others. Jesus did have mercy, but that mercy came with a question: "What do you want me to do?" And they both said, "We want our sight back." Out of compassion, Jesus touched the men's eyes and healed them.

White Peacemakers, mercy is one of the bedrocks of my approach to teaching anti-racism. But mercy is not irresponsible kindness. Jesus' mercy was coupled with a question—he knew that healing without understanding the depth of your condition and the thing you need to be made whole will not bring you shalom. So he asked the men, "What do you want me to do?" They told him, he healed them, and when they saw clearly they followed him.

There is a cost to being made whole that is required, though—you have to be humble enough to ask and still enough to be touched. If you can do this, then you will see. If you can do this, you'll honor the mercy given to you as not an entitlement, but a gift along your way to freedom.

When a White woman touches my hair, I realize she doesn't see, she doesn't understand, and so I offer her mercy. So yes, White Peacemaker, you may touch my hair, but have you counted the costs?

## *Breath prayer*

———

Heal me, LORD, and I will be healed;
save me and I will be saved,
for you are the one I praise.

—JEREMIAH 17:14

Jesus
*INHALE, EXHALE*
Touch my eyes and help me see

16

# Confessions of a Judgmental Ally

Do not judge, or you too will be judged. For in the same way you judge others, you will be judged, and with the measure you use, it will be measured to you.

Why do you look at the speck of sawdust in your brother's eye and pay no attention to the plank in your own eye? How can you say to your brother, "Let me take the speck out of your eye," when all the time there is a plank in your own eye? You hypocrite, first take the plank out of your own eye, and then you will see clearly to remove the speck from your brother's eye.

—MATTHEW 7:1-5

I've made assumptions and perpetuated harm to other marginalized groups and individuals and I've been lovingly corrected:

I've assumed my gay friends who just got married wanted kids.

I've done the cost-benefit analysis about posting anything in solidarity with a marginalized group because "I'm a 'kingdom person' and we don't get political."

I've called a person in their fifties a boomer.

I've been afraid to get pregnant because I didn't want to have a baby with Down syndrome.

I've noticed a building was not accessible and didn't talk to the property manager because inserting myself would take too much time . . . and energy.

I've talked about the joys of pregnancy in a room full of women, ignoring the reality that someone may be struggling with infertility.

I've celebrated my sex life without taking into consideration the pain of my single friends.

I've asked my sons to help me move furniture and my daughter to clean the kitchen.

I've assumed the strong woman pastor was in it only to prove her worth and stick it to the man. Or even worse, was a bitter woman hiding her dysfunction behind church piety.

I've been surprised when I befriended a gay pastor who loves Jesus and prays for me daily.

I've asked a Korean mom to help me find a math tutor for my son and I wasn't surprised when she suggested her daughter.

I've called a Puerto Rican man Mexican.

I've called a Japanese woman Chinese.

I was surprised when a White-passing woman told me she identifies as Latina.

I've used the wrong pronouns when meeting a transgender person.

I've said, "Thank you, ma'am" to a woman, assuming her gender.

I've called my friend into environmentally safe cleaners, "crunchy."

I've rolled my eyes when told we're having dinner with vegetarian friends.

I've shared grammar memes just to prove I know how to use the word *whom* correctly.

I've celebrated when a prosperity pastor was found having a "moral failure."

I've been judgmental. I have biases I need to interrogate and undo. I want to be considered an ally to all these people, but I cannot see how their shalom has been violated and honestly judge the situation with my own prejudices in the way.

The first act of peacemaking for me is paying attention to my own privilege that often comes in the form of a plank in my eye. I cannot see the suffering of others well as long as it's securely lodged in there. So I offer myself grace and receive forgiveness. I remember to accept help and guidance from people—even people I would judge, for they have insights and wisdom I will never have. I invite people in to hold me accountable, and I let the Holy Spirit check me when I am tempted to use my privilege to judge instead of seek justice.

I've been a bad ally, it's true. But I'm trying and I'm trusting that the Lord will help me become a more faithful peacemaker.

# PART IV

# Ain't Gonna Let Nobody Turn Me Around

# 17

# Marchin' Up to Freedom Land

*Leveraging White Privilege*

White Peacemaker, I want to share a letter I wrote to my friend Rachel almost two years after she passed unexpectedly. This book has gone through three drafts, and the most recent one before it settled into what you're holding in your hands was one where I had letters to White Peacemakers from the past—Mr. Rogers; Dietrich Bonhoeffer; two really amazing abolitionist sisters, Angelina and Sarah Grimke; and this one, to my friend Rachel Held Evans. Rachel was an amazing thinker, leader, and challenger. She was a megaphone for mercy and justice to so many who felt like Jesus had given up on them.

The first time I "met" Rachel was on her blog. I think it was one of her Sunday Superlative posts where she collected the best things she read on the Internet and shared them with the world.

A friend of mine loved one of those posts, so she shared Rachel and in doing so shared hope. I had all but given up on White people at that time, but was cautiously encouraged by Rachel, who was at the beginning of her anti-racism journey. I could tell by how she was sharing resources and saying things like "I had no idea . . ."; "I'm really trying . . ."; "things have got to change . . ." Rachel was a woman with many online friends and a large online ministry, so she and her best friend Sarah started a conference, Evolving Faith, to call them in. I was a part of the first conference, where I spoke about enemy love and anti-racism.

By the time Evolving Faith had its first conference, Rachel and I had forged a sweet online connection. She would share my work and encourage me in emails. However, the last conversation I had with Rachel wasn't at Evolving Faith, where I told the story at the beginning of this book on how I chose empathy toward the coach who called my son a n*****. The last conversation I had with Rachel was at the church where I'm now one of the pastors. Woodland was hosting a conference on God, the Old Testament, and nonviolence, and T. C. and I were in town from Los Angeles for it (and a job interview at the church where my husband now pastors). She was eating pizza and I was off in another room talking to someone. T. C. was looking for me and walked into the room where Rachel was and instantly recognized her. So he stopped Rachel mid-greeting and said, "I've gotta grab Osheta, she'll be so upset if she doesn't get a chance to say hi to you in person." Until now, we'd only been online friends, never chatting "in real life." T. C. found me, and I couldn't believe how lovely Rachel was in person. We talked about writing and our favorite books and of course peacemaking.

Peacemaker, I want to begin our final stretch together sharing with you a letter I wrote to Rachel because she is one of the best White Peacemakers I've ever met. In my life. Hands down. She embraced this work with a kind of resolve I knew came from Jesus. I wish she were here. I wonder what she would have said the day Big George died. I know it would have been incisive and tender. It would have been rooted in truth. It would have sounded like Jesus.

This opening chapter of Part 4 is called, "Marchin' up to Freedom Land" from the Spiritual, turned protest anthem, "Ain't Gonna Let Nobody Turn Me Around" because that's my hope for you. I pray for you often that you'll have the stamina and resolve necessary to resist white supremacy culture. I want you to know and be confident in your unique contributions to this work. Part 4 is about taking what you have and using it to bring change. Can I tell you something: the concept of white privilege has been wildly misrepresented and often been used to shame you. It doesn't mean that you as a White person have never experienced hardships and it doesn't mean that you're entitled to anything because of your skin. What it is, is an opportunity for you to reject the individualism of white supremacy culture and begin to think more systemically, more holistically, more community-minded. It's an invitation to understand the long-term and societal implications of America's Original Sin and begin peacemaking. Want to know what this might look like? Read on, Peacemaker, and find your place in this revolution for peace.

❊   ❊   ❊

Dear Rachel,

I was utterly exhausted when I went up to my room at Montreat. The night before Evolving Faith 2018 I had a complete come-apart with my husband because you and Sarah had asked me to come speak and I realized the night before flying to North Carolina the magnitude of the ask and the madness of my saying yes. "What in the ever-loving heck did I agree to!" I cried to T. C. For a good hour I didn't know what to wear to speak for twenty minutes on peacemaking and relationships to hundreds of wanderers, questioners, and doubters. I kept throwing outfits in my suitcase, pulling them out to try them on, and then throwing them back in. I couldn't make a decision about what to take, so I took waaaaay too many outfits and books. I knew I had overthought to the fullest when I got to the airport to meet up with Jeff and Jen and realized I had brought a full-on suitcase and they were managing with sensible carry-ons. I was exhausted and I felt out of place and out of sorts.

When I walked into the charming guest room, I saw at the foot of my bed a basket with some Evolving Faith swag, a gift card, and a little note from you and Sarah.

"Osheta, thank you for coming to Evolving Faith. We're so excited you're here. We wanted to give you a little gift card to thank you for coming and acknowledge that as a woman of color you're giving a lot to be here. Please use this gift card on something for you for your self-care. Love, Rachel and Sarah."

I'm a crier, so I don't think it has an impact for me to say I bawled holding that card, but I never got a chance to tell you how much that meant to me. It was a tangible representation of the kind of White Peacemaker I've always known you to be—thoughtful, present, prophetic, kind.

It made me think of that time when I was catching so much flack online for something I wrote about race and you sent me an email that said you saw me and you were grateful for the ways I kept showing up to speak on race and to not give up.

At your funeral, I found out (not surprisingly) that I was one of several Black writers you championed. You gave, Rachel, for the cause of anti-racism. You gave your voice, your influence, your time, your money, your energy, your prayers. You gave so much and you were never ever performative about it. It was an overflow of your love for Jesus. You embodied Auntie Maya Angelou's axiom, "When you know better, you do better."

Rachel, do you remember when you asked me to share on your site my thoughts on when evangelicals remain silent about issues of race? I had never in my life as a writer been so surprised and so humbled. I expressly didn't want to talk about race, but as my practices of peacemaking required me to be at peace in this Brown body, I began to turn a critical eye toward white supremacy, and then I couldn't stay quiet. But I never expected a White woman from the South to invite me to share my thoughts on race. You did. That short reflection I wrote for you unlocked peacemaking in this area for me in a deep way. If it were not for you, Rachel, I can one hundred percent say I probably wouldn't have forged on and formed my anti-racism peacemaking ethos.

So back to Montreat. That night I had a second come-apart because now I just wanted to make you and Sarah proud and relieved for inviting me, but I also wanted to be true to myself as a peacemaker, so I scrapped my previous twenty-minute reflection on Jesus and peacemaking and decided to tell every-one about my son and the coach who called him a n***** and how relational wholeness looked like loving my enemy through accessing empathy. I know I couldn't have done that without your support, your note that said you empathize with me as a Black speaker in (what would end up being) a pre-dominately White space, and your reminder to take care of my body—to take time to be human.

At the airport on my way home, I used that gift card to buy a bottle of perfume. It was the kind of purchase I would never make—especially for myself. Oh, buy it for my friend who had been eyeing it for weeks? Sure. My daughter? In a heartbeat. Myself? Never. But your encouragement to honor this body God gave me echoed in my ears as I tried it on and fell in love with its musky, sweet scent. I bought that perfume and I still have it today. I wear it most days—even in this corona lockdown reality. I bought the matching shower gel for myself the day after I got home from your funeral.

That was a come-apart kind of day for me, too. I couldn't believe how sad I was because of your passing. I sat in that sanctuary with hundreds of your Beloveds and I just grieved. I grieved the loss of future conversations and I grieved for your children. I wished more than ever I told you how much you meant to me and how grateful I was for your leadership. I was so honored to be in that room and see so many Black and Brown leaders who, like me, loved you dearly.

I'm wearing that perfume now and it makes me think of that passage in Ephesians that says, "Therefore be imitators of God, as beloved children. And walk in love, as Christ loved us and gave himself up for us, a fragrant offering and sacrifice to God" (5:1-2 ESV). You imitated God's sacrificial love and radical hospitality, and every time I catch a whiff of this perfume that I love so much, that I bought because of your thoughtfulness, I thank God for your secret gift of compassion and care. Thank you for being a peacemaker. Thank you for living out the kingdom. For every community-facing and public way you showed up, I've learned there were at least ten quiet ways you were present. You didn't have to. In fact, no one would have faulted you for staying out of the conversation about race altogether or, even worse, proclaiming at every chance all that you were doing.

There's a certain Jesus story I think of when I think of your leadership as a White Peacemaker. In Matthew 8, Jesus was coming down the mountainside with a large crowd following him, and a man with leprosy, that horrible skin disease that made people outcast and marginalized, came to him. He knelt before Jesus in desperation and said, "Lord, if you are willing, you can make me clean." Jesus was willing, and he cleaned him of his leprosy.

The thing I've always thought about leprosy is that it can take a long time for symptoms to occur before people realize they have it—and when they do, it's evident to their community. In a lot of ways, white supremacy is like that, I think especially for White people. It takes some time for it to come to the surface and it often takes a community around you to point it out. Sometimes, a person with leprosy would ignore the symptoms and get others sick. This is not unlike Whiteness, don't you think? A White person who is not willing to acknowledge their own vulnerability to racism can cause so much harm. But the good news is, we have Jesus, right? The leper was healed by Jesus and he was now lesion-free. But Jesus told him, Don't tell anyone. Go to the priest, show yourself, give, and go on your way. There's something I can't stop thinking about: Jesus in his instructions told the man: There are aspects of this healing that are just between you and me and then there's some that should be shared.

I think of how you, Rachel, did the hard work of being healed from your own racial biases and blind spots and how you appropriately shared what God was doing in your life, but more importantly you lived as a healed and hopeful White Peacemaker. You, like the man with leprosy, became a co-conspirator with Jesus for your healing, and then you took that healing back into your community.

You are a disciple of Jesus. I think that's why I trusted the Evolving Faith family with one of the hardest stories about race I've ever told.

If I could have one meal with you, I think I'd like to make you gumbo because I'm writing this letter to you in the winter and you said once that you associate seasons with meals—strawberry salad for spring, burgers on the grill for summer, pumpkin everything for fall, and of course, pot roast for winter. Well, for me winter calls for soups and stews, so if it's okay, I'll make my White Ally gumbo for you. It is practical, no-nonsense, adaptable, flavorful as all get-out, and comforting. I kinda feel like that describes you and your ministry, Rachel. We'd talk about our favorite Jesus stories, and Kamala Harris, and the end of *Game of Thrones*, because I have questions and I'm sure you have answers.

I'd play you "Ain't Gonna Let Nobody Turn Me Around" and I'd tell you about how I was so exhausted with writing this book that I took a long drive in the country and heard a version of this song performed by Joan Baez and Mavis Staples. It was Joan's birthday concert and she had invited Mavis Staples, one of the voices of the civil rights movement, and when I heard her and Joan sing—I pulled over and began weeping. I was listening to shalom. Two gifted women, using their literal voices together to proclaim justice, resolve, and perseverance. And in a lot of ways, this is the calling of a White Peacemaker, a calling you lived so beautifully, to make room for people of color, to invite us in, to harmonize with us, and to march on together to freedom land.

Finally, Rachel, when I pray for White Peacemakers, I pray for them to have your humility and your commitment to Jesus, our Good Troublemaker. I pray for them to have a healthy sense of their Belovedness, as I know you had, and the courage to proclaim the Belovedness of others, as I saw you do time after time. I pray for them to use their resources and their gifts for the kingdom—even if it is scary. I also pray for their children, as I pray for yours. I pray that the next generation of peacemakers will do even more than you or I ever could.

Coming apart at the seams with gratitude,
O

## 18

# Free, Black, and Southern

We were finally getting out of the city! Six months into the global pandemic, my husband and I looked at each other and said, "We need a break!" We needed to be out in nature, running around, and away from Zoom meetings. We desperately wanted just a few days to not worry about masks or hand sanitizer. We loved our neighbors enough to stay home and keep our bubble as closed as possible so we didn't spread the virus, but we were spreading discontent and crabbiness with each other nearly every single day.

The denomination my husband is ordained with owns a beautiful property just two hours out of the Twin Cities. I planned everything, from the packing to the meal prepping, and miracle of all miracles we got on the road within an hour of our planned time. We had to take both of our cars—my husband had the kids in the SUV and I followed in our sedan.

About an hour into the trip, after we exited the main highway to the country roads leading to camp, I realized we needed something for dinner that I hadn't picked up earlier, so I texted my son to let his dad know I was going to stop at a grocery store.

Tyson called me, "Okay, Mom, you be careful though."

With the rise of White nationalism and images of White young men marching across southern college campuses chanting "Blood and soil" (a racist Nazi slogan) and "Jews will not replace us," Tyson was particularly afraid of White spaces, especially small rural towns, especially like the ones we drove past on our way to the cabin. When he found out I was taking the SOMA group down South for seven days, he was furious with me. "Mom, are those White people going to protect you if something happens?" I tried to comfort him—I really did want to convince my young biracial son that his Black mama would be okay—but the truth is, I was afraid, too.

I, however, had no idea what fear was when I told Tyson I'd be fine and I'd see them at the cabin.

I pulled over to the side of the road, turned down the Penny and Sparrow playlist I was blasting, and searched for a store. The first one that came up was in a small town just fifteen minutes up the road.

The town was everything you'd expect of a rural community of less than four hundred people. There was one main intersection. One bank. One post office. Three churches—go figure.

And as I entered the town I started to do the calculation that I always do when I go out as a Black person in rural environments. I am so aware that I stick out.

That I am not the norm.

That I am the outsider of outsiders.

I love the city. I love her energy. But I love the cabin. One day I hope to have a hobby farm. I'm healed in nature, which means I'm often retreating the stress of the city to towns where I'll be forced to navigate my Blackness in that predominately White, probably prejudiced space.

One of the very first things I saw as I drove into the town was White men sitting outside on their porches.

And even though I'm married to a White man, I have a deep discomfort around White men whom I do not know, especially in big groups. I do this thing in my mind. Intellectually, I know, I know that it's unlikely anyone wants to hurt me and it's unlikely that I would be hurt. Yet because of the trauma that's been passed down to me, because of the generational conditioning from my ancestors who had to be on high alert at all times when their rural existence was threatened by White men, I pay special attention when I'm in those spaces.

Above the crooning voices of Penny and Sparrow, I heard the rumbling of a massive pickup truck pulling up to the stop sign at my left, and I looked over and it was filled with three White men and the most precious little dog I've ever seen. And waving from the bed of the truck was the largest Confederate flag I'd ever seen.

I'm not even one hundred percent sure why, in 2020, we still have this deep affinity for a flag that's not the American flag. As an Anabaptist woman, I don't really have a whole lot of affinity for any kind of flag, but the desire to fly the Confederate flag really confuses me. That flag has been connected to so much violence. I know the argument is that it's a symbol of southern history, but then why were three Minnesotan men waving the Confederate flag?

That flag has been waved and flown as Black bodies dangled from southern trees and Black families were chased out of their homes. It's a symbol of terror.

And I was staring at it, while waiting at a stop sign, in Minnesota, in 2020.

It was streaming from the big old pickup truck, which as a Texan, I had to give it to them. It was a nice truck. The kind of old-time truck you see on farmhouse decor throw pillows. You could easily replace the flag with a whole bunch of pumpkins and have yourself a very basic pumpkin spice–scented tableau.

I paid attention to everything while waiting at that light for them to come to a complete stop.

I waited to see which direction they were going to go, if they were going to turn their turn signal on, if they were going to make a right-hand turn to go in the opposite direction. I paid attention because I just wanted to know, I wanted to be aware of what these men were going to do. I wanted to know how their actions would affect me.

Flying that flag was a caution to me, even if they never woke up that morning hoping to make a Black person uncomfortable with their flag. The flag told me to beware—they were the kind of White men who saw no problem with the history of domestic terrorism associated with that flag. Could they be a terror to me that afternoon?

I looked at them and one of them turned.

I nodded, hoping to disarm them, show my humanity, relieve the pressure building in my chest, and they didn't respond.

When it was my turn to go, I drove past them through the intersection. They did not have their turn signal on when we were at the intersection, but just as I expected, they turned and followed closely behind me.

Being in a small town, the grocery store wasn't far down the road, less than two minutes, but when I turned on my signal to turn into the parking lot, hoping that the men would just go around me and continue on their way, they followed behind me.

And at this point, I was getting really, really nervous and really afraid. I didn't know what to do.

I kept hoping that it was just a coincidence. Everybody needs to go to the store. This is a tiny town and is probably their only grocery store. I truly hoped that they were getting dog food for that sweet little dog.

I pulled into a parking spot right in the front of the store, and this is when I knew that these men noticed me and my otherness.

This is when I knew that these men knew to some extent the intimidation of the flag they flew.

They pulled up behind me and blocked my car in.

Me and my tiny little Mazda and them in that big, antique, glorious truck.

They just sat and waited.

They waited. And I waited.

They waited a little bit longer and I waited a little bit longer.

I grabbed my phone and I fiddled around, acting like I was looking for something, maybe a recipe, maybe a grocery list.

Finally, I didn't want to risk one of them coming up to my window, so I grabbed my wallet and my mask and jumped out to go into the store.

"Osheta, you have five minutes, girl. Five minutes to get in and out. This is not your weekly Target run; you don't need anything other than a frozen lasagna. Get out of this town as fast as possible."

The music playing on their radio turned up just a little bit louder.

Not enough to disturb the peace, just loud enough to communicate that they saw me. And I should see them.

Right before I stepped into the store, the driver revved the engine loud, laughed, and sped off. Peeling out of the parking lot altogether. I watched them make a hard right turn and head back to that intersection, the intersection where they first saw me, an outsider.

The same intersection I needed to pass by to get to camp.

I messaged two of my dear friends, Mary and Shawna.

I asked them, please pray for me.

I told them as much as I remembered of the interaction.

I just wanted to get my lasagna and get back to my family.

Both of them texted back within minutes. They were praying and asked me to keep them posted once I got to camp.

I got out of the store. And I got to that intersection as fast as I legally could because I didn't want to get pulled over in this town unnecessarily.

And I could not breathe. I held my breath and my chest was pounding and my ears were buzzing and I just needed to get to the lake and to stand in the water and wash away the terror of this moment. I wanted to scream underwater and exorcise the demons of the South from my healing place, the cabin.

It wasn't until I was a good thirty minutes outside the town, nearly to camp, that I took a full, deep breath. Nothing physically happened to me, but the intimidation of that flag and those men has filled my nightmares ever since.

❈   ❈   ❈

Writer and historian Jemar Tisby says, "For black people, the South is our homeland away from home. We were divorced from our native soil on the African continent and shipped to agricultural regions of North America; the Deep South is as close as many African Americans will get to their past."[1]

It's true, and even though God has called us to live in Minnesota, I've been trying to hold on to the best of my southern heritage everywhere I go. But what can I do then when everything from the South that I love is tainted with racism?

❀   ❀   ❀

I called my friend Jerusalem over Zoom. Jerusalem is a pastor in Arkansas who loves all things southern; she went through a phase where she always wore aprons over her outfits. She has a twang that just envelops you with love, and she cares about farming.

"I feel like an outsider. I'm Black and southern, but so many stories about Black people in the South are so wrapped up in racism. White supremacy has stolen my ability to be free, Black, and Southern."

"Yeah, I get that," she replied, "but you know what, I'm really learning so much about Black farmers and I want to tell you that part of you being your whole self is allowing yourself to love your southern heritage. God placed you there."

"Yeah, and all my ancestors are from the South. I'm like one hundred percent sure there are sharecroppers and previously enslaved people in my ancestry."

Jerusalem nodded. "So, what can I do?"

I shrugged. "I don't know, I guess give me permission to be fully Black and southern. Like, there's this Black-owned company I want to buy cotton from. They make these really beautiful centerpieces with cotton they harvest from their land, and I think I need to begin reclaiming my southern heritage by having that centerpiece in my living room."

Jerusalem agreed. I bought the centerpiece. It wasn't harvesting season yet, so I had to wait.

❀    ❀    ❀

In some ways, this book is rooted in the beatitude "Blessed are the peacemakers" because every aspect of the Jesus way brings shalom, God's peace in this world of immense brokenness. Where our world champions war, we choose nonviolence. Where we would be tempted to divide, peacemaking reconciles. Where there has been great dehumanization, we seek to rehumanize.

But there's a specific calling for you, White southern Peacemakers, that I think about often.

When you, in your social location of the South, do this work of anti-racism, you are right in the thick of this battle. The South has been the place of the fight for Black dignity's greatest casualties and victories. You have the Edmund Pettus Bridge in Selma, Alabama, where hundreds of Black protestors were assaulted on March 7, 1965, for marching in support of voting rights for all African Americans, a day remembered as Bloody Sunday. You also have the victory of just fifty years later at the 50th anniversary of the marches, when John Lewis, a civil rights leader and Georiga's 5th District representative, who was convinced he was going to die on Bloody Sunday, introduced the first Black president. Because so much of our country's imagination about white supremacy involves the things they've seen in the South, You, southern White Peacemaker, have a specific calling to write a better future. You can through your peacemaking destroy the root system running deep in the South that produced the strange fruit of racism and ignorance. It looks a lot like Jerusalem believing me about my fears of the Confederate flag and telling me a story about the South that included Black farmers, black resilience, and black faithfulness. Not everything Black and southern is tragic. Knowing that Jerusalem is collecting these stories not only for her dismantling of white supremacy in her life but to encourage her Black brothers and sisters to fully own and love their southern heritage is one of her many everyday practices of peacemaking. When White people have been responsible for so much displacement and abuse, to have a White woman, a White southern woman, no less, speak up and speak life—well, it was truly healing.

We need to clear out space to make way for the kingdom roots of God's shalom that Jesus, our common Lord, lived and died violently for. His blood seeped into the ground to create a new way of being that's marked by unity, sacrificially loving one another, and eagerly empowering every. single. image bearer—regardless of the color of their skin. Peacemaking begins with honestly looking at the past and dreaming together what a future together can be. My centerpiece came, and it was more beautiful than I could have imagined. I took a slip of paper and wrote the word *free* on it, then mixed it up with the cotton balls.

Free. Free to be Black. Free to be out in nature. Free to love my southernness. Free to be at peace. Free. Absolutely free.

# *Breath prayer*

If my people, which are called by my name, shall humble themselves, and pray, and seek my face, and turn from their wicked ways; then will I hear from heaven, and will forgive their sin, and will heal their land.

—2 CHRONICLES 7:14 KJV

Merciful One

*INHALE, EXHALE*

Heal our Land

**19**

# Two Scoops of Justice and Peace, Please

The first time I ever had a bowl of Blue Bell cookies and cream ice cream, I was at a sleepover my mom forced me to go to. Even worse, when she dropped me off at Jessie's house, she reached across me, pushed the lock in the door down before I could get out, and said, "Listen, unless you're bleeding or a bone's been broken, do not call to come home. Try to stay. Have fun."

Like most quiet and shy twelve-year-olds with a mother who was friends with everyone, stranger to none, my social life was her constant project. I was occasionally forced to "make friends" with the children of my mom's coworkers, which is why on November 12, 1993, I was leaning up against Jessie's couch with the biggest bowl of cookies and cream ice cream, watching Steven Urkel transform into Stefan . . . Urquelle.

Watching *Family Matters* wasn't my idea, although I was super happy when Jessie's mom interrupted our awkward *Seventeen* magazine–based small talk with, "Hey, girls, why don't we order pizza and watch something Osheta would like. It's Friday night. *Family Matters* comes on, right, Osheta?" This was before I met my husband and became the gentle smart-aleck I am now, so I nodded enthusiastically as if to shake out of my mind her casual racism. "Well, at least she didn't offer me Jell-O," I thought, "or even worse . . . watermelon."

Jessie didn't really know anything about the show but she didn't seem to care anyway; she had a massive obsession with Devon Sawa, the human boy manifestation from the Casper movie, so she cut out pictures for a wall collage from her back issues of *Seventeen*. (Did I mention Jessie's mom was my mom's supervisor and had the nicest house I'd ever been in? I mean . . . Jessie had an allowance and back issues of *Seventeen*. I was lucky to get one in the checkout lane on Mama's payday.) She cut out Devon and smooched his papery face when she didn't think I was looking. I, however, ate cookies and cream and hoped Jessie had some weird weekend bedtime like nine o'clock or, even stranger, had a reason to be up early the next day, like soccer or Girl Scouts.

We did have to go to bed early, which was fine by me. Karate. Jessie the collage-making, Canadian heartthrob–loving, straight-A student was into karate and she had a meet at nine in the morning. Glory be.

As the family got ready for Jessie's meet, Mama came to pick me up. In the passenger seat I pulled out my flip pad, where I wrote down everything I wanted to remember about the night, like how cute Jaleel White was without glasses, and a word Jessie's dad used for "weird" . . . cattywampus, and the name of the ice cream: cookies and cream. Mama was a solid Neapolitan lover, dad Rocky Road. That's all we really had in the house. I never even looked at other flavors because I knew Mama wouldn't get them.

"Mama, before we go home we need to stop at the store. I had the best ice cream in the world." Mama looked out the corner of her green eyes and sucked her teeth. "Really?"

"Really. It's cookies and cream and I know you don't want food going to waste so I promise I'll pay for it myself just in case no one else eats it and . . . and . . . and . . . my period is coming on Wednesday, I need to be ready!"

She laughed and turned the car on the main street of our town in the direction of the HEB to get my very first half gallon of Blue Bell. "The best ice cream in the country."

❀    ❀    ❀

"Mama! It's the best ice cream in the world. In the whole world. I've never tasted anything so delicious, it makes me so happy, please, please, please, please, can you come out now . . . we're going to miss it!"

Tyson, seven years old, ran inside from playing with his friends to beg. We call him King Superlative for obvious reasons, and today's effusive pleases were because his little ears heard the ice cream truck in the neighborhood, its melodic chimes serving as his own personal siren's call. My friend Sam used to tell her children that when the truck drove through the neighborhood playing music, it was to alert the children they were out of ice cream and to not come up to it when it stopped. Brilliant. I wish I had told my kids that, but like the overeager mom, one afternoon when it parked at the corner, I gathered my kids and cash to run to the ice cream truck. They had the best cookies and cream bars—they were no Blue Bell, but you can't get Blue Bell in Boston and that is a travesty beyond comprehension that I simply do not have enough time in the book to talk about. Well, maybe I know where Tyson got the whole superlative thing from.

We stood in line behind the other overeager parents, waiting for our turn, when three-year-old Trinity began singing along to the ice cream truck song, "Do your ears hang low? Do they wobble to and fro? Can you tie 'em in a knot? Can you tie 'em in a bow?" And in that way three-year-olds do, she repeated the song over and over and over for the rest of the week until the ice cream truck came back to our neighborhood again.

❀     ❀     ❀

"Oh my gosh, Mom! Look! Look!" Trinity is fourteen now and obsessed with TikTok. Nearly every day of the pandemic she shared some one minute of nonsense paired with really horrible but catchy music.

The video she's showing me is of a woman teaching about the ice cream truck song.

"Did you know that it's so racist?" She goes on to talk about how the original song came from a nineteenth-century song, "Old Zip C**n," which evolved from an even older traditional British song, "The (Old) Rose Tree. "The Old Rose Tree" was hummed by Scots-Irish settlers in Appalachia as "Turkey in the Straw":

> Turkey in de straw, turkey in de hay.
> Turkey in de straw, turkey in de hay.
> Roll 'em up an' twist 'em up a high tuc-ka-haw
> an' twist 'em up a tune called "Turkey in the Straw."

Eventually the words changed to reflect their new life in the American colonies. In this iteration, it was an innocent work song, but in the late 1820s the rise of minstrel shows gave it a new life that reflected not the work of the people but, unfortunately, the racist worldview of the people. George Washington Dixon, in blackface and dressed up in nice clothes and using an "uppity" vocabulary, created the character Zip C**n, the urban counterpart to Jim Crow, another famous minstrel character who was often portrayed as slow and backwards. The lyrics Dixon would sing to the tune of Old Rose Tree were

O ole Zip C**n he is a larned skoler,
O ole Zip C**n he is a larned skoler,
O ole Zip C**n he is a larned skoler,
sings possum up a gum tree an coony in a holler . . .

The song makes fun of a Black man's attempt to become educated and successful in the world after he was freed.

The minstrel shows became a popular form of entertainment in the nineteenth century. And at the turn of the twentieth century, a new rendition came from Harry C. Browne, an actor and banjo player from Massachusetts.

The song opens with a call-and-response:

Browne: "You n***** quit throwin' them bones and come down and get your ice cream!"

Black men (incredulously): "Ice cream?!"

Browne: "Yes, ice cream! Colored man's ice cream: WATERMELON!!"

And then the chorus:

N***** love a watermelon ha ha, ha ha!
N***** love a watermelon ha ha, ha ha!

For here, they're made with a half a pound of co'l.
There's nothing like a watermelon for a hungry coon.

The TikTok teacher stopped the video and played the ice cream truck jingle and it was the exact same melody.

The song became the school rhyme my daughter and I always thought was "Do your ears hang low?"

Thanks to this TikTok exposé, we weren't thinking of droopy dogs with funny ears but rather how racism is normalized and casually instilled in children—wrapping it with sweetness and fond memories. I was sick to my stomach thinking of all the summer afternoons we'd had rushing to the ice cream truck as it ambled down our street, digging for dollars in my purse, coins in the couch, and making the children promise to do chores in exchange for me treating them. Learning the history behind it tainted all those memories. I felt angry and betrayed. I also completely believed it—white supremacy will find its way in.

My daughter and I stared at each other in shock. It never even occurred to us that there would be anything racist about the ice cream truck jingle. Never mind that when my oldest brought up that Aunt Jemima reinforces mammy stereotypes, I explained we still use Aunt Jemima because she reminds us of our family's matriarchs: Grandmama Mary and Great Aunt Ona. On the rare Saturdays she had home from working at Walmart, my own mama would make Aunt Jemima pancake mix and cuddle next to us while we watched cartoons. I never want to believe racism, and I make excuses for it when I see it.

This song, like Aunt Jemima, is a part of American culture; it's been normalized and its racial history has been whitewashed with cream and sugar.

"Mom!" Trinity said, "you have to share this, you just have to!" But here's the thing about being a Black woman attempting to dismantle racism on social media: there are just some things that will not be heard from me by White people. They will take my bringing up a story like this as me playing the "race card." This hurts so much, White Peacemaker, because my lived experience is a dynamic race card—everything is about race because I move through this world in a racialized, Brown, plus-sized body. When a person of color brings a truth like this, we're called divisive, and it's often completely ignored. No, I needed a co-conspirator for justice. I needed Amanda.

❀    ❀    ❀

"Hey . . . Amanda," I typed into a DM on Instagram.

She didn't reply. Amanda often sets really healthy social media boundaries, so I decided to send her a text just in case, and yes, y'all . . . I know that's full-on boomer behavior.

"Hey . . . Amanda," I sent in a text.

"Hey!"

"Check your Insta. I'm wondering if you'll do something for me."

I found the ice cream truck story on Instagram and shared it with her.

"Would you maybe make one of those White people anti-racism classes you do on your stories about this?"

She left me on "seen" for five minutes, I assumed to watch the video.

"Of course! I'm on it!" she wrote back.

My friend Amanda looks like a fairy . . . there's really no other way to describe her. She's got these really beautiful green eyes, brown hair that looks almost black, and a mischievous nose. She also smirks like no one's business. See . . . a fairy! You look at Amanda and know she's capable of goodness and troublemaking all at the same time.

I think of Amanda when I read Jesus' teaching that the kingdom of God is made up of people with an unrelenting desire for righteousness. Righteousness is often thought of as a personal posture of devotion to God—are you in right relationship with God? Do you form your life around the things that matter to God?—which is true, but only partly. The word Jesus uses, *dikaiosyne*, is actually a word that describes God's heart for justice. It's another refracted light of shalom: right relatedness between us and God and us with one another. This beatitude sort of lays the groundwork for Matthew 22:37, "Love the Lord your God with all your heart and with all your soul and with all your mind."

Amanda has an insatiable appetite for righteousness—especially when she's practicing anti-racism peacemaking. She's the kind of White Peacemaker this world needs. She has an inner sense of justice that is incapable of staying quiet. She's inflexible on seeing racism be exposed for all the ways it's brought and continues to bring harm.

I think Amanda loves righteousness because she views anti-racism as her practice of faithfulness toward people whom God loves. As she puts it, she "yells at White people" because oftentimes those of us on the margins can't speak truth without being ignored or attacked. Amanda is trying to be like Christ and suffer for the sake of shalom. And for her White siblings, she wants you to see the importance of your collective liberation. How, when you're set free of the oppression of white supremacy, we're all set free.

So she makes these incredible Instagram stories on her account.

She made one about the ice cream truck jingle. People called her out for it. She just shrugged and made a new one the following week. Dear White Peacemakers, you get to usher in the kingdom of God when you speak up. Speak to each other. When you learn something has racist roots, expose it, and hold those in power accountable until they fix it. You may be thinking, "Osheta, really? It's just an ice cream jingle." But here's the reality: even benign things cause small rifts between us.

The righteousness God calls us to requires us to address these small rifts before they become divisions, and we must do our best to bridge the divide. This Black Peacemaker is praying for you to be brave with each other. Say the hard things. Push instead of pull back. Build a culture of shalom-seeking as White image bearers.

❀  ❀  ❀

In August 2020, Good Humor learned about the history of the jingle and commissioned RZA, founding member of the Wu-Tang Clan, to write a new jingle. Their press statement said:

> We know ice cream trucks are one of the joys of summer, but did you know that the origins of a familiar ice cream truck tune are actually not joyful at all? "Turkey in the Straw" is a 200-year-old song with surprisingly racist roots—it first became popular in minstrel shows and can still be heard in ice cream trucks today. . . .
>
> While Good Humor did not create "Turkey in the Straw" or other ice cream truck jingles, the brand is using its influence to acknowledge the song's history, educate drivers and fans, and help the ice cream truck industry remove it from use.

[A company spokesperson said,] "Good Humor invent-
ed the ice cream truck and is the maker of some of today's
most iconic ice cream truck treats. And while we have not
owned ice cream trucks since 1976, we wanted to be part
of the solution and offer ice cream truck drivers a jingle
that can bring joy to every community."[1]

When I bring up the need for White people to learn history
and teach each other, to leverage your voices and influences,
I often hear, "I had nothing to do with that!" But accepting
blame is not a prerequisite for seeking righteousness—if that
were the case then Jesus would have never gone to the cross.
Jesus the sinless, perfect one saw great injustice and said, "I'll
go first. I'll do what I can to make it right." Are you willing to
go first, White Peacemaker?

❦      ❦      ❦

I have never heard Amanda say a single racist thing, yet she
continues to go first. I know she teaches her children how to
be White Peacemakers. She sees that they are light-years ahead
of where she was as a child and she knows they'll be influential
to move the needle toward righteousness. She is being filled in
this hard work.

So as soon as this pandemic is over, I'm going to grab some
cookies and cream (it won't be Blue Bell, but oh well) and
I'm going to sit with my friend. I think after the year (and
counting) we've had, we're allowed all the ice cream, anytime,
in copious amounts. It'll be sweeter and definitely not ruined
by racism because I'll be with one of my favorite White Peacemakers for righteousness.

# *Breath prayer*

———

For he himself is our peace, who has made the two groups one and has destroyed the barrier, the dividing wall of hostility.

—EPHESIANS 2:14

Jesus

*INHALE, EXHALE*

Be our Peace

## 20

# When "Black Lives Matter" Sounds Like "I Love You"

Blessed are those who are persecuted because of righteousness, for theirs is the kingdom of heaven.

—MATTHEW 5:10

Dear White Peacemakers,

In the days after George Floyd was killed, my husband invited Der, a Hmong American pastor serving at our church as a pastor-in-residence, to come with him to a peaceful protest. One of the officers who stood by while George begged for his life until his final breath was a Hmong American man named Tou Thao. Der felt that it was important to be a voice of comfort because he knew so many members of the Hmong

246

community were grieving right alongside us. I could hear T. C. on the phone with Der discussing the details of the march.

"Yeah, bro, I love the idea for the sign you're bringing. Thanks for making it. I'll see you in a few," T. C. said.

I followed him into our room while he got ready. "Der's making a protest sign?"

T. C. held up a T-shirt and a collared shirt. "Which should I wear?" he asked, seemingly ignoring me.

"Um . . . it's wicked hot, wear the T-shirt. Babes! Der's bringing a sign?"

He pulled on the T-shirt that said "Obey" on the front in silver letters and nodded. "Yeah. It says Hmong Americans for Black Lives."

I sucked in my breath. "Oh really? That's a huge statement given Tou Thao's role in the murder. Are you worried for him?"

T. C. sat next to me on our bed and shrugged. "Yeah, but I'm worried for me. I'm worried for you. I'm worried for our kids. I'm worried about the teens on my caseload. There is a lot to be worried about. But I'm also really thankful that he's willing to march with me and for you and every other Black person we love."

I put my hands in his and rested my head on his shoulder. "Welp . . . we should probably pray before you go, right?"

"Yeah, I mean we're pastors and all . . . ," he said, resting his head on top of mine.

Later that night, T. C. sent me a picture of them holding signs—Der's of course said "Hmong Americans for Black Lives" and T. C., a White man, held up, "George Floyd bears God's Image." Tears welled up in my eyes as I realized what I was looking at: two men standing up for Black lives, and neither one of them was Black. They were putting their bodies on the line to protest what happened to a Black man in our city when they didn't have to. This was Christlike solidarity.

As Der and T. C. were walking back to their cars from the rally, a Black man rode up to them on his moped, pointed at Der's sign, and expressed to him how much that particular sentiment from a Hmong American man meant to him.

Der did receive a great deal of backlash for his sign from members of the Hmong community. They said things like "The Black community hasn't done anything for us, why put yourself out there like that?" It didn't help that Der's picture was shared in various places, opening up the Lors to more attack. The backlash was so great that, Alice, Der's wife, requested prayer for protection for her family. When T. C. checked in on Der in the days after, he kept reiterating that he wouldn't change a thing about his decision, Black lives matter and Der wanted to do everything he could to proclaim that truth. He was willing to be persecuted for seeking righteousness because we have to have, as Der says, "a better vision of humanity." Dear White Peacemaker, sometimes saying "Black Lives Matter" when there's been a great injustice sounds like "I love you." It's a costly kinda love, a humbling one, but it's a cross-shaped, sin-exposing kind of love.

With Love,
Osheta

❀　❀　❀

Without a doubt, whenever I use the hashtag #Blacklivesmatter, I receive several variations of this one question:

Osheta, how can you be a peacemaker and support such a violent, anti-Christian, God-hating organization?

I have a strict no-arguing-on-the-Internet rule, so I often use a Google number I have set up specifically to encourage dialogue with my online friends when they ask me a question that requires kindness, nuance, and humility. One such conversation was with a man named Trevor. Trevor, a sixty-five-year-old born-and-raised Midwesterner, heard me give an interview with a Christian peacemaking organization where I said, "Black lives matter" and he wanted to "share his thoughts."

Instead of the phone call, he opted to meet over Zoom. "That way we can see each other, Pastor," he said in his email.

He joined me from his kitchen with his grandchildren's art on the fridge behind him and his cat pacing back and forth in front of his screen.

"Sorry about that, Pastor," he said as he moved his cat to his lap.

I for one welcome our feline overlords, so it didn't bother me at all. My own cat assumes every Zoom meeting is an invitation for him to show off his impressive tail-swiping abilities.

"No worries, Trevor! Thanks for joining me."

When I do these calls, I always let the other person talk first.

"Tell me about how you received my comment. I want to know everything," I started.

Sure, I know the gist of their questions. I've been having these conversations for years, but not once have I seen great connection when I jump right in to share facts and figures. Remember, anti-racism peacemaking is humanizing work, so I focus on stories—hearing theirs, telling mine, learning from those in the past—for stories unveil our complexity and our beauty more than the latest Reuters report. When I make space for storytelling and unhurried sharing, we become disarmed. I can hear the humanity in them and hopefully they'll hear the humanity in me.

Trevor was raised in a rural Minnesota community where, as he told it, "the Blacks and Whites, we got along okay. They never played the race card and we never bothered them." But then he moved to the city for work and began to notice "a different kind of Black. They seem so agitated all the time and it just seems to me that Black Lives Matter is just another thing for them to use to be all up in arms about. No one knows for a fact race has anything to do with all these boys being pulled over by the police, so I just can't get behind that organization."

I took a sip of my water and nodded.

"Yes, you know, I've met some really nice police officers and I even know some police officers who I think believe they would never treat a Black person differently than a White person. I've had some really bad experiences, too. Would you mind if I share with you a story?" He agreed, and I told him about bringing my kids home from the youth retreat.

"What I'm wondering, Trevor, is why do you think that police officer pulled me over?"

He shrugged. "Maybe she had a bad day or needed to hit a quota. Maybe she was really concerned about your boy?

I took a sip of water again. "Maybe, but do you wanna know something I used to do when my husband and I served in an under-resourced neighborhood in New Orleans that I'm not proud of? When I would be walking hand-in-hand down the street with our two-year-old son, if a group of Black boys was coming toward me, I'd pick him up and move to the other side of the street. I'd smile at the boys and wave because my husband worked with a few of them at the community center, but something in me was really uncomfortable. I think I was a little bit afraid and so I did what I could to make myself feel a little safer, a little more powerful."

"Hmm . . . ," he said.

"Trevor, do you think maybe police officers, because they're human beings, are subject to that same kind of impulse to try to make themselves feel safer, more powerful, and maybe it's even greater because they're doing it for the whole community?"

"Hmm . . . ," he said again. I wasn't sure if this was usual Swedish Lutheran neutral emoting or if I'd lost him or, even worse, offended him.

"Well . . . maybe. Maybe." He went on to tell about how his wife used to feel unsafe around a Latino man and when they got to know him, they felt silly.

"Well, Trevor. What I think Black Lives Matter is doing is helping us see that police are not doing a great job ignoring those fearful impulses and Black people are suffering because of it. Can you tell me of another organization you can get behind that is proclaiming that Black people are subject to violence because of unfounded fears, and that their innate human dignity should be protected, and that anyone who violates that should be held accountable?"

He thought for a minute. "Well, not off the top of my head."

"Do you think the work Dr. Martin Luther King did was important?" I asked.

Trevor nodded emphatically. "I think some of these activists need to learn a thing or two from him."

"You know what, I actually think they were both doing the same thing."

White Peacemakers, before I tell you more about my conversation with Trevor, I want to address something else that concerns me. We have got to be careful we don't romanticize Dr. Martin Luther King Jr. I grew up with stories about Dr. King that celebrate his mountaintop message of "I have a dream," but it wasn't until my later twenties that I learned Dr. King spent time in jail for his commitment to civil rights. It wasn't until I made a commitment to listen to or read "Letter from Birmingham Jail" for a whole month that I realized that in his day, even among White pastors of the South, many of whom Dr. King would have thought of as peers or contemporaries—"my dear fellow clergyman" he called them—he was viewed as a dangerous anti-Christian radical leader stirring up trouble.

Dr. King says,

> You deplore the demonstrations taking place in Birmingham. But your statement, I am sorry to say, fails to express a similar concern for the conditions that brought about the demonstrations. I am sure that none of you would want to rest content with the superficial kind of social analysis that deals merely with effects and does not grapple with underlying causes. It is unfortunate that demonstrations are taking place in Birmingham, but it is even more unfortunate that the city's white power structure left the Negro community with no alternative.[1]

You might even highlight to me Dr. King's commitment to nonviolence, and King himself would agree with you:

> You may well ask: "Why direct action? Why sit-ins, marches and so forth? Isn't negotiation a better path?" You are quite right in calling for negotiation. Indeed, this is the very purpose of direct action. Nonviolent direct action seeks to create such a crisis and foster such a tension that a community which has constantly refused to negotiate is forced to confront the issue. It seeks so to dramatize the issue that it can no longer be ignored. My citing the creation of tension as part of the work of the nonviolent-resister may sound rather shocking. But I must confess that I am not afraid of the word "tension." I have earnestly opposed violent tension, but there is a type of constructive, nonviolent tension which is necessary for growth. Just as Socrates felt

that it was necessary to create a tension in the mind so that individuals could rise from the bondage of myths and half-truths to the unfettered realm of creative analysis and objective appraisal, so must we see the need for nonviolent gadflies to create the kind of tension in society that will help men rise from the dark depths of prejudice and racism to the majestic heights of understanding and brotherhood. The purpose of our direct action program is to create a situation so crisis packed that it will inevitably open the door to negotiation. I therefore concur with you in your call for negotiation. Too long has our beloved Southland been bogged down in a tragic effort to live in monologue rather than dialogue.[2]

Dr. King got into what future congressman John Lewis, one of his protégés, called "good trouble." But he did it in a way that angered, confused, and inconvenienced White people. King used direct action to expose racial oppression and force the community to deal with it.

Black Lives Matter, in a lot of ways, is continuing the work of the civil rights movement.

Both movements ask us to be uncomfortable for the sake of justice.

I've already talked about this, but we can be tempted to think that the "righteousness" Jesus is talking about in Matthew 5:10-12 refers to personal piety, or our personal relationship with the Lord, and not social relationships or systems of oppression that keep people from experiencing Jesus as anything but the Good Shepherd. It's so important as peacemakers to note that in the Greek language of the New Testament, the word rendered "righteousness" here could just as easily be translated "justice." So an appropriate translation could be "Blessed, seen, favored are the ones who are persecuted for seeking justice."

When I think of justice, I worry that you, White Peacemaker, will get hung up on arguments like "Marxism" or "communism" or "anti-gospel." White supremacy has a high value on the written word: if someone has researched it, written about it, and can refute it, then White people tend to believe it over the lived and shared experience of others. Even if multiple stories refute an idea that's been codified by academia, you are tempted to explain away those stories and stick to something you've read. That makes so much sense, given that a great way to reinforce a social structure that will ask you to reject your natural inclination to empathy is through data and studies and papers written by people you assume are much smarter and much more educated than you. And once you have a good chunk of information to discredit a narrative, that is what you'll rely on to avoid any kind of change. Listen: I do this too. It's one of the lingering effects of the Enlightenment era.

We could have a really fun thought experiment about the virtues and vices of various philosophical ideas, but justice and creating a just society should not and cannot be up for debate. Justice simply means to make whole. If we believe God's shalom is wholeheartedness in a broken world, then we must be wholeheartedly for justice. In Amos 5:21-24 (ESV), God says:

I hate, I despise your feasts,
    and I take no delight in your solemn assemblies.
Even though you offer me your burnt offerings
    and grain offerings,
    I will not accept them;
and the peace offerings of your fattened animals,
    I will not look upon them.
Take away from me the noise of your songs;
    to the melody of your harps I will not listen.
But let justice roll down like waters,
    and righteousness like an ever-flowing stream.

Justice is God's idea. It is a part of his character, and one way we can worship him in spirit and in truth is to seek it. To God, justice is as essential as moving water: it purifies and satisfies.

My favorite definition of justice came from Judge Marilyn Milian, the first Hispanic judge to preside over "the People's Court." Whenever someone appears and asks for an exorbitant amount, she almost never gives it to them. "I'm here to make you whole," she's said. "Justice means I give back to you what has been taken away from you. You don't get to get rich off the justice system. It is here to make things right and bring back fairness to you and the defendant." If the dispute is decided in favor of the plaintiff, the defendant has to repair the damage and the plaintiff gets a reasonable settlement. This is justice, a reasonable balancing of the scales when our sinfulness has caused harm.

For first-century Judeans like Jesus, the concepts of righteousness and justice weren't compartmentalized the way they are in modern Western cultures. For Jesus and his contemporaries, a person's righteousness was tied not only to their "vertical" holiness but also to their "horizontal" holiness—what we could easily consider as "justice."

This significantly affects how we might view "persecution because of righteousness."

Instead of imagining a pious person being picked on for their love for God, we might instead imagine a person being reviled for speaking out on behalf of people who are mistreated in society. We might think of someone being spoken ill of because they are "a friend of sinners," or someone who prioritizes love and grace over "law and order"—someone like Jesus.

We should always remember to keep Jesus' teachings in the context of his ministry. Jesus was someone who was persecuted because of his righteousness, and his righteousness entailed calling for and demonstrating justice.

Jesus' teaching "Blessed are those who are persecuted because of righteousness, for theirs is the kingdom of heaven" invites us to consider how important it is to be among those who suffer because they bring justice, because they are in good, good company, because they are following in the steps of Jesus, and even as they suffer, they will experience the kingdom of God.

The kingdom of God isn't a fantastical way of talking about our personal piety, as if we need to dress it up with fairy tale language to give C. S. Lewis and Tolkien a run for their money. The kingdom of God describes the community of Jesus followers who completely reorient their lives to look like Jesus *and* it describes the countercultural movement of the values of Jesus as lived out in his followers. So we are the kingdom of God and we advance the kingdom of God.

Shalom is the texture of the kingdom of God, and we get to be ambassadors of grace, mercy, love, peace, and yes, y'all . . . justice. But ambassadorship ain't easy. Jesus, our example, bled and died, not because he was a great teacher but because he challenged the oppressive Roman Empire. Every time Jesus spoke of the kingdom of God, it was as if he was holding a massive protest sign that said "Defund the Roman Guard," or maybe in language we'd understand today, "Say Their Names" (speaking of all the marginalized and neglected). Jesus says, When you are persecuted because you've exposed injustice, then you are doing this peacemaking thing right. You're blessed, seen, honored, empowered by God.

❊   ❊   ❊

I'm going to say something that you're not going to like: If you pull away from the Black Lives Matter movement, which is arguably the most impactful expression of the fight for human dignity of this moment, because it comes in a package you don't like, then you don't have enough proximity to the pain of white supremacy. If you resist aligning yourself with Black Lives Matter and the conversation about racism turns into a fun thought experiment or a lively debate on Facebook about philosophical ideas and not a visceral pain in your gut for the extreme loss of life and liberty for Black people in America, then you are in danger of worshiping of god of Intellect and not Jesus, the humble suffering servant. Jesus, who was persecuted because he defended his people when everyone else wanted him to defend their ideas or politics.

Be so very careful, friend, that you don't put up unnecessary barriers to you living in right-relatedness with your Black and Brown brothers and sisters. Racial righteousness is not personal, it's communal, it's systemic, it's a reorienting of this world away from the violence of white supremacy to the healing of shalom. I love what psychologist and professor Chanequa Walker-Barnes says in *I Bring the Voices of My People*:

> The *telos*, or divine "endgame," for racial reconciliation is not restored relationship between Whites and people of color. It is not, as one ministry colleague, activist Onleilove Alston, once sarcastically described it, the image of "a big Black dude and a White dude on a stage, hugging it out with a single tear rolling down their cheeks." It is the establishment of a just world, one in which racial inequities have been abolished. This means that the current practices, policies, and societal norms that disadvantage people of

color or advantage White people must be abolished and corrected. Further, there must be intentional, sustained, and large-scale effort to remediate the economic, educational, political, social, physical, and psychological harm inflicted upon people of color by racism.[3]

This is what an invasion of the kingdom of God looks like: we turn violent systems of oppression upside down, like Jesus flipping over tables, disrupting the systems built on power and greed that lull us into indifference, that reward us for our defensiveness. I say no more, White Peacemakers. No more arguing over whether we should say "Black Lives Matter," because it's not even a question in God's mind. And here's another thing: Every single one of those leaders of Black Lives Matter is made in God's image. They are his Beloved too. They have been led by the Spirit to seek justice and call you to repent.

I know when you're looking at the news and you see what looks like looting and violence sanctioned by Black Lives Matter leaders, it reinforces your belief that this movement is godless and anti-Christian because it doesn't have the stated commitment to nonviolence of the civil rights movement of the '60s.

I agree that no one should lose property and no police officer should be in danger because of an anti-racism demonstration. However, Black Lives Matter as an organization does not condone or encourage violent resistance. In fact, a study by the Armed Conflict Location and Event Data Project (ACLED) reports that 93 percent of all the Black Lives Matter protests in the wake of the murder of George Floyd were peaceful.

More than 2,400 locations reported peaceful protests, while fewer than 220 reported "violent demonstrations." The authors define violent demonstrations as including "acts targeting other individuals, property, businesses, other rioting groups or armed actors." Their definition includes anything from "fighting back against police" to vandalism, property destruction[,] looting, road-blocking using barricades, burning tires or other materials. In cities where protests did turn violent—these demonstrations are "largely confined to specific blocks."[4]

If peacemaking is our goal, then we would do well to acknowledge the peaceable efforts of Black Lives Matter at their protests. We should offer grace when we see violence and know that it is not the rule but the exception. Wasn't it King who said, "I think that we've got to see that a riot is the language of the unheard"?

A profound act of peacemaking is to hear the cries of suffering and move toward relieving that suffering, even if that means we'd have to suffer, like my friend Amy.

❀     ❀     ❀

"Okay, but it's negative fifteen degrees out," T. C. said, curled up on the couch, sipping a cup of chicken broth. He'd been in and out of the hospital for the past three weeks with an unknown stomach issue. Finally, the doctor suggested it was better for him to rest at home but come back if he spiked a fever again. Thankfully, he was keeping broth down, and his temp was a gloriously average 97.5 degrees.

"Yeah, but I really want to be there for Amy," I said, pulling on my knit hat and puffy coat.

"Have you even met this woman?" he asked.

I grabbed my purse. "No, but she was charged for filming a police stop with three officers pointing guns at two unarmed Black men. I can't run around here talking about White Peacemakers needing to show up if I don't show up for them."

He put his cup down on the coffee table and waved me over for a hug. "All right, but don't get yourself in trouble. I'm too weak to come get you out of jail."

I hadn't planned to say anything to the judge—just go, sit in the galley, and pray.

Five months before her court date, Amy, a local pastor, noticed a traffic stop that seemed to be escalating unnecessarily. She pulled over and went live on Facebook for over four minutes, calling out to the police, "How about you put the guns down?" and "They're being compliant!" At one point, Amy even advocated to the police for one of the men who was trying to get out of the car but was afraid of the drawn guns. The shaky video, shared with me by another pastor in the area, showed Amy a good fifteen feet from the action, out of the way of the police, but close enough to hold them accountable. Later on the officers issued her a citation for obstructing a legal process.

Driving nearly an hour to the courthouse, I was completely aware of how weird it was that the first time I'd meet Amy would be outside a courtroom, but a White Peacemaker was being unnecessarily persecuted for her commitment to protect Black lives, and nothing, not my social anxiety or even a Minnesota polar vortex, could keep me home.

The ACLU got involved and after months of fighting in court, the charges against Amy for recording a traffic stop were dropped. Amy doesn't have a record, but this experience cost her greatly. Financially, she had to invest in a lawyer; emotionally, she was anxious about the outcome; relationally, some friends disagreed with her. In a lot of ways she suffered, and her suffering reminds me of something James Cone says in *God of the Oppressed:* "Faith is born out of suffering, and suffering is faith's most powerful contradiction. This is the

Christian dilemma. The only meaningful Christian response is to resist unjust suffering and to accept the painful consequence of that resistance."[5]

That same day I saw a picture from Louisville, Kentucky, protesting the shooting of Breonna Taylor, a twenty-six-year-old unarmed Black woman who—still in her bedclothes—got up to investigate when the police forcibly entered her apartment without adequate notification and was shot eight times. Breonna bled to death while her boyfriend was arrested for firing his weapon at the police. When I saw her picture, I couldn't help but think, "Gosh she reminds me of my cousin. Actually . . . she kinda looks like me."

I wanted to protest Breonna's death, but I was worn out from all the other protests of the summer. But, when I saw that picture, it was as if a weight was lifted from my soul. The nonviolent, direct action demonstration on my screen told me, "Don't worry, Osheta, the White Peacemakers have got this."

The picture shared by the Kentucky National Organization for Women was of White women standing in front of Black and Brown demonstrators.

The Facebook caption read, "6th and Jefferson in Louisville. This is a line of white people forming a barrier between Black protestors and the police. This is love. This is what you do with your privilege. #NoJusticeNoPeace #SayHerName #BreonnaTaylor."

These were women willing to be persecuted for righteousness. They were literally putting their bodies where their values were: protecting the dignity and worth of Black and Brown people and expecting more from the systems that they have benefited from. They put their bodies on the line because they knew those systems would protect them, and they stayed there until the Black leaders had their chance to speak. They were told to do this extravagant act of righteousness by one of the Black Lives Matter leaders.

Anti-racism is an embodied practice, and Black Lives Matter invites us in many ways to practice anti-racism peacemaking for the humanity of Black people. We are no longer three-fifths of a human, no longer property, no longer criminals. Our lives matter. The question is then, White Peacemakers, are you willing to suffer to make sure we live in a world that never forgets our *imago Dei*?

## Breath prayer

———

Not only so, but we also glory in our sufferings, because we know that suffering produces perseverance; perseverance, character; and character, hope. And hope does not put us to shame, because God's love has been poured out into our hearts through the Holy Spirit, who has been given to us.

—ROMANS 5:3-5

Holy Spirit
*INHALE, EXHALE*
Give me hope

# What We're Not Going to Do

## *A New Orientation to Anger*

You have heard that it was said to the people long ago, "You shall not murder, and anyone who murders will be subject to judgment." But I tell you that anyone who is angry with a brother or sister will be subject to judgment. Again, anyone who says to a brother or sister, "Raca," is answerable to the court. And anyone who says, "You fool!" will be in danger of the fire of hell.

—MATTHEW 5:21-22

May 6, 2020

Dear White Peacemakers,

I couldn't sleep at all last night. I'm deeply, deeply disturbed by the murder of Ahmaud Arbery by two White men while he was out for a Sunday afternoon jog. Father and son Gregory and Travis McMichael profiled, chased down, harassed, and murdered Ahmaud with a shotgun. They shot him point-blank with a shotgun. Let that sink in. Neither suspect has spent a day in jail. Let *that* sink in. Okay . . . White Peacemaker, what are you going to do? You see, I can't do anything more with this today—it's almost too much to process. Again. I'm going to have to pull away and grieve, so it's time for y'all to step up. Let the Spirit empower you to make peace and demand justice for Ahmaud. I'll promise you this, though, I'm a Black Peacemaker, so I'm going to try to hold in tension my desire for justice for Ahmaud, a Beloved Black man who experienced unspeakable trauma, who experienced a modern-day lynching, and a kind of compassion for the McMichaels, who were so consumed by their sickness of racism that they took his life. Holding this tension is going to be difficult, but it's necessary because I will not let my anger consume me. I have no more words, just a short prayer:

Lord, have mercy
Lord, bring justice
Lord, weep with us

#Irunwithmaud
Osheta

❀ ❀ ❀

Here's a situation that often comes up. I'm going about my everyday business around the house—laundering the clothes, washing the dishes, yelling at the dog to stop chasing the cat, reheating my cup of coffee for, oh, the fifth time of the day, you know basic mom-at-home stuff, when I finally sit down from all the puttering around to play on the Internet. I want to see if Amy's had her baby, if Kurt's turned his manuscript in, if Steph's releasing a new fun T-shirt to raise money for hungry kids in the Twin Cities. I love the Internet for all the ways it connects me to the people I love doing the things that make them come alive. Then I scroll through the updates from friends until I start to see a common hashtag, the name of someone, usually a Black, unarmed man or woman, usually police are involved, usually the details are murky—was there a gun, was there a chase, was there probable cause for self-defense?

"He was shot, while running," my friend Rachel posted. "I run all the time. #justiceforMaud," I read on one of these mid-puttering breaks. My coffee grows cold while I begin the spiral. First I look to a few credible accounts on Twitter to see if they are reporting the same thing I've read from my friends. Then I check my favorite public theologians to see if they are leading a lament in light of the news. If they are, then I know it's true. White supremacy has claimed another Black life.

I've told you how I've learned to accept that grieving is a part of my life as a Black woman in America. Once I've gone down the spiral, I know my plans for a day of quotidian bliss are ruined. I must begin some version of the five stages of grief. I'm past denial, but the one that's going to really get me, the one that I have to prepare for is right around the corner. It's about to slam into me with such a force I'll feel it in my gut, I won't be able to breathe, I'll have to pace around the room: the anger.

Anger. White Peacemaker, anger always trips me up. It poses a very real threat to my whole "peace of Christ be with you" vibe.

Anger has come to sit by me. I have to give her appropriate attention. If I don't, she'll fade into the background, her fiery eyes watching me, watching the snowball of pain and everyday annoyances, watching the vulnerabilities of my family members. Just when I've forgotten she's there, when I have begun to believe she never really came to visit. I tell myself, that was just her quirky cousin Passion—Passion I can accept; Anger, nope. This is the exact moment that Anger will rush into the room, crashing over me and toward the ones I love.

I slam cabinet doors, and throw pens and growl, literally growl, when I can't find my keys. I'll say things like "What the hell is wrong with you all?" and "Why am I the only one around here who cares?" My family will look at me like I've lost my mind, and to be honest, I think I have, maybe just a little bit. I think every time I see another picture of a Black person killed by White hands, the trauma of it chips away at my sense of safety in this world—if that isn't a form of madness, then I don't know what is.

The only thing I've learned in order to stay sane and whole-ish in the spiral is to give each stage of grief its appropriate time:

I have to allow myself to be in denial and cling to whatever innocence I still have.

Then I have to allow myself to be angry, because unchecked anger becomes violence, and in the kingdom of God, we turn our swords into plowshares.

❦    ❦    ❦

Jesus teaches a different orientation to anger in our passage for this chapter, one that is a warning to not let anger dehumanize others and call them fools. *Raca*, the Aramaic word Jesus uses here, can be translated as "empty-headed" or "foolish." Think of Vizzini holding Buttercup captive in *The Princess Bride* when facing off with the man in the black mask (Westley, y'all . . . it's Westley and if that's a spoiler then I'm sorry . . . also what are you doing with your life that you haven't seen *The Princess Bride?*). Vizzini uses convoluted thought experiments in an attempt to trick Westley into taking a poisoned goblet of wine. Finally, Westley makes a decision and Vizzini begins yelling at him, "I switched the drinks when your back was turned, ha ha, you fool!"

This kind of self-righteous, othering posture—even when we've been wronged, even when our anger is completely justified—is antithetical to the way of Jesus.

When I learned of Ahmaud Arbery's killing, Anger sat beside me. I watched the video of Ahmaud running away from Gregory and Travis McMichael, father and son, who after seeing Ahmaud jogging in their neighborhood and checking out a construction site, loaded up their truck with Travis's shotgun and Gregory's service revolver from when he was on the police force. Filmed by their friend William Bryan, the viral video released months after his death shows nothing short of an execution. Some have called all of what Ahmaud endured on February 23, 2020—the being profiled because of his skin, the chase, the several attempts to block him in the neighborhood (without which he could have gotten away easily), the shooting, and then Travis's hateful words of "f\*\*\*ing n\*\*\*\*\*" as Ahmaud lay dying on the street—a modern-day lynching.

I was angry.

So incredibly angry.

And I wasn't the only one.

I posted the Dear White Peacemakers letter at the start of this chapter on social media with a slideshow comprising three things:

- A video from Toni Morrison reflecting on the madness of racism when asked if even she, Toni Morrison, respected and known and often Beloved, still experienced racism. Her thoughts stayed with me all day as I was processing my anger: "[The question to ask is] 'How do you feel?' . . . Don't you understand that the people who do this thing, who practice racism, are bereft? There is something distorted about the psyche. It's a huge waste and it's a corruption and a distortion. It's like it's a profound neurosis that nobody examines for what it is. It feels crazy. It is crazy. And . . . it has just as much of a deleterious effect on White people. And possibly equal [as it does] Black people."

- A graphic with various calls to action seeking justice for Ahmaud.
- A picture of Gregory and Travis McMichael both in their hunting gear, having just taken down a stunning deer.

I wasn't sure about posting the third picture. I was so angry at them that I didn't want their picture on my social media. But because I didn't want their picture on my account is exactly the reason I knew I had to post it. One intentional practice of peacemaking I do to cultivate empathy for White people who are still stuck in racist thoughts or committing racist deeds is to go out of my way to humanize them. I look at pictures of them—not the mug shot or the terrifying ones that are shared by news outlets, because those are chosen for the express purpose of making them look guilty; rather, I try to find pictures of them with family or friends. I know White people have always "been humanized." Because of white supremacy, White people and Whiteness are the standard of humanity. This isn't a practice I prescribe across the board for all peacemakers at all times, it's just my personal commitment to have a first line of defense against enemy-making, retributive anger. I have to remember that they are human, that they are made in the image of God, that they are Beloved, and that they are not too far gone for redemption. So I posted the picture of the McMichaels, turned my phone off, and went about my afternoon to continue rumbling with my anger.

Others were angry too.

"They need to be put to death."

"I hope they get what's coming to them."

"White trash supreme."

"Bastards."

"White trash dogs."

"Hillbilly racist a-holes."

These were a few of the comments posted under the picture of Travis and Gregory on my Facebook account. Y'all . . . I was horrified and a little energized. These people, mostly White, were saying the things I wanted to say about a father-son duo who hunted down a Black man as if for sport, as if he was nothing more than a prized buck. But I'm a kingdom ambassador, an anti-racism peacemaker.

I know that kind of anger, the kind of anger that seeks to humiliate, is particularly dangerous to me in the aftermath of racial trauma.

Psychologist Leon F. Seltzer says,

> When you experience anger, it's almost impossible not to feel like a victim, for virtually all anger can be understood as a reaction to what feels threatening or unfair to you. In such instances, you feel unjustifiably attacked, taken advantage of, betrayed, violated, or powerless. And your anger, essentially retaliatory in nature, agreeably serves the function of restoring to you a sense of righteousness and control, even dignity and respect. Added to this, the energizing surge of adrenaline accompanying your eruption

further accentuates your sense of "wronged virtue." So naturally, you feel morally superior to whoever or whatever provoked you in the first place.[1]

It's pretty difficult to love someone you feel morally superior to and even more difficult to be discipled by Jesus, who according to Philippians 2:6-8, embraced humility and suffering instead of humiliation and subjugation.

> Who, being in very nature God,
>     did not consider equality with God something
>         to be used to his own advantage;
> rather, he made himself nothing
>     by taking the very nature of a servant,
>     being made in human likeness.
> And being found in appearance as a man,
>     he humbled himself
>     by becoming obedient to death—
>         even death on a cross!

I knew I had to craft a response to everyone who was posting attacks and slurs about the McMichaels. So I posted this to everyone:

> Hey, y'all . . . no, this isn't cool. They are loved by God too—even though they did something terrible. I'm praying for their hearts to soften and for them to be held accountable, because I believe they are not too far gone for redemption. Y'all . . . even as God is grieving Ahmaud's death with us, God also deeply loves Gregory and Travis and delighted when they woke up this morning. I'm not going to delete your comments because they are an honest expression of your pain . . . but what we're not going to do is undermine our peacemaking with hate.

I posted this because I couldn't let the conversation keep filling up with White Peacemakers practicing retributive anger.

I couldn't allow myself to foster that space online, because I was actively trying to evict it from my heart.

❀    ❀    ❀

I know you might say it's completely okay for me to give in to my angry feelings—Jesus flipped tables in anger, right? Well, let's really talk about that, because I'mma be real with y'all . . . this is my kind of Jesus, the gadfly for justice Jesus, who's not having it with oppressive shenanigans. I love it when Jesus tells rich people to sell their stuff, and shocks the self-righteous Pharisees by forgiving a woman caught in some form of sexual violence. Give me Jesus who was looked down upon because his mama was unwed when she got pregnant and his father was a common tradesman. Forget Buddy Jesus, I want Gadfly Jesus. I have a feeling, y'all, that Jesus really was "that" guy, the one who didn't let those around him forget that they were a part of a bigger story, that their lives and actions have impact, and I love it.

Jesus cleared the temple because the temple system had become corrupt. Money changers were charging exorbitant rates for worshipers to purchase animals to sacrifice, and at that time, Passover, thousands of people in Jerusalem had come to the temple to be purified. And instead of removing as many barriers as possible for people to worship, those in power and those who stood to profit institutionalized economic injustice, and Gadfly Jesus was not having it. So when he fashioned a whip (which based on its description was a cord and ropes), it was more like a broom he used to shoo the animals out of the temple. Then he flipped over the tables and he exposed the money changers for their greedy, dehumanizing actions.

Anti-racism is the world of being, as Dr. King describes it, a gadfly for justice. It will require us to feel intensely, and our anger is a natural response. It requires us to take that adrenaline and channel it toward actions that will challenge systems and expose injustice.

I want to be angry at the systems and I want to disrupt those systems in direct action like Jesus, but I never, ever want to weaponize my anger toward others. And listen, I know on face value when you read of Jesus clearing the temple it seems like Jesus' anger was a retributive kind—he showed up, saw something that deeply angered him, and reacted. But this is not consistent with the life of Jesus, which was radically, uncompromisingly, creatively nonviolent, even to death on a cross.

Our anger should never be used to inflict pain on people. Where is the logic in that? I'm so angry about violence toward one person that I'll turn and seek violence toward another. No, we must be resolvedly, meticulously, wholeheartedly nonviolent—even when we don't know what, as Mr. Rogers says, to do with the mad that we feel.

In Mark's account, Jesus went to the temple, looked around, then came back the next day to clear it. Jesus was, as peacemaking priest John Dear puts it, "meticulously nonviolent." Meticulously nonviolent. That is my goal when Anger comes to sit beside me. I want to be thoughtful, responsive, and as nonviolent as possible. Which means I cannot allow myself to speak hateful or insulting words about people who are complicit to racism. Jesus, even in his initial anger at what he saw, took a beat, and then responded.

There is a massive difference between retributive, reactive anger and the kind I feel every single time another Black person is killed. If I want my anger to look like Jesus' and to accomplish the same kind of direct disarming and dismantling of oppressive systems that he did when he overturned the tables in the temple, then I need to entrust myself—anger included—to the Holy Spirit to help me practice anti-racism peacemaking with the same commitment to human flourishing as Jesus.

I'm angry about racism and the lasting influence of white supremacy. So. Very. Angry. I'm angry at every act of violence toward Black and Brown people. I'm angry at every careless word. I'm angry at biases and microaggressions. I'm angry at the fear that keeps White Peacemakers quiet. I'm angry that we're influenced by scarcity that keeps us from taking risks that might result in healing. I'm incredibly angry. But my anger doesn't give me permission to sin. It doesn't give me permission to take it out on White people. It doesn't give me permission to mistreat and believe the worst about them. It just doesn't. My anger is not holy like God's—I cannot always trust it to burn up all that is dross and leave only the gold.

So my job as a Black Peacemaker, a peacemaker committed to anti-racism, is to be for every single image bearer in this fight and to take all these big feelings of mine—all my anger, all my fear, all my sadness, all my perceived smallness—and give it to God. My job is to ask God to do what only he can do—turn that anger into a holy passion and then point me toward the appropriate tables to flip over. You know those tables. I've named a few of them here, but let me be super clear here that the first tables I'mma flip over as we dismantle white supremacy are scarcity, racial biases, and violence.

Each one benefits a few at the expense of the many, and those systems need to come crashing down.

So, White Peacemaker, I try so hard to be mindful to direct my anger toward the right places—systems and not people. Because what we're not going to do is undermine peacemaking with our anger.

# *Breath prayer*

———

A gentle answer turns away wrath,
but a harsh word stirs up anger.

The tongue of the wise adorns knowledge,
but the mouth of the fool gushes folly.

The eyes of the LORD are everywhere,
keeping watch on the wicked and the good.

The soothing tongue is a tree of life,
but a perverse tongue crushes the spirit.

—PROVERBS 15:1-4

Rabbi

*I N H A L E ,    E X H A L E*

Teach me the words of Life

**22**

# Forgiving While Black

For if you forgive other people when they sin against you, your heavenly Father will also forgive you. But if you do not forgive others their sins, your Father will not forgive your sins.

—MATTHEW 6:14-15

October 3, 2019

Dear White Peacemakers,

I am raising two Black boys to be peacemakers and practice enemy love. I am as passionate about shalom and the kingdom of God as they come, and I would never in a million years condone Brandt Jean's act of "forgiveness" to them. In fact, I'd encourage them to sit in their sadness, process their anger, and pray fervently—but publicly forgive? No. Not as Black men. Not as they are coming of age in this country that has consistently policed Black grief and promoted fear of Black anger. I've worked too hard to teach them to love their Black identities, stand up for their liberation, and seek shalom for *all* people involved in a conflict. White Peacemakers, you need to learn to sit in the pain of this event and not rush to the "joy" or, quite frankly, the relief that the hug gives you. The hug, while arresting in its mercy, only serves to short-circuit any progress toward dismantling white supremacy. This is what we need right now. We need to focus on dismantling the very racism and fear of Black men that took Botham Jean's life. Remember this: forgiveness is not reconciliation. We are called to be reconcilers. So, Peacemaker, listen to the people of color in your contexts—if we're concerned about this, maybe you should be too.

Truth *and* Reconciliation,
Osheta

❀    ❀    ❀

Forgiveness.

When I think of "the Hug Heard around the Internet" from Brandt Jean, Botham Jean's brother, to Amber Guyger, the White police officer who shot Botham in his own apartment because she was (allegedly) confused, I can't help but wonder if that was an emotionally healthy choice. Did he perform this act of forgiveness to satisfy his faith community or as an impulse to please the White people in the room? I wonder this because forgiveness can happen without the public performance of reconciliation.

Is it appropriate to offer tear-filled statements and hugs without (1) any indication that the root issue is going to be addressed; and (2) a clearly communicated plan of restoration? I don't think so.

In anti-racism circles, forgiveness can be a bit of a land mine. Some anti-racism educators aren't in favor of teaching forgiveness because Black communities have been forgiving White people for centuries, but to what effect? Writing in 2015 about how the members of Mother Emanuel AME Church offered unmerited grace and forgiveness to Dylann Roof just hours after he murdered their loved ones, author Roxanne Gay even says, "Black people forgive because we need to survive. We have to forgive time and time again while racism or White silence in the face of racism continues to thrive."[1]

Some say forgiveness is the only way we'll move forward. Forgive and forget, that's what the Bible teaches, right? No, there's actually a quite significant difference between forgiveness and reconciliation. Both are important aspects of calling towards anti-racism peacemaking. The question is, White Peacemakers, do you care about forgiveness and reconciliation as equally important parts of the process? We cannot have one without the other.

Forgiveness is a choice, and I believe Brandt Jean is free to make that choice. However, how he modeled that choice in such a public way, in the moment, was problematic because he didn't invite or maybe even couldn't allow White onlookers into the whole process of reconciliation that includes forgiveness. You see, Amber Guyger didn't have the chance to really show the Jean family that she'd interrogated her own biases and recognized the depths of her sin. She was caught, she was on camera, and she gave the appropriate statement of regret. The kind of commitment it takes to justify such an act of reconciliation, well, there wasn't enough time for that. There wasn't enough time to work through all the trauma, to be vulnerable and honest with each other. There wasn't enough time to hold the police department accountable for their participation in covering it up. There wasn't enough time to examine the working environment Amber Guyger was in and if it somehow contributed to her inability to think rationally at the end of her shift. There were so many things necessary for the Jean family and Amber Guyger to explore before they could be reconciled. There are also historical power dynamics to think about here.

When something horrible happens and White people are the first to say we should forgive, what the Black community is being called upon to provide isn't necessarily forgiveness, because that can be done quietly and without fanfare. No, what's being asked for is to assuage white guilt by performative reconciliation.

What I mean by performative reconciliation is that, in this context, the hug was a deeply intimate and impactful gesture. A hug is a symbolic act of protection and acceptance, a taking into your space another person and offering them comfort. Why were White pastors so excited about a Black man hugging a White woman? Because the reconciliation theater of the hug gave them something to reflect back on when they think of Botham Jean's horrific case. The hug overshadowed the horror of another unarmed Black man killed by a White officer. It overshadowed the white supremacist reminder that Black people are not safe, even in our own homes, enjoying a bowl of ice cream. It even overshadowed the deep-seated pain and loss and calls for justice from Botham's mother, Allison! Ms. Allison Jean clarified to reporters that while Brandt was at a place where he could publicly forgive, she was unable to forgive Amber Guyger in that moment. To that I say as a wholehearted Black Peacemaker: Amen, Sis! Just because she didn't offer forgiveness immediately doesn't mean she never would. She chose to take the necessary time, to work through her pain, and I'm hopeful at some point she will offer Amber Guyger words of forgiveness and acts of reconciliation when she's ready.

I think part of the problem is our fast-paced, news-driven age. We've been conditioned to think that a story like this, one that's so horrific and so shocking, needs a pretty bow to wrap it up so we can hurry along to some version of happily ever after. That's what the Hug did.

But this is not the way of Jesus. When Peter sinned against Jesus by denying him three times, I believe Jesus had already forgiven him. Jesus was the one who told him that he would do it and Jesus offered a blanket prayer of forgiveness from the cross. I think there's something to be said about being a person who moves with forgiveness in their heart like that. It's as Maya Angelou says, "You can't forgive without loving. And I don't mean sentimentality. I don't mean mush. I mean having enough courage to stand up and say, 'I forgive. I'm finished with it.'"

I believe we can access grace and forgive immediately. But I also think that because you have love in your heart, because you understand the gravity of the sin and the damage it has caused, then you will know that a restoration process is required. For Peter, part of his restoration process was walking with Jesus along the beach and telling him three different times that he loved him. And what did Jesus say to him? "Then feed my sheep." Our faithfulness to Christ is never separated from our loving care of each other. This is the hard work of reconciliation. This is anti-racism peacemaking.

In this chapter's teaching from the Sermon on the Mount, Jesus is not suggesting a kind of quid pro quo where God will do for us if we do for others. Rather, Jesus is teaching us about the deeper grain of love by which the Father in heaven has ordered the world. God is love and God's world runs according to love. When we follow the way of Jesus we are remade in love, and love flows through our lives. When we grasp that sin no longer has any hold over our lives, we are freed to release others from sin's grip. When we live in love, we no longer have space for unforgiveness. This is why I deeply believe Brandt Jean, a follower of Jesus, could forgive Amber Guyger.

Forgiveness, however, is not the same as reconciliation, and the two must be distinguished. While forgiveness is vital to a life lived in love, we must also love ourselves enough not to subject ourselves to ongoing retraumatization. Jesus' way of love opens the door to reconciliation, but it's not a guarantee. People are also free to continue in their sin, and it isn't healthy for us to join ourselves to them while they are in that state.

For example, in the context of marriage, Paul advises Jesus-disciples this way: "But if the unbeliever leaves, let it be so. The brother or the sister is not bound in such circumstances; God has called us to live in peace" (1 Corinthians 7:15). Reconciliation is predicated on repentance. In fact, if a person has not repented, there may even be reason to withhold public forgiveness so that the sin is not excused or justified. "If your brother or sister sins against you, rebuke them; and if they repent, forgive them" (Luke 17:3). Some do not respond well to the confrontation of their sin.

Public performance of forgiveness/false reconciliation may also be problematic if it is presumed to be required and if unacknowledged power dynamics are at play. Black Americans are often celebrated for their public forgiveness, yet the power dynamics are rarely acknowledged. Is the same public forgiveness enthusiastically offered to Black offenders by

White victims? I worry that if Black people are expected to publicly forgive quickly and unconditionally, the underlying ideologies that produced the crime or harm will never be adequately exposed and rooted out. This turns something beautiful like the Hug into something ugly: cheap grace.

Cheap grace is the opposite of what Jesus taught. He called disciples into a life of deep self-examination and subversive social engagement. He called disciples to "take up their cross and follow me." This "taking up" of "the cross" that Jesus spoke of wasn't a bum knee or an annoying mother-in-law. No, the cross was a device used by the empire of Rome to terrify would-be revolters. The cross was Rome's way of saying, "We're in charge and if you try to come for us, we'll crush you!" Jesus knew that his way of love was so countercultural, so radical, that it set him on a collision course with the powers that be, and would ultimately get him killed. When he called disciples to join him in his mission, he wanted them to know they were signing up for a similar fate. To follow this path, disciples would have to "count the cost." Were they truly willing to lay it all on the line to follow Jesus? Were they willing to give up what meant most to them? Now, if Jesus' idea of "grace" was to invite disciples into a life of radical surrender and dangerous risk, where do we get the idea that grace is "free" and forgiveness is easy?

When cheap grace is normalized, societies quickly devolve. That's what happened in 1930s Germany. "Cheap grace" is what German pastor and theologian Dietrich Bonhoeffer called the way the German Christian church had compromised with Nazism. In that society, grace was reduced to an empty religious word and forgiveness was a legal fiction bestowed by God upon everyone unconditionally. But what about the atrocities committed by churchgoing Christians? What sense does it make that God's grace enabled German Christians to feel justified while they slaughtered their neighbors? That's why Bonhoeffer famously wrote,

> Cheap grace is the preaching of forgiveness without requiring repentance, baptism without church discipline, Communion without confession, absolution without personal confession. Cheap grace is grace without discipleship, grace without the cross, grace without Jesus Christ, living and incarnate.[2]

You see, White Peacemakers, forgiveness is inextricably tied to communion. It isn't an abstract declaration pronounced over you or me divorced from our actual heart condition, our actual words, and our actual deeds. Jesus didn't teach that forgiven people robotically forgive others. No, he taught that forgiving people get forgiven, as we become conduits of forgiveness when we are rightly related to others. But being rightly related to others isn't easy, and doesn't happen quickly.

Forgiveness is something that we need to do for our own spiritual health. It may be necessary for us to release someone from an emotional debt we're carrying around so that we can heal. But it may be just as necessary for us to require demonstrable repentance of those who have caused a rupture in relationship. Premature reconciliation isn't wise when the other person hasn't changed. Reconciliation in that case could signal that the behavior that caused the rupture in the first place wasn't all that bad and becomes enabling. This is what happens on a societal scale when Black Christians are expected to forgive quickly, even before there have been tangible signs of repentance. White Peacemakers, I need you to know that people of color are tired of being abused and then told we need to forgive and embrace our abusers. This is another form of abuse.

When White Christians weaponize reconciliation against people of color, especially people of color who are holding them accountable to our calling to follow the Jesus way, then they have lost all moral authority to speak on receiving God's grace or repentance. They have not loved their Black and Brown siblings because they do not pay attention to what we need to be truly healthy in our forgiveness and ready for reconciliation.

Instead, we need true shalom—the kind of shalom that can be produced only when the Spirit has superintended a process of reconciliation that exposes and roots out the underlying pathologies that produced the behaviors that produced the harm. We need a process of reconciliation that includes taking ownership of un-Christlike ways of thinking about our sisters and brothers, about our neighbors, and about anyone who is different from us. We need a process of reconciliation that names and shames the lie of white supremacy. We need a process of reconciliation that includes concrete commitments to new patterns of thinking and new ways of living together. We need a process of reconciliation that includes restoration. Shalom means "nothing missing, nothing broken." We can't have shalom if we put a bandage over a gaping wound and call it healed.

I don't know Amber Guyger personally, but I've known many Amber Guygers over the years. She likely had no clue how deeply she'd imbibed the lie of white supremacy until it was far too late. She likely thought she was actually quite a compassionate and caring person. She likely thought she didn't "see color" and that Botham Jean's race had nothing to do with her thoughts or actions. So many of the Ambers I've known don't. Yet once they're sitting in their version of that courtroom, reevaluating their choices, they realize they've been duped. They've been lied to. They've had racist ideology so deeply implanted in their brains that they didn't even realize it was there.

If I love Amber with Christ's love, I don't just want to place a bandage over the gaping wound that is now her relationship to the Jean family. I want her and them to be made whole. I want there to be restoration. That's going to require some ruthless self-reflection, some concrete steps of change, some dying to herself, some "taking up" of "the cross." All the hugs in the world won't create shalom if she isn't transformed in the process.

## *Breath prayer*

All this is from God, who reconciled us to himself through Christ and gave us the ministry of reconciliation: that God was reconciling the world to himself in Christ, not counting people's sins against them. And he has committed to us the message of reconciliation. We are therefore Christ's ambassadors, as though God were making his appeal through us. We implore you on Christ's behalf: Be reconciled to God.

—2 CORINTHIANS 5:18-20

Jesus, the Lord Who Sees
*I N H A L E ,   E X H A L E*
Show me the Restoration Way

# 23

# White Saviorism and Black Joy

The eye is the lamp of the body. If your eyes are healthy, your whole body will be full of light. But if your eyes are unhealthy, your whole body will be full of darkness. If then the light within you is darkness, how great is that darkness!

—MATTHEW 6:22-23

Dear White Peacemakers,

Today I dressed up to write this letter. I know you can't see me and it's weird to curate an outfit simply to write a letter, but didn't I tell you this book would be a little weird? I'm in a good mood today. I just had the most glorious cup of coffee from the Starbucks Reserve line and my writing chair is toasty from my cat napping in it while I went to pick up the coffee (drive-through, friends, there's still a pandemic out there). I'm wearing a cozy sweatshirt that says exactly how I feel: "Joy is

Resistance." It's red buffalo check because . . . Minnesota, and it's a little larger than my regular size so I can get away with wearing it out and about with leggings. Later on I'm going to get my hair braided, so I'll be not only cozy, but cute. Y'all . . . the Lord is good and his mercies endure forever!

I'm in a good mood in this good Brown body and today I really want you to know that for every grieving day, I can point to three or four days just like this one. Good days. Joyful days. Days that make me feel human. And that's really important for you to know, White Peacemaker. That this work of anti-racism isn't just a response to the gory but also a responsibility to protect the glorious. To remember that Black and Brown people are holistic beings. We contain multitudes. Our stories are greater than our struggles. If all you see is our pain, the dark side of being a person of color, then all you'll do is respond with sympathy and pity. Maybe even a twinge of saviorism and self-righteousness. I don't want that for you, so let's talk about joy, Black joy to be specific, and let's figure out how you can cultivate a practice of subversive joy alongside us.

Cheers and changes,
Osheta

❀    ❀    ❀

My friend Emily says that every time she sees me, I'm dancing. "It's like you've always got music in your head, Osheta." It's true. I don't mean to do it, I just . . . dance. I was listening to a podcast a while ago about the leaders of the civil rights movement and one of the guests made a point to talk about the dance parties the leaders would randomly have in the evening after strategy sessions. The speaker went on to say that maybe they knew something about the human body that we didn't—that when we are in bodies that are holding trauma, that are vulnerable every single day, when grief and anger take up residence in our guts, movement gives us a release, movement builds our resilience. It gets us grounded and free in these good bodies. I thought of Emily when I heard him say that. I also thought of my college dance teacher, Ms. Chapman. Ms. Chapman looked like Carole King and talked like Ms. Patty from *Gilmore Girls*. Even with her diminutive frame she took up the whole room. One day in class after we warmed up and stretched, she gathered us to the middle of the dance floor.

"Little birds," she started. (That was her name for us— something about us owning the space we're in, even the vast air around us. "Soar into your leaps, little birds," she'd yell nearly every class). "Today, we're going to trust our bodies. The dancer that does not trust her body cannot partner with it to create. That's what you are, little birds, creators with your bodies."

She and her assistant taught us sixteen counts to take across the floor, starting on one side of the dance floor, then dancing the counts, well . . . across the floor. Chapman was partial to us going across in small groups of three so she could critique us as we moved.

"Contract! Release! Step back and trust your body and spatial awareness!" Ms. Chapman yelled from across the room, wrapped in a bohemian scarf with her curly hair piled in a messy bun on top of her head.

Before my group's turn, I just closed my eyes and pictured myself moving, unbothered and unafraid. My body had been training all week and Ms. Chapman was a good teacher—I trusted her, the space I was in, and this body. We crossed the floor, the three of us, and at the end, Chapman yelled,

"YES, LADIES! Do it again, watch little bird in the middle"—
me—"she fully trusts her body!" and, y'all . . . that was the
worst thing Chapman could have done. Singling me out put
pressure on my creativity—it forced me to prove that this
body had trained and was good and that I did have something
worth paying attention to.

Being Black in predominately White spaces feels like that.
When I'm with White people I trust or even when I'm alone
in such spaces, I trust myself, I know I am fearfully and won-
derfully made . . . I know that full well. I'm creative and joyful
and liberated from the White gaze, but then when I'm in spaces
where a White person is watching me, waiting for me to prove
my place, waiting for me to fail, doubt creeps in and I become
disengaged. I become whatever it is the White people want me
to be—so I can gain their approval even if every bone, cell,
neuron, and fiber of my body is screaming, "No, Osheta, stop.
Trust us. We're not made to bend and break to make someone
else feel whole."

Sometimes, asking us to share our traumatic race stories
on panels and podcasts, for articles or commentary, in small
group or on coffee dates—sometimes it feels like you're rob-
bing us of our liberation. It seems like you don't care if we're
grounded in these bodies, finding joy and peace within them,
finding beauty in our cultural expression, finding a sense of
place in the stories and traditions of our ancestors. Those don't
seem to be the stories you want to engage with. Maybe you
don't want us, just want our tragedies. It feeds your "why"
with a bittersweet taste, and I'm just wondering, can't you be
motivated to dismantle racism with the same fervor when you
see us joyful?

White savior complex is at the core of this curation of Black
Pain and neglect of Black joy.

A white savior complex is formed when White people cling to a narrative that people of color need their help in order to have a better life. The White person always has the answers, resources, connections, and the person of color always has to come into the White person's world in order to receive help. You don't see the White "savior" have any meaningful change of perspective about the community or thoughtfully engage in the culture the person of color comes from because by the end of the book, movie, missionary testimony, or lesson the person of color has ascended to some version of Whiteness—they've changed the way they speak or eat, where they live or whom they interact with. Very rarely will you even see the person of color share with others the insights given to them from the White savior because the narrative wants you to believe that only a White person can be of help. The White protagonist in this story got to help a person of color, so now you, White person, go out and find your own Black problem to fix.

Teju Cole, a Nigerian American novelist, describes white saviorism this way: "The White Savior Industrial Complex is not about justice. It is about having a big emotional experience that validates privilege."[1]

I know, White Peacemaker, that attempting to become someone's savior is the furthest thing from your heart. Jesus gives a caution on our gaze that serves as a safeguard from white saviorism—cultivate a healthy, holistic view of people of color and our cultures. This requires you to examine any biases you may have about Blackness and Black culture—do you think rap music is grimy and raunchy, or brilliant and prophetic? Do you think natural hair is interesting and ethnic, or beautiful and ingenious? Do you love Beyoncé only because she makes you feel sassy, or do you allow her to help you appreciate Black history? If you believe that the creative Spirit of God is at work in and through communities of culture, then you'd celebrate with us as often as you lament with us.

Jesus says, "The eye is the lamp of the body. If your eyes are healthy, your whole body will be full of light. But if your eyes are unhealthy, your whole body will be full of darkness. If then the light within you is darkness, how great is that darkness!"

Where we place our focus forms our imagination. If we focus exclusively on depictions of Black Americans as victims, we will miss the amazing joy that fills our lives. Focusing on Black joy is powerful and important for building a counter-narrative to the daily rehearsal in the media of Black death and Black victimhood. When we let light into our eyes it illuminates the truth.

❊    ❊    ❊

When I suggest celebrating Black joy as a practice of anti-racism peacemaking, I sometimes get this response:

"But, I was told Black art . . . music . . . church . . . isn't for White people. We don't get to engage with it, because White people have appropriated so much."

What I think is important here is to understand the difference between appropriation and appreciation.

For example, you can and should appreciate the wonder that is *Black Panther* and the fictional African country of Wakanda, but because it has cultural, historical, and ancestral significance to Black people, especially Black Americans who often feel disconnected from our African roots, you probably shouldn't do the Wakanda salute.

And I think that's the most difficult aspect of learning how to celebrate Black joy—it requires you to ask the Black people in your life how they feel and what they think is appropriate.

It means inviting them in as you process your own appreciation and asking them to hold you accountable if you ever veer into appropriating.

A simple gut check to see if you're appropriating is, Did you cite your sources? Did you point to the person or community of color from where that art came and are you willing to put some respect on their names by crediting them? Can you decenter yourself and not be celebrated in the sharing of it? Are you engaging in that art to seem cultured, cool, or woke, or are you comfortable diverting the praise or "likes" away from you and toward the original creators? This is rooted in something really sinister, friends. On the plantation, every good thing that came from the enslaved community was taken by the White owners, and they often profited or received the praise for it. African people were brought to the American South and forced to work its land in part because the climate and soil was similar to that on the West African coast. The ingenuity they had from working their own land in Africa free and at peace was now constrained to a white supremacist economy. White communities flourished and the American dream was purchased by enslaved peoples' blood, sweat, tears, and suffering. Recipes that are passed down in White Southern families often were the culinary brainchildren of their brilliant enslaved cooks. White Peacemaker, you must learn how to appreciate without appropriating. You must right this wrong! Then you can celebrate wholeheartedly, like the Dragon Breath Prayer Warriors on Juneteenth.

❀　❀　❀

I planned the morning with one thought in mind: be as wildly, supremely joyful as I could. Everything from the prayers written by Black ministers to the playlist (including "Freedom" from Beyoncé) needed to not only spark joy but ignite joyfulness in me, and so much so that the women who joined me every morning for Breath Prayers felt it.

It was Juneteenth, one of the most notable Emancipation Days for enslaved peoples in the United States. I say "one of" and not "the" Emancipation Day, because as the Civil War came to a close in 1865, the news of the Northern defeat of the Southern Confederacy spread slowly to the enslaved population in remote areas. Because they didn't know the war was over and slavery ended, thousands of the people still lived as if they were not free. The idea that they could be freemen and women was ridiculous. I'm from Texas City, Texas, a small town about thirty minutes away from Galveston, one of those remote areas. What's so fascinating to me about Juneteenth is that it's not the celebration of an "official" act like the signing of the Emancipation Proclamation or even the ratification of the Thirteenth Amendment, which made slavery illegal in the United States. Juneteenth is the day the news of freedom finally made it to people who were waiting and were given a reason to celebrate.

My godmother, Hilda, sat me down one June morning when I was ten years old and said, "Child, do you know what today is?"

Hilda is a Black Puerto Rican woman. Her skin a dark mocha, closer to mine than my own mother's, who with her green eyes, red hair, and Irish cream skin often passed for White. I think this is why anytime Hilda paid attention to me, I felt a little more seen. My mother saw my soul and called out the good in me, knowing I'd become a woman who'd love others. Hilda saw my skin and called out the beauty, hoping I'd become a woman who'd love myself.

"Sheek (my nickname), today's Juneteenth. It's the day Black people knew they were free! This is history that happened just up the road. Black slaves were set free. You know what I'm going to do? I'mma make a 7-Up cake and heat up some tamales. We must celebrate."

We danced in the living room and ate cake. I honestly didn't understand the importance of Hilda teaching me. I was just super excited for cake on a weekday morning, but I think Hilda's experience as a Puerto Rican, an American who is not fully treated as such, an American who is still waiting for her reason to celebrate along with this country, made her want to instill in me a reverence for Juneteenth.

Fast-forward to me sitting at my laptop, hair wrapped up in a scarf, waiting anxiously for seven in the morning and Breath Prayers to start so I could celebrate Juneteenth with my friends.

This was the first Juneteenth since George Floyd died, which meant more White people than ever were paying attention and joining Black leaders to celebrate Juneteenth, but many not knowing how. I announced on my Instagram account that I would be hosting a morning breath prayer time centered on Juneteenth. The Dragon Breath Prayer Warriors were all about it. They started putting little dragon emojis in the comments and said they couldn't wait.

I planned the Juneteenth celebration, but I knew more than anything I just wanted to have a good time, so I asked them, "Would y'all be okay with me just playing "Freedom" by Beyoncé? Can we just listen to it together?"

YES (dragon emoji)

PLEASE DO (heart, dragon emoji, woman in red dress)

Bring it on, Osheta! (dragon emoji, dragon emoji, dragon emoji)

I played it and grinned and moved even though I knew White people were watching, even though I felt ridiculous doing it all by myself in the little farmhouse I'd rented for the week to write. I invited the Dragon Breath Prayer Warriors into Black joy and they came right in.

Later on, I received several messaged from DBPWs thanking me for the opportunity to celebrate Juneteenth. I told them they as White Peacemakers are always welcome to practice subversive joy. There's always enough room on the dance floor.

## *Breath prayer*

———

The Spirit of the Lord is upon me,
because he has anointed me to proclaim good news to the poor.
He has sent me to proclaim liberty to the captives
and recovering of sight to the blind,
to set at liberty those who are oppressed.

—LUKE 4:18 (RSV)

Liberator

*I N H A L E ,   E X H A L E*

Set the captives free

## 24

# Breathing Room

Do not store up for yourselves treasures on earth, where moth and rust consume and where thieves break in and steal; but store up for yourselves treasures in heaven, where neither moth nor rust consumes and where thieves do not break in and steal. For where your treasure is, there your heart will be also.

—MATTHEW 6:19-21 NRSV

At this moment, my friend Steph is slightly annoyed with me. She's told me over and over again to call her physical therapist and get a massage. She's set up her credit card with them; she's told me exactly how to make the appointment; she's reminded me a few times just to make sure I knew that at some point she'd really like to pay for me to practice self-care. Steph is one of four White Peacemakers who circle around me making sure I eat well, get enough sleep, have breathing room in my budget for little luxuries like pedicures and Starbucks coffees. Breathing room. That's the phrase that came up in my Zoom class right after George Floyd's death.

When I taught anti-racist peacemaking to a group of about forty White students online, I avoided talking about reparations. I was still in process about what I believed about it, but one of my students emailed me before our final class and said, "Pastor Osheta, I've noticed you didn't talk about reparations as an aspect of peacemaking and I'm just curious, why? How can someone live at peace when there is a significant gap in income and access? I keep thinking of George Floyd saying he can't breathe as a metaphor for how the Black community feels and I think me as a White person offering a financial commitment in response to hundreds of years of free labor enslaved Africans gave to create American wealth would give them some breathing room." Well . . . dang. I had to do my homework and quick because it's true, we cannot have an honest conversation about anti-racist peacemaking without discussing reparations. It's biblical, it's a reflection of our value systems, it's historical, and it's the exact kind of thing that will ruin a holiday gathering. "Hey, everyone, wouldn't it be nice if we had three fewer presents so that Black and Brown people could have the same as us this fine Christmas morn?" Yeah, no . . . but even still, White Peacemakers, let's try to get our minds around God's dream for our finances and our anti-racism.

The concept of reparations in America is a fairly simple one to understand, which means it's massively hard to execute, according to Ta-Nehisi Coates in a reflection on his popular article "The Case for Reparations." In an interview a few years after that article was published, he said,

> The case I make for reparations is, virtually every institution with some degree of history in America, be it public, be it private, has a history of extracting wealth and resources out of the African-American community. I think what has often been missing—this is what I was trying to make the

point of in 2014—that behind all of that oppression was actually theft. In other words, this is not just mean. This is not just maltreatment. This is the theft of resources out of that community.[1]

When we discuss reparations, we're actually talking about a heart condition before we discuss the logistics of it because reparations is simply the act of repairing harm that has been done by paying money or helping those who have been financially impacted by a wrong. A court settlement is a form of reparations that we are all comfortable with. You break it, you bought it—another form of reparations that is common in our culture. However, when we start talking about reparations on a larger scale—communally or nationally, and especially when the case for reparations is rooted in repairing racial harm—there seems to be a barrier in understanding or even empathy. I wonder if it's because in your hearts, White Peacemakers, there's an unhealthy attachment to money, generational myths of exceptionalism, and the status quo.

After the emancipation of enslaved peoples, there was one form of reparation that, had it come to fruition, could have closed the current wealth gap between Blacks (average net worth $17,150) and Whites (average net worth $171,000[2]): forty acres and a mule. During the Reconstruction era of 1865–77, the government attempted to repair some of the damage done by slavery, but not everyone was in love with how African Americans were integrating into society and advancing. For the first time there were Black congressmen, Black people were able to build lives apart from White control, thriving Black communities began to emerge, and all this change was just too much, so Congress voted to end it, military protection and support was pulled from the South, and the rise of racial terror ushered in the Jim Crow era.

But Congress wasn't opposed to offering government help to White Americans. As the program that would provide forty acres and a mule to freed families waned, the Homestead Act of 1862 was awarding White families with farmland—mostly taken from Indigenous People. According to the podcast *Science Vs*, "one scholar estimates that a quarter of the U.S. adult population in the year 2000 could trace some of their money to this act. And that's just one way that the federal government ultimately helped a lot of White people get land and get wealth—and didn't help a lot of Black people."[3] So if there isn't a moral or even logistical problem to providing land and resources to people to help them gain wealth and stimulate the economy, then what's the problem? Again, it's a heart thing. I wanna go back to the Jim Crow era and I want to highlight to you the behavior of White folks toward Black folks trying to live in peace in many small southern towns. I want to look specifically at a county in Georgia called Forsyth County.

In 1900, Forsyth County was the site of one of the most prolific expulsions of Black residents in U.S. history. Instigated by a White woman who was viciously attacked by an unknown assailant, because of some circumstantial evidence and racial bias, members of the White community in Forsyth believed the attacker had to be Black. There was an extrajudicial lynching of a man who had nothing to do with the attack, and when the woman died of her injuries, the violent fervor increased. A group of White men called the Night Riders began terrorizing Black residents. They would tell them they had twenty-four hours to leave their homes and if they didn't they would come back and shoot up the place. In his book *Blood at the Root*, Patrick Philips describes one particularly horrifying practice by the Night Riders:

Joel Whitt, a local white man who was twenty-three in 1912, said that in the beginning, the night riders used gunfire and torches. . . . But later, Whitt recalled, "Certain men would go to a black person's home with sticks tied up in a little bundle [and] leave 'em at the door." By late October, if you made such a thing and placed it outside the cabin of some last, proud black farmer, by sunup he and his whole family would be gone.[4]

Y'all . . . can you believe this? I can't even believe it. White residents would go to their Black neighbors' homes and leave a marker for the Night Riders, asking them to at best shoo the family away, at worst and more likely to kill them in the night. For simply wanting to put down roots and make a life. For simply wanting the freedom to grow whatever crops they wanted, work whatever trade they wanted, raise their children in their home, teaching them their culture and traditions. The driving away of Black people from land is an example of how white supremacy reinforces the narrative that we do not deserve a comfortable, dignified human existence, because we are not human.

Repair must be made because it's biblical and just. Jesus not only taught us to examine our hearts to see what we truly treasure, but modeled this kind of examination in how he called disciples to himself. We can see this in his encounter with the tax collector Zacchaeus. This man isn't a mild-mannered pencil pusher. He's not an accountant; he's a mobster. Not only does he collect Rome's exorbitant taxes, but he adds his own cut on top. Over many years, he's systematically defrauded hundreds of people. But his wealth doesn't fully satisfy him; he still feels empty. That's why when the famous rabbi comes to town, he suddenly becomes a tree-climber. He may be a criminal, but he still believes there's hope for his soul. Jesus sees this man seeking him out and decides to invite himself over for dinner. In the presence of Jesus' holiness, Zacchaeus declares how grateful he is to be unconditionally forgiven for all his sins. He tells everyone that no matter what has happened in the past, Jesus has convinced him to move on and never look back. Right? That's how the story goes, doesn't it?

No, not at all. Jesus' gracious presence in Zacchaeus's home actually moves Zacchaeus to right wrongs, to repair damage— namely, to repay those he's defrauded. His repentance must be concrete if it's to mean anything. If his soul is to be redeemed, he needs to be free of the burden of guilt that his crimes have caused. He needs reparations as badly as those he cheated and from whom he stole.

What does it mean for you to embody repair? What would it look like for you to make amends for the fact that 12.7 million Africans from West Africa and West Central Africa were stolen from their homelands? They were trafficked in the transatlantic slave trade, shipped to the Americas, and many of them died in the Middle Passage. They were stripped of their cultures, their families, their bodily autonomy. They were fed scraps from the tables and their bodies received whatever violence—sexual, physical, emotional—that their White masters desired. What does that look like to say, "I will use my resources, time, energy, and influence to repair the harm done to another human being by making amends to their descendants"?

Well, first, I think we need to deal with Jesus' words here in the Sermon on the Mount. White supremacy culture says your value is defined by what you can take and keep, but the kingdom of God says you already have value apart from anything you own and therefore you can be open-handed with the things of this earth—your land, your savings, your disposable income, your connections, your vacation properties, everything that creates your earthly net worth could and should be available to God, and if your heart is seeking first the kingdom of God, then, White Peacemaker, that means you'd be willing to part with those things to some degree to make financial reparations available to descendants of enslaved peoples. I fear though, friends, that Ta-Nehisi Coates may have an insight as to why this isn't happening on a national scale, but more so, I think this is also an indicator of why the church isn't the forerunner of modeling reparations: "For Americans, the hardest part of paying reparations would not be the outlay of money. It would be acknowledging that their most cherished myth was not real."[5]

Income inequality is a vital aspect of systemic racism. Wealth is tied to power, and power is necessary for the continuance of a racial caste system. When Jesus warns his disciples against storing up treasure on earth, part of this warning is about inequities in society. In America, we've been taught to accumulate as much wealth as possible without ever questioning its morality. The American dream has its roots deep in Native genocide, baptized violence, and labor exploitation. We must dream a new dream, one that repairs harm done, restores trust, and reorients our priorities to put people over profit.

White Peacemakers, reparations on a systemic level of change can look a bunch of ways and I'm willing to leave that up to economists who are a lot smarter than me to suggest how to apply it. But I think it's time, Peacemakers, to not be afraid of the conversations and to begin to cultivate small practices of reparations to and for the people of color in your lives. At the end of the day, it's an integrity issue—whom do you love and where are you putting your security? Are you willing to do whatever you can to repair the damage, heal the breach, and give breathing room? Reparations is one way you can practice peacemaking that will leave a generational legacy of shalom where there is currently a legacy of hate and violence. The choice is up to you, my friends.

# *Breath prayer*

---

Sell your possessions, and give to the needy. Provide yourselves with moneybags that do not grow old, with a treasure in the heavens that does not fail, where no thief approaches and no moth destroys. For where your treasure is, there will your heart be also.

—LUKE 12:33-34 (ESV)

Lord of Justice
*I N H A L E ,   E X H A L E*
Here am I, send me

# Please Kneel for the Kingdom Anthem

When you pray, don't pile up a jumbled heap of words! That's what the Gentiles do. They reckon that the more they say, the more likely they are to be heard. So don't be like them. You see, your father knows what you need before you ask him.

*So this is how you should pray:*
*"Our father in heaven,*
*May your name be honored,*
*May your kingdom come,*
*May your will be done*
*As in heaven, so on earth.*
*Give us today the bread we need now;*
*And forgive us the things we owe,*
*As we too have forgiven what was owed to us.*
*Don't bring us into the great trial,*
*But rescue us from evil."*

Yes: if you forgive people the wrong they have done, your heavenly father will forgive you as well. But if you don't forgive people, neither will your heavenly father forgive you what you have done wrong.

—MATTHEW 6:7-15 (KINGDOM NEW TESTAMENT)[1]

Dear White Peacemakers,

I have a confession: I think I'm a terrible American. Want proof? Okay. The first time I had an apple pie was at my college best friend's house when I made an off-handed comment that I didn't understand the saying, "as American as apple pie." She stared at me, "Wait . . . wait . . . are you saying that you've never had an apple pie or you just don't like apple pie? Either one is bonkers, but I need to know what I'm working with here." I shrugged and said, "I've never had apple pie. Why is it the quintessential American dessert?" That weekend Heather and her mom made me try three different kinds of apple pie. I was proved wrong. Apple pie is life. I now make it every autumn at least once a week. The apple orchard is my happy place and flannel is my all-American uniform. Even after getting my dessert life right, I'm still a terrible American. I'm so bad at being an American that only recently did I decide to vote, because a big part of me didn't really care about democracy or policies. I mean, on some level I cared because I live in this country. I'm a part of this society and I do want to effect real change. But on the other hand, I really glommed on to a mistaken notion of what it means to be a "kingdom person," and slowly a gnostic kind of belief system crept in, to where I stopped being concerned about the "cares of this world" because "heaven in my home." I stopped paying attention to politicians and their campaign promises. They seemed divisive and disingenuous. My political stance was solidly self-contained: I'll do what I can in my little pocket of the world, and that has to be enough. And I think in that way, I'm kind of a perfect example of an American because I individualized everything around me: what are my core convictions, what do I feel comfortable with, what can I accomplish and accomplish well. This individualization is as American as . . . well, apple pie, and is what white supremacy thrives on. In the fine print penned by White men afraid of giving up power was this Faustian deal— we give up our soul, our empathy, our ability to connect with those who are different, our commitment to the greater good, and in return we'll have untold wealth for a few people. We'll tell them that if you have wealth, it is because you made it happen for yourself. If someone is not thriving, it is their fault. This rugged individualism is in every *i* dotted and *t* crossed. We as peacemakers must take the metaphorical pen out of the hands of people unwilling to access humility and empathy and we must be a part of rewriting the next great American story. Not because we want America to be great again, but because we want the souls of all image bearers to feel their worth and know the deep soul-nourishing shalom of God. This American context is the place where we've been called to make peace, and so we must figure out how to be in this world, but not of this world of dominion and violence.

White Peacemaker, because of what I know I'm capable of, I fear that when you hear me say "kingdom person" or you think about your peacemaking as embodying the kingdom here on earth as it is in heaven, you'll shy away from American political life. But you with your voice and your skin privilege are needed. You have access to rooms that I don't. You have influence in predominately White spaces that I'll never have. There's an authenticity to your engaging in anti-racism that some White people will never assume in me simply because when I advocate for anti-racism, I have a vested interest in it. I need you to show up. We need you to show up. I think we need to think of our ambassadorship as two parts: our kingdom identity and our covenant to God and each other. Kingdom so that we never lose sight of what we're building in our contexts, and covenant so that we never lose sight of for whom and why we're building the kingdom. Kingdom and covenant. This is how you show up, shored up and ready with a strong sense of your kingdom identity and a strong call to action. There's really no other text that better prepares us to be kingdom people in this American context than the Lord's Prayer. The Lord's Prayer has become my national anthem, my healing mantra, and my call to action. So let's look at it together, but first let me tell you about the only time I've walked out of a church service.

Apple Pies and Ballot Boxes,
Osheta

❀    ❀    ❀

I'm not the protesting kind, the find-a-cause-and-fight-for-it kind, or the poster-making-party kind. Even though I love a good rhyme, I'm not even the pithy-political-chant-creating kind. No, I prefer to be more of an under-the-radar radical, if you will. I'll give money or like your political Facebook statuses. I may even change my profile pic, if I'm feeling especially feisty—just don't ask me to speak up and definitely don't ask me to make a stand—I'm too afraid of offending someone.

Lately, Jesus has been challenging me on this. "Osheta, you can't have two masters. You can have your quiet comfort or the cross—but you must choose."

❀    ❀    ❀

"What do you think he'll preach on?" my husband asked after we loaded our family up for church in our red minivan.

We were on vacation and one of our favorite things to do if our trip falls on a Sunday is visit a local church for a glimpse into the body of Christ that calls our vacation community home. Since we love visiting churches, we're fairly laid back with our Sunday worship preferences. Does your church have smells and bells? Cool. Having encountered Jesus across denominational lines and traditions, our threshold for discomfort is fairly high. We hope only to experience Jesus wherever we go.

This flexibility—this openness to trying new ways of connecting to the heart of God—has served us well.

We've been encouraged by liturgy and loud worship bands. We've experienced what some may call "the joy of the Lord" in the choreography of worship—the stand up and sit down, the kneeling and jumping. We sense the provision of God for his children when passing the peace or the plate. If Jesus is worshiped, the logistics of how they "do" church is just not a sticking point for us.

This posture helped when we found out that the church we visited wasn't having children's program that morning. We shrugged it off, pulled the kids aside for a little family rally, then loaded them up with clipboards and coloring sheets.

When the pre-service contemporary Christian "muzak" had a few country renditions of some of my favorite Hillsong worship choruses, I just smiled and thought, "Yep. I can totally see everyone in this room rocking out to this Spotify playlist of Dolly Parton meets Darlene Zschech."

When the greeter's southern twang rivaled mine—y'all, I darn near dropped my Bible. A for-really-real southern accent in New England? "Oh come here, brother, and let's trade sweet tea recipes!"

With my kids drawing dragons and zombies on a Zacchaeus coloring book, and my husband studying the bulletin,

I settled into the cushy chair with hope and gracious expectations. The music died away and the chatter quieted as the "Welcome" message on the screen up front cut away to a video of a waving American flag. I gasped. Then the words to a famous patriotic song flashed on the screen. My husband and I made eye contact over our children's bowed heads. Although we're laid back with our preferences, we're pretty inflexible about our principles. The chief ones being we're Jesus followers first, Americans second, and Sunday morning is never a place for patriotism.

*What should we do?* my wide-eyed gaze asked my husband's.

As far as I saw it, we had two options: we could sit quietly in the back while good, well-meaning believers led us in the worship medley of empire and nationalism on the day we traditionally set apart for the Lord, or we could actually follow through with our conviction that as Jesus followers, we cannot "serve two masters," so we should leave. Singing to the glory and wealth of one nation while standing under the shadow of the cross felt like a crossroad. It felt like a betrayal. It felt like a teaching moment.

Daughter, you can have your quiet comfort or you can have the cross. Choose this day whom you will serve.

"Let's go," I said over the chords of "My Country 'Tis of Thee." My husband nodded and gathered up the children closest to him.

We walked out of the service, even while latecomers were rushing in, even after the greeters called to us, "Y'all aren't staying?" We walked out of the service even though it felt rude and ungrateful to those sweet, sweet people.

I walked out of the church service when asked to stand and sing patriotic songs, even though I'm not the protesting, political kind. It's true I'm not, but I'm not the patriotic kind, either.

When I walked out of that church, I chose the kingdom of God over America. It's one thing to quote John 3:16 and hum "He's Got the Whole World in His Hands," but if we're ready to conflate worship of our country with worship of our King on a Sunday morning, do we really believe in unfailing, incomprehensible love for all people—American and Iraqi, South Korean and Russian, Israeli and Palestinian alike?

When I chose Jesus, I chose the way of his cross that breaks down barriers and nullifies the power of empire.

Empire says, "Rome and Rome alone can offer peace. Romans and Romans alone have the answer." The way of the cross says, "All are welcome to find peace here. All are infinitely worthy of love." The way of the cross asks me to remember my true citizenship, every single day—and maybe even twice on Sundays.

I think it's important for us to know that when we choose Jesus, we're not choosing the conquering political leader his disciples hoped he'd be; we're choosing the humble King, riding in on a donkey, betrayed by his own followers, crucified on a Roman cross, resurrected to overcome the enemy of the world and inaugurate his kingdom on earth as it is in heaven.

I wanna sing about that old rugged cross, not rockets blasting in the air.

I worry about good and earnest believers who view serving God and country as one and the same. When we as followers of Jesus lift up our voices to sing of the virtues of our home country in the space and time that should be dedicated to him, we are offering our voices to the enemy. We're joining in the brazen battle cry of the world against our King who died not just for good, God-fearing Americans, but for every person, in every nation, regardless of their alliance or antagonism toward this country.

On the cross, Jesus was crowned Prince of Peace, and his kingdom is not of this world. As kingdom people we have to live this countercultural message of love, and I'm sorry, but singing a rousing patriotic theme or even saying the Pledge of Allegiance muddies that message.

It waters down the upside-down, direct act of nonviolence, exposing the powers for who and what they are.

When I walked out of that church, I made a choice. I chose Jesus over country. I chose truth over lies. I chose to honor my identity as Beloved kingdom woman over lukewarm American believer. I chose the cross over the American flag.

I chose the shalom of God over the manufactured peace of empire.

And I'd do it all over again—even though I'm not the protesting kind.

❀   ❀   ❀

The Lord's Prayer is Jesus' own creative and kingdom-focused practice that he gave us so we can grow in our kingdom allegiance. By praying the Lord's Prayer regularly, we reinforce the values of the kingdom of God in our hearts so that we can live out our Christian vocation as kingdom ambassadors in whatever country and context we're in.

It's interesting that the Lord's Prayer is found in Matthew because Matthew's main goal in his gospel is to help us see how Jesus is the Messiah, how Jesus is Emmanuel, God with us. Jesus lives out this kingdom way, and as he draws people to him, he's drawing them to learn and listen and look at him. When I think of Jesus, I think of a true leader, one who says, "This is the way and I'll go first."

And so all throughout Matthew, we see Jesus talking and ministering and living this kingdom way. But toward the beginning, we get the Lord's Prayer. One of my favorite scholars said this was actually a strategic act by Jesus as a rabbi, as a teacher, because he basically gave his followers the lay of the land. "This is where we're going in my ministry." And then he lived it out every single day. He taught it to them all the way to the cross and then the resurrection. Jesus taught them the Lord's Prayer so that it would be in their minds as they were ministering next to Jesus, and it became real and more relevant as they walked alongside Jesus. The Lord's Prayer helps us embody what Jesus says in Matthew 22 are the two greatest commandments: "'Love the Lord your God with all your heart and with all your soul and with all your mind.' This is the first and greatest commandment. And the second is like it: 'Love your neighbor as yourself.' All the Law and the Prophets hang on these two commandments" (vv. 37-40).

These two commandments are kind of like kingdom and covenant. They're our ways of living out this DNA of spiritual life. The Lord's Prayer reminds us of our relationship to God and our responsibility to each other. It's our way of committing to Jesus' greatest commandments. And again, when we regularly pray the Lord's Prayer, we become more aware of the kingdom of God and our call to live it out. And this is what I learned when I started to pray the Lord's Prayer. You see, when I began to pray the Lord's Prayer, his own words that he crafted to help take the big ideas of kingdom and covenant and make them real to me, I began to see how the Holy Spirit would open my mind to the love of God and give me a love for others that I never had. Stories from the Bible where God showed up began to become real to me, like the ways that he loves like a father does, the ways he provided, the forgiveness he offered, and the ways he invited people to go on a mission with him.

The Lord's Prayer opened my eyes to see that kingdom and covenant were part of the whole narrative of Scripture, and as I practice anti-racism peacemaking I hold these two concepts in my mind. It keeps me focused and balanced.

As anti-racism peacemakers, let's break the Lord's Prayer down line by line:

*Our Father in heaven.* The Lord's Prayer famously begins with "Our Father," not "My Father." It's a reminder that we share a common experience and, as Christians, a common Father. The work of anti-racism isn't self-help; it's the work of bringing the human family back together. Beginning with "Our Father in heaven" reminds us that we need help in this work. We cannot and should not expect to show up at the family reunion without our Father there bringing us to the table, setting a meal before us, mediating our conflict, offering healing and new life. It's super important for me to pray this line of the Lord's Prayer when I experience trauma from white supremacy and I'm tempted to otherize White people, because they are my siblings.

*May your name be honored.* How we engage in the work of anti-racism is important, because we want to honor God's name.

We want the way that we oppose racism to reflect the non-violent love of God revealed in Jesus. More Christians will want to join us in this work if they see it as God-honoring. Anti-racism peacemaking honors God the way Jesus did: by challenging oppressive systems, graciously loving sinners, and calling disciples to leave their self-interest behind and follow him to the cross. That's what's needed in this moment in history.

*May your kingdom come, may your will be done as in heaven, so on earth.* This is basically saying, "Lord, let my 'say so' be aligned with your 'say so.' May I look for ways to live out the culture of the kingdom here and now." It's a way of saying: May I desire your greatest desire that heaven and earth wouldn't be these separate things, but rather that heaven and earth would be, as I've heard N. T. Wright teach it in his class on the Lord's Prayer, "a single bond, deeply connected, interwoven." When we live out anti-racism as a practice of peacemaking, people can see the kingdom of God in such stark contrast to the kingdom of this world. When Jesus teaches in Matthew to seek first the kingdom of God and all these things will be added unto you, I wonder if he was reminding them of this line from the Lord's Prayer. I wonder if Jesus knew that his disciples lived in a world rife with preoccupation and that the potential to worry about so many things could be overwhelming. This call for the kingdom to come on earth as it is in heaven may be Jesus' way of helping us focus. Are we seeking shalom in our relationships with God, with ourselves, with each other, and then with systems of the world? Good—then the kingdom of God is in our midst.

*Give us today the bread we need now.* Okay, raise your hand if you've ever felt that learning about anti-racism is a tidal wave of heartbreak, challenge, insights, and expectations. Raise your hand if you've blown your book budget regularly getting resources to understand each nuance of the anti-racism conversation. I mean . . . you're holding a book like that in your hands right now. Do you have both hands raised? And you're still reading a book at the same time? Wow . . . you're amazing. But seriously, there are so many good books, classes, dialogues, small groups, podcasts, documentaries, lectures, articles, experiences, and so much more for you to learn, and it can seem like you don't have enough time to take it in or that all you're doing is studying—you're not living it out. This request for the anti-racist peacemaker to receive only today's bread is a reprieve from the "do more" to prove your commitment to anti-racism. As I named in the first part of this book, I worry, friend, that we're building a legalistic practice of "read this, say this, protest here," which is always shame-laden and hustle-bound. Trusting God for our daily bread here can mean that each day we're open to whatever invitation to dismantle racism God places before us. It'll look and taste different, but it'll be that day's bread, and that's really good news.

*And forgive us the things we owe, as we too have forgiven what was owed to us.* We've already talked about this but it cannot be overstated: forgiveness is one of the cornerstones of true peacemaking. This is a hard one, but it is the bedrock of our kingdom ethic. Forgiveness is so different from the way the world works. The forgiveness of God changes the very foundation of our relationships, it transforms our relationships, it changes the dynamic in our relationships. There's no longer a quid pro quo. It reminds us that we don't have everything figured out. At the same time, we must be mindful that forgiveness can also be weaponized, especially in interracial relationships.

*Don't bring us into the great trial, but rescue us from evil.* If forgiveness was hard for us to get our brains around, this one might make our heads explode.

The traditional way we've said it, "Lead us not into temptation, but deliver us from evil," has a picture of God in it that's very troubling. It's as if God were going around putting sin and temptation in our path and being like, "Let's see what they're going to do." But what we need to do is get that picture of God right out of our minds, because we started this prayer saying that God is a God of love and justice. We're committing our allegiance to a God who's lived with us, loved us, died for us, and overcome sin and the grave for us. So if that's true, then "Don't bring us into the great trial, but rescue us from evil" cannot mean that God tempts us or sets out to trick us into sinning. God is not capricious. So the temptation here isn't something God is putting in our path, it's something we're bumping up against every single day as we live in this world.

When we commit ourselves to the kingdom of God and our covenant with each other, we're going to face opposition. The enemy is going to say, "Oh, really? Watch this!" Want to know how I know? I started this book in January, then the pandemic happened. Then a series of racially charged events happened. Then I was harassed by White supremacists in Minnesota. It seems to me that I've faced my greatest trials when I've stood up and said, "I'll resist white supremacy and call it out wherever I see it." We need to change the way we think about this line—to shift from asking God, "Oh, please don't hurt us" to asking God, "Please be with us through opposition." We cannot overcome the enemy on our own, so Lord, protect us, be with us, and fight alongside us when the enemy comes against us—especially in this holy work.

This idea of rethinking the way that we pray the last line of the Lord's Prayer isn't new. Actually, the pope recently suggested changing it from "lead us not into temptation" to "do not let us fall into temptation," for he says a father doesn't lead his children into temptation.[2] The Father helps pull you up immediately when you have been tempted. It is Satan who leads into temptation; that's his department.

❀  ❀  ❀

My son reminded me the other day that after we walked out of that church I said something to him about Jesus that he won't ever forget. He told me I'd said, "Jesus loves every person in that room, but his heart breaks when we don't love him back, when we love our country more than him." For me, loving my country goes only as far as my believing in her ideals and holding her accountable to them. I like what James Baldwin once wrote: "I love America more than any other country in the world, and, exactly for this reason, I insist on the right to criticize her perpetually."[3] My dual citizenship between kingdom and America allows me to seek this country's shalom without overidentifying with it. At the same time, I can hold the ideals of this country in light of the ethics of the kingdom, and where America fails, I know I have a better, truer, more just course of action to move toward.

We have to choose, Peacemaker. Jesus, our Prince of Peace, and his kingdom, or America. We can't have both in equal parts. One must be subject to the other. So I pray the Lord's Prayer every day to help me stay focused. And sometimes (especially during Sunday and Monday night football), I pray it twice.

## *Breath prayer*

The coming of the kingdom of God is not something that can be observed, nor will people say, "Here it is," or "There it is," because the kingdom of God is in your midst.

—LUKE 17:20-21

Jesus

*I N H A L E ,   E X H A L E*

Your kingdom come, your will be done

**2 6**

# Amen!

## *A Benediction*

We've come to the end of our time together, Peacemaker. I'd like to send you back into the world with one last Spiritual. This book was birthed in my heart as I sat in that prayer vigil for the Charleston Nine and watched the two women, one Black, the other White, sing to each other. If you were truly here, by now Fenway would have made you his best friend and snuggled up against you—partly because you are amazing and he's a very good judge of character, but partly because I would have offered you the comfy throw to keep you warm during our chat, and that's his favorite. We'd have had plenty of cups of coffee and then switched to tea and then water because it's late and skin care and insomnia are real things when you're pushing forty. "Hydrate or die-drate," as they say. But it's time for you to leave, so I'm going to ask you to push Fenway out of your lap and stand in front of me as I sing this benediction over you. If you were here, you'd sing the amens and I'd sing the verses.

"Amen!" was one of the slave songs that celebrated when someone made it to freedom. The news would come from a visiting enslaved person, and as it passed from one to another, the fields and slave quarters would begin to fill with triumphant "A-a-a-men! A-a-a-men! A-a-men! Amen! Amen!"

It's a call-and-response song: One sings amen, the other sings a story about Jesus—his birth, his life, his death, and his resurrection. It's a call to all those with the temerity to believe in the promise of peace because Jesus went first and secured that everlasting peace, shalom. Everything we do on this road of peacemaking is following in his legacy. We're walking the road he paved for us. We bring the air of the kingdom here with every prayer, every conversation, every protest; every moment we use our breath to dismantle racism, we are resisting the knee of white supremacy. For every Black man or woman hung by a noose or dying on a sidewalk who gasps, "I can't breathe," we get to breathe for them.

So, lean in close and receive this song as a jubilant benediction reminding us of the life of Jesus, our model for anti-racism peacemaking.

Amen!

See the little baby,
Amen
lyin' in the manger
Amen
on Christmas mornin'.

Amen, amen, amen.

See him at the temple,
Amen
talkin' to the elders;
Amen
how they marveled at his wisdom,

Amen, amen amen.

See him at the Jordan
Amen
where John was baptizin'
Amen
and savin' all sinners.

Amen, amen, amen.

See him at the seaside,
Amen
talkin' to the fishermen
Amen
and makin' them disciples.
Amen

Amen, amen, amen.

Marchin' in Jerusalem,
Amen
over palm branches,
Amen
in pomp and splendor.
Amen

Amen, amen, amen.

See him in the garden,
Amen
prayin' to his Father,
Amen
in deepest sorrow.

Amen, amen, amen.

Led before Pilate,
Amen
then they crucified him,
Amen
but he rose on Easter.

Amen, amen, amen.

Hallelujah!
Amen

He died to save us all
Amen
and he lives forever.

Amen, amen, amen.
Amen, amen, amen.

Go in peace, White Peacemaker, to dismantle racism with grit and grace.

# By the Waters of Bde Maka Ska

I'm sitting by Bde Maka Ska (Be-DAY Mah-KAH Ska) thinking about our time together in this book, about all the ways I've encouraged you to be a White Peacemaker and the promises I've made to you as you do this work. But as I'm praying and thinking, I notice the ripple of the water and the swooping of the birds, and a flyer twists and swirls on the ground, animated by the wind. A winter event is happening at the lake, and the name of Bde Maka Ska is a Dakota word that means "White Earth Lake."

The Dakota people who used to live along the shore of the lake gave it its original name, but in 1839, it was changed to honor the seventh vice president of the United States, John C. Calhoun. While this in and of itself was a deep cut of white supremacy to the Native People who lived here, to add salt to the wound, Calhoun was a pro-slavery segregationist. I looked at the Dakota word and thought of the Dakota people, whom I don't know very much about. I know there's a solidarity that comes from both of our people suffering from white supremacy. However, the extent of their pain, the impact they've made on this state that I love so much, their culture and history, are all mysteries to me. What are my calls to action to come alongside them and reject apathy, disarm my fragility, and leverage my privilege? These are all questions I think of regularly as a happy Minnesotan; I love this land and I want to honor those who love it, know it, praise God for it, on a deeper level. And so, the work continues. I'm putting my hands to the plow to keep learning how to practice anti-racism and peacemaking for as long as I'm on this earth. I want to be an ambassador of the kingdom of heaven, bringing its shalom to dismantle white supremacy every single day, with grit and grace, hope and honesty, love and reconciliation all the days of my life.

# Note to the Reader

Like most pastors, I get to hold the stories of those who are hurting, questioning, or processing. I hold these stories with reverence, honoring that for a moment—some stories are only for that moment of care—I'm invited into their story as they entrust it to me to help us move from brokenness into wholeness. I take this part of my calling seriously.

I'm also a pastor who happens to be a writer too, so stories sometimes take on a different function, they invite me in to learn more about myself, about the world, and they ask me to pay attention to anything that may help someone else—in particular you, my dear reader. The stories in this book are told to the best of my memory while honoring the amazing people who let me share their lives with you. Identifying details have been changed to protect them, and some timelines have been condensed for narrative flow. I chose to root this book in stories because like Toni Morrison, my favorite storyteller of all, I am an optimist. I believe that we learn best from watching others succeed and fail and not necessarily when we pontificate endlessly on obscure theological ideas.

If this book has inspired you to know your Black friends' stories more, can I offer you some advice? For their sake and for your shalom, would you ask them with an open hand? Until things change, until generations of resetting and reframing happen, you as a White person will have this unfair power dynamic. If you ask a Black person, especially one who loves you, to do something, they may say yes even if they don't want to. For many of us, that's part of our HIPP—historical, intergenerational, persistent institutional, and personal trauma. So, I hope you invite them in with all the outs possible. "Hey, I read this book on anti-racism and peacemaking and I have some questions. Would you be interested in processing them with me? If not, it's totally okay. But let me know." Then, when y'all meet, pay for dinner and send them something to help them practice self-care. It is a unique physical stress, one unlike any I've experienced before, to unpack racism with a White Peacemaker. So take care of the Black people in your life well.

Also, these stories and approaches to anti-racism are mine and mine alone. Not every Black person feels the same commitment to White Peacemakers that I do and not every Black Christian is obligated to interpret Scriptures the way I do. My theological framework as an Anabaptist has put a high emphasis on nonviolence, love of enemy/other, embodied discipleship, and cross-shaped love. Not all Black Christian thinkers agree with me, and that's completely okay. There's a particular strategy of divide and conquer that occurs when White people compare Black thinkers, and I'm going to ask you to be really careful about that.

When I think of this landscape of anti-racism, I'm reminded of something Paul wrote to the church in Corinth. There were various leaders, Apollos, Cephas (Peter), and, of course, Paul. Each leader had their own distinct personality and teaching style and it was causing the church to split into factions and claim their leader was the best leader. Paul, writing to the church, warned them of letting this prevent them from being a witness. He spoke of the unique calling each leader had to advance the work of the gospel. "What then is Apollos? And what is Paul? They are servants through whom you believed, as the Lord has assigned to each his role. I planted the seed and Apollos watered it, but God made it grow. So neither he who plants nor he who waters is anything, but only God, who makes things grow. He who plants and he who waters are one in purpose, and each will be rewarded according to his own labor. For we are God's fellow workers; you are God's field, God's building" (1 Corinthians 3:5-9). This is how I feel about Black leadership and White Peacemakers. You may really resonate with me, but I am but one fellow worker with others. I'm grateful for their witness, scholarship, and mentorship. When you're leaning into the work, if you find one of our teachings/approaches works best for you, then follow that teacher/thinker, support that person (financially), and learn from their teaching. But don't compare that leader to someone who maybe rubbed you the wrong way or with whom you disagree.

Black leaders get to be on the journey, too. We get to express our full humanity by doing this work from a place of authenticity to ourselves, our experiences, our core convictions, and our commitment to Jesus.

Thank you for understanding, and thanks for reading this book.

Yours always,
Osheta

# Acknowledgements

If after reading this book you wonder if the Beloved Community actually exists, and if so, what it might look like. It looks like:

Dayna Olson-Getty writing me back saying, "I think there's a book here for White Christians; let's work on this together." Meghan Florian's eye for structure, love of words, and relentless optimism. The whole Herald Press team helping me write the book of my heart with utmost integrity.

Marla Taviano accepting my proposal and becoming my "book wife," answering texts, responding to calls, holding space, fixing wonky sentences. Dawn Rice, Heidi Tungseth, Laura Mitchell, and Mariann Reardon showing up for Sunday Zoom meetings to help me process chapters. Mary Van Sickle walking around Central Park to help me narrow down *all my ideas* to one hopeful call to White Peacemakers: Become the Beloved Community. Paul Eddy and Greg Boyd inviting me to listen to and learn from their expertise and experience as White Anabaptist theologians with a heart for racial justice. Katherine Willis Pershey, Amanda Ginn, Jerusalem Greer, and Emily Morrison allowing me to share how we've linked arms against racism as friends and peacemakers. Abby Trout and her prayers. A dozen White Peacemakers writing the name of this book on a piece of paper and sending it to me to remind me I'm not alone. Kevin Callaghan's trust and his copy of *The*

*Beloved Community*. Di Kistler's tears and tender heart. Rob Kistler's prayers and prophetic words. Shawna Boren's protective care. Dan Kent's curiosity. Naomi Krueger's encouragement and insight. Lauren Rotach's texts of encouragement. Samantha's hospitality, offering her guest house so I could write—and play with her goats during my breaks. Everyone in the "Help Osheta Write" group who read passages, gave feedback, and posted hilarious GIFs. The PAX team, Josh Buck, Michelle Reyes, Andrew Rillera, who made it possible for me to grieve and process George Floyd's murder so I could write this book. Haley Stewart for praying to the Saints for me. Aundi Kolber asking me, "Where does it hurt?" in that way only a skilled therapist can. Nina my spiritual director over the summer. Jen for breakfast and her mentorship over all these years, even from afar.

My children, Tyson, T. J., and Trinity, who each committed to giving up their mom for several months. It looks like them going with the flow, cleaning up the house, making their own dinners (and lunches), and giving me all the grace I needed (especially during the edits).

My husband, T. C. Moore—my best friend and favorite conversation partner. He held me in the middle of the night while I cried—maybe over something heartbreaking I just wrote, read, or was preparing to share. Often, he resisted my insecurity and fear with compassion and wisdom. "You've got this, babe" was his ever-ringing benediction as I went to write.

Wanna know why I believe we can build the Beloved Community and dismantle racism? Because I've seen it, lived it, and benefited from it every day from every single one of these people.

# Notes

## COME TO THE TABLE

1  Angela Lee Duckworth, "Grit: The Power of Passion and Perseverance," TED Talk, 6:01, April 2013, https://www.ted.com/talks/angela_lee_duckworth_grit_the_power_of_passion_and_perseverance.

2  Mark Charles and Soong-Chan Rah, *Unsettling Truths: The Ongoing, Dehumanizing Legacy of the Doctrine of Discovery* (Downers Grove, IL: InterVarsity, 2019), 124.

3  Glen H. Stassen and David P. Gushee, *Kingdom Ethics: Following Jesus in Contemporary Culture* (Grand Rapids, MI: Eerdmans, 2014), 180, quoting Joseph Kotva, *The Christian Case for Virtue Ethics* (Washington, DC: Georgetown University Press, 1996), 8–9.

4  James Baldwin, "Dark Days," *Esquire*, October 1, 1980.

5  William Stringfellow, *Free in Obedience* (Eugene, OR: Wipf and Stock, 2006), 52. First published 1964.

6  Nell Irvin Painter, "Why 'White' Should Be Capitalized, Too," *Washington Post*, July 22, 2020, https://www.washingtonpost.com/opinions/2020/07/22/why-white-should-be-capitalized/.

**CHAPTER 2**

1 Henri J. M. Nouwen, *Life of the Beloved: Spiritual Living in a Secular World* (New York: Crossroad, 2002), 30–33.

2 Nouwen, 135.

**CHAPTER 3**

1 Walter Wink, *Jesus and Nonviolence: A Third Way* (Minneapolis: Fortress Press, 2003), 13.

2 Wink, 16.

**CHAPTER 4**

1 Martin Luther King Jr., "The Role of the Church in Facing the Nation's Chief Moral Dilemma" (address, Conference on Christian Faith and Human Relations, Nashville, April 25, 1957), in *Symbol of the Movement: January 1957–December 1959*, vol. 4 of *The Papers of Martin Luther King, Jr.*, ed. Clayborn Carson (Berkeley: University of California Press, 2000), 190.

2 Charles Marsh, *The Beloved Community: How Faith Shapes Social Justice from the Civil Rights Movement to Today* (New York: Basic Books, 2005), 2.

3 Osheta Moore, *Shalom Sistas: Living Wholeheartedly in a Broken-hearted World* (Harrisonburg, VA: Herald Press, 2017), 31.

4 Henri J. M. Nouwen, *Life of the Beloved: Spiritual Living in a Secular World* (New York: Crossroad, 2002), 44–45. Emphasis in the original.

5 Marsh, *The Beloved Community*, 3.

6 Marsh, *The Beloved Community*, 3.

**CHAPTER 6**

1 Brian Engelhart, "White Apathy and the Crucifixion," *The Jesuit Post*, August 21, 2020, https://thejesuitpost.org/2020/08/white-apathy-and-the-crucifixion-know-justice-know-peace-a-jesuit-antiracism-retreat/.

**CHAPTER 7**

1 Richard Rohr, "Transforming Pain," Center for Action and Contemplation, October 17, 2018, https://cac.org/transforming-pain-2018-10-17/. Adapted from Rohr, *A Spring within Us: A Book of Daily Meditations* (Albuquerque: CAC Publishing, 2016).

2 Brené Brown, *Rising Strong: How the Ability to Reset Transforms the Way We Live, Love, Parent, and Lead* (New York: Random House, 2017), 50.

3 This quote is often attributed to artist and activist Lilla Watson. Watson, a Murri (Aboriginal Australian) woman, was a part of the 1970s activist group, and has specified that it was crafted as part of a collective process.

## CHAPTER 8

1 Marissa Evans, "The Relentlessness of Black Grief," *The Atlantic*, September 27, 2020, https://www.theatlantic.com/ideas/archive/2020/09/relentlessness-black-grief/616511/.

## CHAPTER 12

1 Jude Ellison Sady Doyle, "Why Are White Women So Terrified of Being Called Racist?," *Elle*, July 27, 2018, https://www.elle.com/culture/career-politics/a22565907/why-are-white-women-so-terrified-of-being-called-racist/.

2 Aundi Kolber, *Try Softer: A Fresh Approach to Move Us Out of Anxiety, Stress, and Survival Mode—and into a Life of Connection and Joy* (Carol Stream, IL: Tyndale, 2020), 72.

## CHAPTER 13

1 Dan Kent, *Confident Humility: Becoming Your Full Self without Becoming Full of Yourself* (Minneapolis: Fortress Press, 2019).

## CHAPTER 15

1 Stephanie E. Jones-Rogers, *They Were Her Property: White Women as Slave Owners in the American South* (New Haven: Yale University Press, 2019), xv–xvi.

## CHAPTER 18

1 Jemar Tisby, "I'm a Black Man Who Moved to the Deep South. Here's What It's Teaching Me about Race," Vox, updated January 4, 2019, https://www.vox.com/first-person/2017/10/31/16571238/black-man-deep-south-race.

## CHAPTER 19

1 "Good Humor and The RZA Collaborate on a New Ice Cream Truck Jingle for a New Era," PRNewswire, August 13, 2020, https://www.prnewswire.com/news-releases/good-humor-and-the-rza-collaborate-on-a-new-ice-cream-truck-jingle-for-a-new-era-301111746.html.

## CHAPTER 20

1 Martin Luther King Jr., "Letter from Birmingham Jail," in *Why We Can't Wait* (Boston: Beacon Press, 1963), 64–65.

2 King, 67–68.

3 Chanequa Walker-Barnes, *I Bring the Voices of My People: A Womanist Vision for Racial Reconciliation* (Grand Rapids: Eerdmans, 2019).

4 Sanya Mansoor, "93% of Black Lives Matter Protests Have Been Peaceful, New Report Finds," *Time*, September 5, 2020, https://time.com/5886348/report-peaceful-protests/. Citing "Demonstrations and Political Violence in America: New Data for Summer 2020," ACLED, September 3, 2020, https://acleddata.com/2020/09/03/demonstrations-political-violence-in-america-new-data-for-summer-2020/.

5 James H. Cone, *God of the Oppressed*, rev. ed. (Maryknoll, NY: Orbis, 1997), xi. First published 1975.

## CHAPTER 21

1 Leon F. Seltzer, "Why You Secretly Enjoy Getting Angry," *Psychology Today*, November 7, 2018, https://www.psychologytoday.com/us/blog/evolution-the-self/201811/why-you-secretly-enjoy-getting-angry.

## CHAPTER 22

1 Roxane Gay, "Why I Can't Forgive Dylann Roof," *New York Times*, June 23, 2015, https://www.nytimes.com/2015/06/24/opinion/why-i-cant-forgive-dylann-roof.html.

2 Dietrich Bonhoeffer, *The Cost of Discipleship* (New York: Macmillan, 1966), 47. First published 1937.

## CHAPTER 23

1 Teju Cole, "The White Savior Industrial Complex is not about justice," Twitter, March 8, 2012, 11:37 a.m., https://twitter.com/tejucole/status/177810262223626241.

## CHAPTER 24

1 "Ta-Nehisi Coates Revisits the Case for Reparations," *New Yorker*, June 10, 2019, https://www.newyorker.com/news/the-new-yorker-interview/ta-nehisi-coates-revisits-the-case-for-reparations.

2 Kriston McIntosh, Emily Moss, Ryan Nunn, and Jay Shambaugh, "Examining the Black-White Wealth Gap," Brookings, February 27, 2020, https://www.brookings.edu/blog/up-front/2020/02/27/examining-the-black-white-wealth-gap/.

3 "Reparations: How Could It Work?" October 30, 2020, in *Science Vs*, produced by Rose Rimler and Anoa Changa, podcast, 28:52, https://gimletmedia.com/shows/science-vs/5whw4ld.

4 Patrick Phillips, *Blood at the Root: A Racial Cleansing in America* (New York: Norton, 2016), ch. 5.

5 Ta-Nehisi Coates, *We Were Eight Years in Power: An American Tragedy* (New York: One World, 2017), 159.

## CHAPTER 25

1 N. T. Wright, *The Kingdom New Testament: A Contemporary Translation* (New York: HarperCollins, 2011), 10.

2 Harriet Sherwood, "Led Not into Temptation: Pope Approves Change to Lord's Prayer," *The Guardian*, June 6, 2019, https://www.theguardian.com/world/2019/jun/06/led-not-into-temptation-pope-approves-change-to-lords-prayer.

3 James Baldwin, *Notes of a Native Son* (Boston: Beacon Press, 1955), 9.

# The Author

Osheta Moore is a writer, pastor, speaker, and podcaster in Saint Paul, Minnesota, as well as a mother of three and an economic justice advocate for women in developing countries. She is the outreach and teaching pastor at Woodland Hills Church and the pastor of community life at Roots Covenant Church alongside her husband. Her work  has been featured on numerous websites and blogs, including *Sojourners, SheLoves Magazine, Deeper Story,* The Art of Simple, ReKnew, and Rachel Held Evans's blog. She is the author of *Shalom Sistas: Living Wholeheartedly in a Brokenhearted World*, published by Herald Press in 2017. Connect with her at Osheta.com and follow her on Instagram @oshetamoore for encouragements to practice everyday peacemaking and invitations for White Peacemakers on their anti-racism journey.